Undocumented Workers' Transitions

Routledge Advances in Sociology

For a full list of titles in this series please visit www.routledge.com

Undocumented Workers' Transitions

Legal Status, Migration, and Work in Europe

Sonia McKay, Eugenia Markova, and Anna Paraskevopoulou

LONDON AND NEW YORK

First published 2011 by Routledge
2 Park Square, Milton Park, Abingdon, Oxon OX14 4RN
52 Vanderbilt Avenue, New York, NY 10017

*Routledge is an imprint of the Taylor & Francis Group,
an informa business*

© 2011 Taylor & Francis

First issued in paperback 2013

The right of Sonia McKay, Eugenia Markova and Anna Paraskevopoulou
to be identified as the authors of this work has been asserted by them in
accordance with sections 77 and 78 of the Copyright, Designs and Patents
Act 1988.

Typeset in Sabon by IBT Global.

Library of Congress Cataloging-in-Publication Data
McKay, Sonia.
    Undocumented workers' transitions : legal status, migration, and work
in Europe / Sonia McKay, Eugenia Markova, Anna Paraskevopoulou.
        p. cm.—(Routledge advances in sociology ; 58)
    Includes bibliographical references and index.
    1. Foreign workers—Europe—Case studies.   2. Illegal aliens—
Europe—Case studies.   I. Markova, Eugenia.   II. Paraskevopoulou,
Anna.   III Title.
    HD8376.5.M37 2011
    331.6'2094—dc22
    2010053533

ISBN13: 978-0-415-88902-5 (hbk)
ISBN13: 978-0-415-85180-0 (pbk)

To migrant workers—documented and undocumented—everywhere

Contents

Tables and Figures

TABLES

FIGURES

Acknowledgements

The authors are grateful to the European Commission's sixth Framework Programme, for financing the study, from which this book grew and to Guilia Amaducci for her support of the research.

This book would not have been possible without the work of our colleagues, in particular, Tessa Wright, for her invaluable contribution throughout the research process since its inception, as well as Steve Jefferys, Leena Kumarappan and Janet Emefo from the Working Lives Research Institute, London Metropolitan University, UK; Manfred Krenn and Bettina Haidinger from Forschungs-und Beratungsstelle Arbeitswelt, Austria; Isabelle Carles and Estelle Krzeslo from the Université Libre de Bruxelles, GEM- Institut de Sociologie, Belgium; Violetta Angelova, Zhelyu Vladimirov, Antonina Zhelyazkova and Mila Mancheva from the International Centre for Minority Studies and Intercultural Relations, Bulgaria; Shahamak Rezaei and Marco Goli, Roskilde University, Denmark; Fabio Perocco, Pietro Basso and Rossana Cillo, from the University "Ca'Foscari" of Venice, Italy; Paolo Leotti and Miguel Pajares, from the Gabinet d'Estudis Socials, Spain.

We would like to give special thanks to the participants in the stakeholders' meetings organised in Austria, Belgium, Bulgaria, Denmark, Italy, Spain and the UK in 2008, for all their advice and helpful comments.

We are most grateful for the contributions of the numerous international and national migration experts who gave us their time and knowledge in providing lengthy interviews.

We can't thank enough Chi Chang, Iris Suen and Joe Hung from the Chinese Immigration Concern Committee in London for securing access to one of the most vulnerable migrant groups in the UK. We are also grateful to the people at Kanlungan—an organisation of migrant workers from the Philippines—for their willingness to participate in the research. We extend our gratitude to our families for their encouragement and understanding throughout the research and writing process.

Finally, we are deeply indebted to all migrant workers who gave generously their time to share with us their personal stories and experiences of work and living conditions. Their patience and friendly attitude made this research possible.

Needless to say, the authors alone take full responsibility for any errors in this book.

1 The Lived Experiences of Undocumented Migrants

> Employers wanted workers, but workers without families, who needed no schools or community services. They wanted workers who could be housed in homeless shelters or packed into trailers like sardines.
>
> (Bacon, 2008: 181)

In his book *Illegal people* (2008), David Bacon, an American journalist, vividly describes the situation of undocumented migrants in the US. Our study leads us to concur with his description also in relation to European-based employers. Those who are undocumented in Europe today fit into Bacon's description for a number of reasons. As migrants they are more mobile than indigenous workers, because they have (at least on first arrival) no ties to specific geographical areas. As undocumented migrants they are less likely, than other groups of migrants, to be accompanied by their families. They generally arrive as adults, so that their countries of origin have borne the costs of whatever education and training they have had; they are over-represented within the under 40-year-old population and thus can be said to be in the 'healthiest' phase of their lives, having overcome childhood illness and not reached the second phase of illness, in middle to old age. They are more 'willing' or 'accepting' of poor living and working conditions, in part because they construct these as temporary challenges, which will be overcome through time and the acquisition of financial security but, more than this, because they have no alternatives. The impact of this model of subservient labour is witnessed predominately, although not exclusively, in global cities, whose economies demand a workforce that is seen as doing low-skilled work (Sassen, 2001; Wills et al., 2010). Increasingly, however, undocumented migrants have been spreading beyond these narrow geographical confines, moving from the principal cities to smaller towns and to more rural areas. In part this is driven by competition for jobs, but they are also responding to an expressed need for 'flexible' workers in rural areas, where the demands of the agriculture and food processing sectors are for workers who can be hired and laid off, dependent on specific production needs. However, moving to smaller localities means undertaking the risk of detection and expulsion and for some of those whom we interviewed for this study, the risks of detection were too great to compromise through moving to such areas even if work might be more plentiful.

International migration has become a highly politicised issue on a global scale, regularly debated by governments at international, national, and local levels. The migration phenomenon has also become a topical subject for the media, often reported in ways that reflect the overall political climate of the time but also the specific opinion of the media and its viewers or readers. Consequently, much of the emphasis has been on policy making, with specific government departments being set up to control migration, assess the scale of it or develop policies that deal with the issue. Although migration policy varies between different states, in our study we have noted an increasing inter-state cooperation, with mechanisms being put in place that have shifted the debate to a more global dimension. These mechanisms include bodies such as the Global Forum on Migration and Development (GFMD); the High Level Dialogue on Migration, as part of the United Nations (HLD); or the Global Commission on International Migration (GCIM). But other organisations, such as trade-focused ones, also now bring migration into their debates, discussing it within the framework of global developments, for example, unrestricted migration and terrorism (Düvell, 2006:7).

Equally, migration has generated a great deal of activity from various nongovernmental organisations (NGOs) in many states, working nationally or internationally and predominately on general issues related to the protection of human and migrant rights. Often this NGO work has a more practical focus, offering help with issues of settlement, housing, employment, language learning courses, education, and health, among others. Trade unions are another example of organisations that have offered their support to migrant workers, especially in relation to employment law and employment rights and by incorporating and promoting relevant policies. Indeed throughout the history of labour movement struggles, migrants have assumed active roles within the structures of trade union organisations and helped mobilised other migrants to participate in trade union activities or struggles, such as strikes. The two-year strike of the Grunwick women workers, which began in 1977 in the UK; the janitors' strikes in the US, from the early 1990s onwards; and more recently, the fight back by African origin migrants working in agriculture in Italy, against the attacks on them in Rosarno, Calabria, all demonstrate the potential power of organisation among migrants. Finally, the phenomenon of migration has always been of interest to researchers, ranging from social scientists, to economists, historians, anthropologists, and demographers. The recent and accelerated trends of migration, as this book demonstrates, have given rise to further interdisciplinary research—both quantitative and qualitative—commissioned either with the purpose of supplying data useful to policy making or for academic purposes or more often as a combination of both.

In Europe today hundreds of thousands of workers live out their lives in the shadows, as undocumented migrants. In many cases this means that they are denied employment rights, have limited or no rights to healthcare[1], are forced to live apart from their families or, where they do manage to reunite with them, have difficulty in finding schools for their children or in securing adequate financial or health provision for their families. They may have arrived intending to stay for a short time, as work permit holders, students, holiday makers, or tourists, but then found that their situations changed as they began to organise their new lives, perhaps meeting partners, establishing new friendships, and developing new visions, all of which would make a return to a previous life difficult. They may also have had long and arduous pathways to Europe, relying on smugglers to arrange their journeys and in the process creating debts which they then find they may never be able to re-pay. They rarely feature in public debates, other than when linking their presence to criminality and illegality, and it is precisely for this reason that we have rejected the use of the term 'illegal' in relation to undocumented migrants, noting that it is perhaps not coincidental, that during the Nazi period it was a term used in relation to Europe's Jewish populations. Defining people as illegal removes elements of their humanity and sends out messages that discrimination and exploitation against such peoples is not of the same calibre as when the same actions are applied to those who are 'legal'. This is why in our research we have chosen to use the term 'undocumented' to describe a variety of experiences relating to the presence of foreign citizens on the territory of a state, in violation of the regulations on entry or of continued residence. It has been argued that the term is ambiguous, as it refers both to migrants who have not been documented (recorded) and to those without documents (passports, etc.), but for us it has been important to capture the diverse experiences that contribute to a person being 'undocumented' while utilising a vocabulary that does not stigmatise individuals whose status is a consequence of the absence of alternatives. Although policy frameworks concerning immigration and migrant regularisation operate both at national and EU level, our research demonstrates that defining 'illegality' or 'illegal status' is not a straightforward question but is linked to the legislative changes that may occur in each country. Moreover, considering that there has only been limited research on the scope and process of irregular migration in the EU, further complexities may arise in attempts at defining who is an 'illegal' migrant. So long as states remain antagonistic to migration, other than when it is believed to serve particular economic interests, it is inevitable that some migrants will try to circumvent the rules and no number of border controls appear capable of completely halting undocumented migration—in Europe, North America, or indeed anywhere in the world—where the advantages that migration brings appear to outweigh the disadvantages that undocumented status confers. In our view it is states that play a crucial role in socially constructing status, through policies of inclusion and exclusion. However, what we have concluded from our research is that these conditions of status are not fixed and that from the many migrants that we have interviewed, both in the Undocumented Workers' Transitions research and in other research (both individually and collectively), we have established that the immigration status attached to individuals is not constant. In more than 200 in-depth interviews conducted with migrant workers in the course of the our study, more than seven in ten had experienced at least one status transition, and some had gone from one status to another more than once, with at least one in five having had documented status before losing it. This has strengthened our conclusion that the status an individual holds is not cemented, in a sense that someone is consistently either documented or undocumented. More often than not they will have shifted between 'documented', 'semi-documented', and 'undocumented' (or what Ruhs and Anderson (2006) refer to as 'compliant', 'semi-compliant', and 'non-compliant'). What we show is that migration status is much more fluid and that many migrants experience changes in their status throughout their period of migration. They may start as documented and fall into undocumented status when a permission to work or a residence permission ends, but equally they may move from undocumented to documented status due to a change in their own personal circumstances (for example, marriage) or a change in the legal regulations permitting migration. As a national expert, commenting to us on the situation in Italy with regard to status, noted:

> Obtaining a residence permit does not necessarily mean escaping illegality: the introduction of the 'residence contract' which demands the satisfaction of specific contractual and residential requirements, has made it far easier to lose one's residence permit and therefore fall back into illegality. (Italy, trade union official)

In other words, what we have conclusively found is that the concept of the 'documented' and the 'undocumented' as being two separate and distinct categories of migrant is flawed and that the focus of states on the 'undocumented' ignores the changeable character of status. In Chapter 3 we place our theory on transitions within a discussion of migration theory in general and of undocumented migration in particular. To do this we first turned to earlier theories on migration, which we have suggested have been premised on attempting to find answers as to why individuals migrate, and it is instructive that it was really not until about 40 years ago that researchers started to try to present an analysis of what happened to migrants within Europe once they had migrated.

For the overwhelming majority of Europe's undocumented migrants it is not a desire to engage in illegal activities that caused their migration, but the combination of unacceptable conditions in their countries of origin and of state policies in their countries of destination that have restricted rights of entry. Our central argument in this book is that workers do not 'seek' to be undocumented. They have to take the legal regime as they find it and as long as states, where opportunities are believed to exist for work and for better prospects, put up barriers that prevent migrants from entering or remaining with permission, some individuals will take whatever routes are available to them. We should not therefore be surprised when we find that false documents are bought by those seeking to better their lives and those of their families through migration. Nor should we be astonished that criminal elements might seek to benefit from the desperation of those seeking such a new life; or that those without the right documents end up working in the informal economies of Europe, beyond the reaches of the tax and social security authorities, but also outside of the protection of other regulatory bodies, like those dealing with health and safety and minimum wages. And, for precisely these same reasons, undocumented migrants are more likely than not to be outside of the areas of influence of trade unions and other collective bodies, making them particularly vulnerable to exploitation by employers, landlords, co-workers and even co-ethnics (Erdemir and Vasta, 2007). Policymakers can address all of these issues but only if they accept that how migration occurs cannot just be on the basis of a set programme determined to satisfy the declared interests of the host country but that undocumented migration will continue to occur, regardless of the attempts by states to exclude or return those without permission to remain. Arguments as to their numbers, whether they are increasing or decreasing, deflect from developing an appropriate and inclusive policy for dealing with those who are here and with those who, whatever the legal regime, will continue to come. This also means that governments need to consider how their own policies—for example, those that have led to the lack of adequate provision for the care of the young, the sick, and the elderly; the privatisation of previously public services; the subcontracting out of all but core activities in many large companies—have created a 'market' for a new army of workers, in increasingly fragmented employment situations, with 'employers' who either do not want to protect them or who do not have the means or the organisation to do so.

We want in this book to recount the experiences of those who are undocumented and to present their stories as told to us. Our specific focus is on their working lives, to bring to the surface that which is more often than not hidden and not admitted, to make it possible to better understand why it is that in Europe today (and, in particular, in Western Europe, in one of the richest regions of the world) some workers earn less than €4 an hour,[2] forcing them to work for long hours in appalling conditions, ensuring that our food gets picked, packed, delivered, and cooked and that the supermarkets can keep prices low in a never-ending spiral of competition; that our homes and offices are not only built and maintained, but are also cleaned; that our children, our sick, and our elderly relatives are looked after; and that our clothes are stitched in dimly lit factories that sit silently in many of Europe's major cities.

The book draws mainly from a two-year study that we undertook between 2007 and 2009. The study, Undocumented Workers' Transitions (UWT), was funded by the European Commission and brought together researchers from seven EU Member State countries which, in different ways, all 'hosted' undocumented migrants. The seven countries were selected to represent varied histories of migration and of undocumented migration in particular. Two of the countries—Belgium and the UK—had colonial histories that had resulted in early migration to them, initially from citizens of their 'empires' and later from migrants more generally. Two of the countries—Austria and Denmark—had also experienced the arrival of migrant workers over many decades. For the remaining three countries—Bulgaria, Italy, and Spain—their experiences of migration were different. Prior to the fall of the Soviet Union there had been limited inwards migration to Bulgaria, and equally its citizens had limited points of exit. Migration, in the form that we acknowledge it today, has been a more a recent phenomenon there, with little existing migration research and with a very limited amount of credible statistical data. Furthermore many of the migrants who were interviewed in Bulgaria perceived themselves to be relatively temporary migrants, looking for the occasion to move further westwards, to countries where they believed that the opportunities were greater. Italy and Spain, in contrast, were countries that had in the past identified themselves with emigration, as generations had left seeking better lives in the Americas or in Northern Europe. However, in the last 20 years, both countries had experienced a large-scale increase in migration, fuelled by a combination of job availability, geographies that assisted access, and legal systems which were initially less structured around the desire to keep migrants out.

Whereas these brief histories might lead to the assumption that what we found, in relation to undocumented migration, would differ widely, the more startling fact is how similar the situation was for those who were undocumented in the seven countries. In terms of country of origin, although there might be differences—for example, larger proportions of migrants from Turkey in Austria and from South East Asia in the UK—what work they performed, and the conditions under which they did this, was remarkably similar. In the seven countries we found that those who were not fully documented were more likely to be working informally and in terms of sectors were more likely to be working in caring, construction, catering, agriculture, and food production. In terms of occupation, the overwhelming majority were in exceptionally low-paid jobs, usually jobs which are regarded as 'low skilled'.

The pre-existence of informal economies also interacts with undocumented migration, and we know that the size/importance of informal economies in different European states affects the size/nature of undocumented migration. Our data confirms that whereas many migrant workers, both documented and undocumented, begin their employment in the destination country by working in the informal economy, for those who are undocumented this remains a sole source of employment throughout their migration. For us it is apparent that the existence of the informal economy is structural, operating within a co-reliant formal economy and that similar patterns of working arrangements operate in many EU Member States, suggesting there are specific production processes that are reliant on undocumented labour. These include fixed processes that are difficult to programme for (as in construction); the outsourcing of welfare (as in elder care); as well as the pre-existence of an informal sector within which local and migrant labour is absorbed. At the same time there are contradictory forces at play. In some sectors undocumented labour is sought out precisely because it is considered as flexible and disposable. However, it is also required for stable and long-term employment, in those sectors (like caring) where working conditions may be poor but where long-term employment relationships are highly prized.

There is currently an extensive and wide-ranging debate, both in the national states and at EU level, on the issue of undocumented migrants. In broad terms the focus has been in portraying the phenomenon as a problem that needs to be managed through stricter border controls and return policies, with, as we will show, a turn away from policies that are aimed at regularisation and at the integration of those who are already in the territory or that provided for some a right of entry for jobs that were defined as 'low skilled'. Thus we hear regularly of plans by states to remove even basic healthcare rights from those who are undocumented and to imprison and to forcibly remove, if necessary. And yet these debates take place at the same time as the EU has formally adopted a Charter of Fundamental Rights which commits it to respect for family life (Art. 3); to the right to pursue a freely chosen and accepted occupation (Art. 15); and which gives specific protection to young workers (Art. 23). These can only be viewed as empty protections, when the conditions of life and of work and the characteristics of undocumented migrants are taken into account.

At the same time, the long-term application of strict migration controls, in combination with the increasing number of persons migrating in search of work, has led to the portrayal of migrants as breaking the law or as those that take advantage of 'liberal' policies so as to claim asylum. This results in both undocumented migrants and asylum seekers being stigmatised as unwanted or problematic migrants. This of itself has consequences, as it provides potential employers with a rationale for the exploitation of such workers. Moreover, it provides the media with an excuse to focus on the undocumented and on asylum seekers, as those who are taking away jobs from local people and who are thus not deserving of support, consideration, or even compassion. As a result, these policies have contributed to the violation of the rights of the migrants concerned, to an increase in racism and xenophobia, and at the same time, ironically, to the strengthening of smuggling and trafficking networks which take advantage of the market for 'flexible employment' and of the need of people to migrate.

The world has changed in many ways since Europeans began to migrate to North America more than 200 years ago and these changes, including new communications and transportation systems, mean that migration does not appear to be associated with the same sense of loss as it has been in previous periods. The notion that migrants can maintain their links with countries of origin are highlighted in the literature on transnational theory, but we question whether, for those who are undocumented, transnationalism can have the same positive meanings, when transport systems may seemingly permit relatively easy travel back and forth but where status means that those who have migrated cannot risk a journey to their country of origin, as the likelihood of return is slight.

As a consequence we have come to the conclusion that state policies, which formally should guarantee the fundamental rights of those within their territories, actively promote the creation of a group of people without social security or fundamental rights (Düvell, 2006) resulting in a pool of workers with sub-standard or no rights and thus obliged to accept work under the most precarious conditions and removed from any labour rights legislation. Of course this does not occur in a vacuum. Undocumented migration in Europe has been on the rise since the early 1980s, as the result of state policies tightening rights of entry to third-country nationals combined with neo-liberal economic policies which have promoted the de-regularisation of the labour market. These operate alongside changes within the labour market, with the promotion of new forms of work organisation, such as outsourcing, subcontracting, flexibility, and casualisation. One outcome is the growth of informal sectors of the economy, even in those countries, like Denmark, the UK, and Austria, where previously informal working was relatively rare. At the same time they have encouraged employers to constantly search for even cheaper and more 'flexible' labour, and by this we mean workers who are willing to work whenever and wherever the employer needs them. Importantly, this permanent search for lower cost labour means that where it cannot be found in the home country, capital is always ready to move its production to another country where labour is seen as cheaper. Indeed the sectors where undocumented migrants are employed within Europe are precisely those (e.g., construction, caring, catering, and agriculture) where the work itself cannot easily be physically re-located.

Most EU Member States have introduced sanctions on employers who knowingly employ undocumented migrants and as we show later in the book, there is now also similar regulation at EU level. Employers use the existence of sanctions as a justification for paltry pay and unacceptable working conditions. Thus although technically it is employers who take risks in employing undocumented migrants, their risks are transferred to the workers they employ, as low pay is their 'insurance' against a possible raid by the immigration authorities; in other words they aim to 'bank' the difference in pay between that provided to the undocumented and that which they might have had to pay to the documented, so that they can cover the costs of any potential sanctions on them. As Bacon asserts, 'workers have paid the price for the enforcement of employer sanctions, not employers' (Bacon, 2008:6). We detail a number of cases where employers seem to adopt such a strategy that, in some cases, can even go as far as indicating to workers that a raid is likely, so as to encourage them to flee before they have been paid for work they have already performed.

We have also felt it important to place current migration within its historical context, and it is for this reason that we have first turned to look at migration in a European historical perspective. Our aim has been to highlight the fact that migration is not a new experience for Europe and at the same time to emphasise that citizens of European states have, through most of their history, been migrants themselves, migrating to North and South America, to Africa, and to South East Asia and Oceania. Indeed the largest migrations of peoples from the mid 19th century to the early period of the 20th century were undertaken by European migrants seeking better lives elsewhere. At the same time what we need to stress is that in theorising their own migrations, Europeans have tended to define them as adventurers and as providing positive experiences, not just for themselves but also for the peoples of the worlds that they reached. Of course this was not necessarily the case, but it does demonstrate a gap between perceptions of emigration and of immigration.

Additionally we wanted to highlight the experiences of women in relation to migration. With the notable exception of a few researchers whom we have referenced in this work, women have been absent from the study of migration, in particular in relation to their employment histories. We were determined to hear the voices of women, as well as those of men, and to understand how legal status affects them. We note the increasing feminisation of undocumented migration and that it is precisely the changes that we have referred to above, with regard to the production of labour, that have created a market for gender-specific work. We also discuss the nature of such work models in relation to family and care in different EU countries and note how migration is shaped by these, what the implications are, and also under what circumstances it differs from that of men. We suggest that for women, migration can be a trap but it can also be a release from the tightened constraints imposed on them, so that it presents an even more contradictory dilemma than it does for male migrants. We also found that women migrants experience migration in a different way and that for them undocumented status brings particular disadvantages, in trapping them in 'out of sight' work where access to external support and advice is non-existent. On the other hand, these forms of 'hidden' working may be thought to offer greater protection from detection by immigration authorities. What we have found is that both men and women reside as undocumented, as well as documented, migrants in Europe today but that within the labour market they occupy discrete roles which mirror those of women and male workers generally, with women being segregated into low-paid work in a limited number of sectors. Thus for women workers, migration does not provide the opportunities to escape from gender segregated employment, and indeed these gender divisions are re-inforced. Where there are specific differences between the genders is in relation to what happens when they do change status, in particular from undocumented to documented.

Whereas for male workers such a transition appears to bring economic and other advantages, in the longer term if not in the immediate aftermath, for women workers, achieving legal status does not seem to permit exit from the trap of work in those sectors peopled by undocumented workers, at least according to our findings.

We could not consider the position of women without also looking at the position of undocumented families, and our research has shown that the consequences of being undocumented has a profound impact on all family members, not just on adult wage earners. Undocumented migrants with children are even more susceptible to labour market exploitation and are more constrained in the choices they can make in relation to work. We have also found more cases of female lone parent migrating, as a means of supporting their children, but that this creates emotional and financial distress, greater than that experienced by male migrants, both due to the nature of their caring relationships with their children and due to the more limited job opportunities they have access to in the destination countries.

We also need to make it clear that ethnicity, country of origin and class, as well as gender, impact on the lives of undocumented workers. In particular, their employment experiences are differentiated, depending on their ethnic origin. Indeed it is clear that racism allocates undocumented status principally to those who are visibly different, whereas for those who appear to share physical characteristics (primarily skin colour) assumptions are more likely to be made that their status is regular. This means that they fall beneath the radar of state intervention and are more able to live their lives in a way that is relatively undifferentiated from that of legally resident migrants. One of those whom we interviewed for our research made the point that due to his forged French passport and the fact that he was blond and with a 'white' complexion and dressed 'like the people of Paris', no one took him to be from Algeria and he therefore had been able to work in sectors where other North African migrants would not have been accepted. We also know that states tend to target those who are visibly different, as evidenced in raids on ethnic-minority-owned businesses in several of the countries in our study, together with an absence of effective state protection in cases of physical attacks on visibly different workers, such as in Southern Italy in early 2010. Analysing our interview data demonstrates that racism colours the experiences of undocumented migrants and that black migrants are more vulnerable to deportation and therefore more 'willing' to work under whatever conditions are obtainable. Furthermore we believe that employers are all too aware of this and utilise it to their advantage.

In the chapters that follow we put flesh to these ideas. We describe the current regulatory systems in Europe as they apply to undocumented migrants and set out the significant range of controls, either operating in relation to undocumented migrants or being considered. We believe that one of the outcomes of the EU's focus on undocumented migrants has been to weaken the powers of national states to set their own priorities in relation to migration. They also have encouraged the institution of systems of control which have implications for all EU residents, as they potentially enable states to monitor us all. In our concluding chapter we draw together our ideas that have emerged from the project and consider what the options for the future are for undocumented migrants in Europe.

2 Migration in a European Historical Perspective

> One of the central ways in which the link between the people and the state is expressed is through the rules governing citizenship and naturalisation.
>
> (Castles and Miller, 2009:16)

The importance of the nation state in determining who is part of it and who is not, as the above quote suggests, is highly relevant to any study of migration. However, migration is not a new phenomenon of social life nor was it one that was the subject of significant state controls and regulations before the start of the 20th century. This point is of specific relevance to the undocumented migration of today, as it is not only part of an overall migratory movement but, we would assert, is the direct result of such controls and regulations. For us, therefore, it has been important to begin by focusing on the key reasons for such a change. How did migration policies move from being very limited in their scope, to the restrictions that we see today? Could the aims of states to limit entry for very specific groups of workers, be seen as solely serving the short-term interests of the labour market? The chapter therefore discusses the main types of migratory movements occurring in the 20th and early 21st centuries, although to place this in its context we also provide a brief overview of migration throughout European history. We have concentrated mainly on European developments, but within the wider context of international migration. We demonstrate that although European policy today is based on keeping people out, for most of their own history Europeans were themselves migrants. As the subject of migration covers many and complicated aspects, we have focused on what we see as the most significant developments that help us in understanding the concept of undocumented migration today.

The chapter specifically focuses on irregular migration from a perspective that views undocumented status as a socially constructed notion, put in place by states to control the number and typologies of entry. And as we shall see in Chapter 5, today there are concentrated efforts by governments to regulate migration at a time that when the irregular movement of people is also high (Castles and Miller, 2009). This poses further difficulties, as whereas the literature on the history of migration is rich, there are limited resources that provide a robust historical background on irregular migration.

Within these limitations and as we shall see later in this chapter, European history of migration consists of two major trends: emigration towards most parts of the world mainly through various forms of colonisation and immigration consisting of inter-European movements of population, as well as migration from outside Europe. Both of these trends have contributed to the policies and general developments of European migration since 1945 and can be distinguished into two broad periods. First are the post-war mass labour migrations of the 1950s to the mid 1970s. These are represented both in migrations within Europe—for example, from Italy to Germany and from the developing world mainly towards Western Europe but also to America, Australia, and New Zealand. This period came to an end with the oil crisis in the mid 1970s. The second period starts from the mid 1970s. This represented a new economic phase globally and in Europe. It has also been a period of rapid political change, especially in Central and Eastern Europe after the 1990s. As a consequence, relatively new migratory patterns have risen, to include the migration (mainly labour focused but not exclusively so) of Central and East Europeans to other European countries, primarily to the EU15 countries of Western and Southern Europe.[1] From the mid 1990s onwards and for the first time, EU Member States located in Southern Europe became the destination choice for migrants, both within the new enlarged Europe as well as for third-country nationals, principally from South America, Africa, and South East Asia. This has constituted a new feature in European migration, as until the 1970s the countries of the Mediterranean were themselves major labour suppliers. Furthermore, the increase in migration movements can be considered as the result of globalisation and the deregulation of the markets, drawing migrant workers, both skilled and unskilled, from outside Europe to seek employment. Finally, political unsettlement in various parts of the world has forced many people to leave and seek asylum in Europe, although this type of migration is neither new nor a particular characteristic for this period only.

A SHORT HISTORICAL BACKGROUND OF EUROPEAN MIGRATION

Throughout history, migration has been a feature of human societies, as for most of our history humans led mainly a nomadic life and the search for food or new resources was the primary motivation for finding new and habitable areas. As populations spread and more permanent settlements started to develop, migration continued to take place, often through more complex patterns of warfare and conquests, slavery and colonialism (for example, Greek or Roman in the ancient period), epidemics or religious opposition (such as the Iconoclasts fleeing the Byzantine Empire).

Similar reasons for migrating populations can also be found in later periods. So in the middle ages and before the industrial revolution four main causes of migration can be distinguished. First, religion, either in the form of religious persecutions or due to the constitution of new religious sects, became the cause of movements of populations within Europe or the emigration of Europeans to America, but also to other parts of the world. For example, the rise of Protestantism through the reformist movements of Luther and Calvin were embraced as a new religion in some European countries but suppressed in others, depending on the preferences of the monarchs. Thus between the 15th and 17th century, religious refugees such as the Huguenots in France, the Protestant Dutch from the South, and the Jews and Moors of Southern Spain (to name but a few) escaped to countries where Catholicism was not the official religion. Religious migration also took place to areas outside Europe, such as the Purists' movement to America or the secondary migration of the Huguenots to South Africa.

The next three types of migration closely relate to the Mercantilist period (which extends beyond the 17th century) and includes economic migration, colonialism, and slavery. First, this is a period of general changes in Europe with a pronounced effect on economic systems. Political and economic transformations were closely related to ideas that gave rise to the new political landscapes, with the creation of nation states as a predominant form of government unit, together with the concept of national sovereignty. This period is characterised by economic expansion and at the same time by the growing intervention of the state apparatus in the national economy.

During this period the demand for labour became the key to economic development, and policies were introduced to prevent people from migrating to other states while at the same time migration from other European countries was encouraged as a strategy to gain additional labour but also to deprive competitors of their own labour (Moses, 2006). Apart from artisan labour, attracting and developing trade became also a strategy to promote further economic migration of the merchant class, especially in central European countries. For example during this period a significant merchant Greek Diaspora was established in cities across the Danube but also in Britain and France.

Second, this period was characterised by intense competition by the main powers such as the Netherlands and Britain and led to the search and exploitation of new resources. Economic and military/naval superiority led to the colonisation of lands in all continents. The main type of European immigration during this period was the emigration of Europeans towards Africa and Asia at first, followed by America and Australia and New Zealand (Oceania) at a later stage. European emigration was either permanent or temporary and included farmers, sailors, traders, administrators, and so forth, not all of whom were nationals of the colonial powers, but included transnationals from other European countries, such as Germans who migrated to the British or Dutch colonies in order to escape poverty (Castles and Miller, 2009:8).

The third type of migration, which came as a consequence of colonialism, was slavery and was used by colonialists as forced labour for plantation and mines in the New World, for the production of tobacco, coffee, cotton, sugar, and the mining of gold. Slavery was used from the late 17th century to mid 19th century and benefited all the colonial powers, but predominately Britain and France and secondarily Spain, the Netherlands, and Portugal. Slaves were either abducted or bought from local traders and then shipped and sold in the Americas. The money was used to buy the commodities (also produced by the slaves) which were then sold in Europe. Overall, millions of Africans were shipped to America and the Caribbean during this period. Slavery as a phenomenon has existed at various stages of human history but the way that the slave trade was organised during this period, the use of racism to justify its existence, and the use of slaves for the creation of new (international) markets is what distinguishes it from previous experiences. Ultimately, it can be argued that slavery has served as the basis of a new economic system and defined current structures of both the economy and society (Castles and Miller, 2009).

EUROPEAN MIGRATION BETWEEN THE LATE 19TH CENTURY AND 1945

The wealth acquired by the colonies and the slave labour led to the industrial revolutions of the 18th and 19th century, in Britain first, followed by other European states a little later. Industrialisation created new economic and labour structures within the states which witnessed mass population movements at national level, as vast numbers of their rural populations left the countryside and moved to industrial cities in search of work. Mass population movements also occurred at European level during this period, as for example Italian immigration to France which gradually grew to reach over 400,000 in 1911 (Bade, 2003). German industrialisation was assisted by over 700,000 foreign labourers such as Poles, Italians, Dutch, and Belgians. Similarly, German, Swedish, and Polish migration occurred in Denmark, while the needs of agriculture in Spain led to inter-regional migration—for example, Catalonian—but also migration from abroad.

Despite the technological advancements, the development of transportation which enabled high mobility, and the work opportunities created by the new industries in Europe, the supply of labour soon superseded that of demand, coupled with a rapid increase in the European population. Unemployment was high and wages very low while recent evidence suggests the extensive use of unpaid child labour as a means of maximising profit (Humphries, 2010). Poverty became widespread, especially in urban cities, and grew disproportionately in size, creating the infamous slums, for example, those in Victorian Britain, whose unsanitary living conditions are vividly recounted in the literature of Dickens in that period.

While European societies were going through transformations from agrarian to industrial economic structures, some at a faster pace than others, economic developments in America led to an increasing demand for workers. The emigration movement from Europe to America that took place throughout the 19th century but concentrated predominately in the later part of the 19th and early 20th century was one of the largest in modern history. This was a period of a world proletariat labour movement that was incorporated in the process of the development of American capitalism which followed the end of civil war (Tsoukalas, 1977). Paradoxically, what enabled this journey were the technological advances of the industrial revolutions that had improved transportation, making long journeys possible for a large number of passengers. The British and the Germans, in the first half of the 19th century, were the first to emigrate to America, followed by the Irish, Spanish, Italians, Jews, Greeks, as well as Greeks from the collapsing Ottoman Empire, and other nationalities from Central and Eastern Europe and the Middle East from the 1850s to the 1920s. America promoted itself as the new land of opportunity and hope with free movement attracting many who sought to improve their futures. European migrants were employed in many sectors: in the heavy steel industry in the North, agriculture in the South, and railways in the North West. Migration to America also included women who migrated as a family, or as young brides, but also as workers. Like men, women worked in factories or ran small businesses, but they also found employment in the care and support sectors. Vecchio's (2006) account of Italian women midwives in the late 19th century is one example of the independent migration of women.

Despite the promotion of America as a haven for migrants from all over the world, in reality work and living conditions were far from favourable and workers from different ethnic groups regularly experienced racism and xenophobia, especially if they came from outside Europe (for example, Chinese workers who worked predominately in the railways). But also Catholics and Jews from Europe and people who had come from Central and Eastern Europe or from the Middle East were the targets of 'nativist' groups, including the notorious Ku Klux Klan. There were many clashes, and racist groups were actively anti-migrant. Such attitudes were also reflected in legislation introduced in the US after World War 1 (WW1), namely, the National Origin Act of 1921, whose purpose was the restriction of migration other than to migrants from Northern and Western European states.

At the same time, the intensification of work in factories, as production increased during this period, and the extensive use of migrant labour also led to the demand for better working conditions and improved pay. Migrant workers actively participated in the labour movement and supported its demands by taking part in strikes. American labour activists, such as Elizabeth Gurley Flynn (the daughter of Irish immigrants herself) organised workers in factories, restaurants, and mines to take part in strikes or to otherwise support the labour movement. Similarly, Eugene Debs, an American union leader and a socialist, who was arrested and sentenced to 10 years' imprisonment under the 1917 Espionage Act, had chosen Canton,

Ohio, to make an anti-war speech urging people to resist military draft. Canton at the time was a town with a heavy steel industry relying mainly on a migrant labour force who were either drafted to the war or worked in an industry that was covering the needs of the war.

From 1918 Onwards

Migration before World War 1 (WW1) and during the interwar period, within and from Europe, followed unpredictable patterns that reflected the general political and economic climate of the time. The main characteristic of this period included a mainly inter-European movement of population, as vast numbers of people were displaced due to the two wars, ideological and political persecutions, racism, the use of forced labour, exchanges of population, or as a result of civil wars. The 20th century is often characterised in the relevant literature as the 'century of refugees'. Another form relates to European states with a colonial past whose power was weakened as their colonies sought and gained independence. Colonial related migration towards Europe included the return of the colonialist population to their countries of origin but also local people who came to Europe as soldiers, as labourers, and in some cases as citizens, for example to the UK and to France, Belgium, and the Netherlands.

Almost every country in Europe was actively involved in the two world wars and even those that remained neutral, such as Ireland, were affected by the unsettling economic and political climate. According to Kennan (1957), at least eight million soldiers and 10 million civilians were the direct or indirect victims of the 20th century wars (cited in Bade, 2003:166). During WW1 and World War 2 (WW2), intensified programmes for the recruitment of soldiers took place throughout Europe at national level and from outside Europe, mainly in the colonies. For example, an estimated 60 million Europeans served in the armies and navies between 1914 and 1918. In Germany almost 80 per cent of the male adult population of serving age was recruited (20 per cent of the total population), in France over seven million, in Russia up to the revolution of 1917 around 15 million, and in Britain over six million (Bade, 2003). Britain and France used their colonies as an additional source for the recruitment of soldiers. In France, African soldiers were used not only for the wars in Africa but also for those in Europe. Britain recruited mainly from India.

Recruitment from the colonies took place also during WW2. Britain produced a series of propaganda posters aimed at attracting recruits from West Africa. Images of slavery were widely used as the theme: 'Britain is your friend and believes in progress for all. Germany is your enemy and believes in slavery for all non-Germans'. The poster portrays a British soldier shaking hands with an African man and a German soldier whipping an African man who is lying on the ground (National Archives, 2008). It is estimated that over four million men and women from the British colonies volunteered service to both WW1 and WW2 (Rogers, 2002). Women from the colonies were recruited and served in Women's Auxiliary Air Force (WAAF) and the Auxiliary Territorial Service (ATS).

In terms of labour migration during the interwar years, there was an overall reduction in international migration, not only in Europe but also in the US. Following the Great Depression of the 1930s, European and American economies stagnated and this led to very high unemployment levels for both existing migrants and indigenous workers. Competition for the few existing jobs gave rise to hostile attitudes regarding the use of foreign labour. Nationalist movements became once more active, and 'aliens' were treated as a threat[2] while racism was often targeted towards specific groups, for example, towards Southern Europeans in America. A more isolationist political climate started to appear, as state intervention and regulation increased during this period and tough controls and quota systems were introduced in order to control people's movements and limit the flows of migration. In post-revolutionary Russia, restrictions on emigration were introduced through complicated bureaucratic processes (rather than an official ban on emigration) (Bade, 2003) as labour demands were high for the accelerated industrialisation programme that was taking place. In Italy, controls were also imposed, as cross-border migration was perceived by the Italian fascist government as a national disgrace that undermined national economic development (Bade, 2003). One exception was France which, having suffered heavy war losses, became the only country in Europe to allow substantial numbers of foreign migrants from Poland, Italy, and Czechoslovakia, as well as North Africa. Even in this case, a system of migration controls was introduced and linked to specific recruitment requirements (Castles and Miller, 2009).

However, during the wars, mass conscription programmes and war losses led temporarily to severe labour shortages in the weakened European economies. Women and young people were employed to fill in the gap, but the pressure was too high and as a consequence governments sought to recruit foreign labour. Companies started to recruit from other European countries but also from overseas. For example, France and Britain recruited from their colonies, and in the case of France labour recruitment also involved countries from Southern Europe such as Greece, Italy, Spain and Portugal. During this time there was also a widespread practice for the use of the forced labour of prisoners of war (Castles and Miller, 2009). In Germany, the Nazi regime extensively used forced foreign labour mainly from the occupied countries. People were moved by force to work at many locations in Germany, but they were kept isolated as the highly racialised regime ensured that they should avoid contact with local German citizens. It was estimated that in 1944 there were almost eight million foreign workers in Germany from 26 different countries; two million prisoners of war and six million civilians were all working in the German war effort (Bade, 2003:206).

Refugees (Ethnic/Religious)

One consequence of the two world wars in Europe was the vast shift of the populations that occurred as borders were being redrawn. Forced movements for parts of the population followed, and as a consequence of political or racial persecutions many people were left stateless. At the end of the 1914–1918 war, the League of Nations called an international conference in 1920 which made a number of recommendations especially with regard to the passport system, which for example, in the UK had been introduced during WW1 to control borders and emigration for security reasons. According to Moses (2006), these restrictions on immigration that were applied during WW1 constituted the basis for the restrictions that are still in place today in all states, as no state allows free access to migrants.

During WW1, the Ottoman and Hapsburg empires began their decline, and new smaller independent states were formed in Central and Southern Europe, although the process had started almost a century earlier. Ethnicity and the ethnic identity (and not always religion) were at the heart of the building of these new states and came to dominate the redefining of the borders, territories, and populations on the grounds of a common ancestry and a common past.[3] Through this territorial homogenisation, concepts of 'otherness' were re-established through concepts of 'belonging' while sealing the fate of minorities in the Balkans and in areas that were previously part of the Ottoman Empire, sometimes through tragic events such as the massacre of the Armenians and other minorities. And an ethnocentric approach, based on the concept of the 'unmixing of peoples' (Marrus, 1985) also found expression in policy making and international agreements that followed the war.

In the Balkans, WW1 was experienced through the two Balkan Wars. The first started earlier in 1912, the aftermath of which resulted in mass and forced population expulsions. The Greek-Turkish war (1920–1922) ended with the signing of the Lausanne Treaty where over a million Greeks from Turkey and half a million Turks from Greece were forced to leave their homes and to be resettled. Similar exchanges, albeit on a much smaller scale, took place earlier between Greece and Bulgaria (the Neuilly Treaty) while Muslims from Yugoslavia, Romania, and Bulgaria were 'resettled' in Turkey. In Central Europe the new national borders that were erected left some minorities vulnerable, for example, Hungarians in the new Czechoslovak Republic (as Czechs and Slovaks had been in the Austro-Hungarian Empire). The defeated Germans and Hungarians were also affected by the outcome of the war and the Weimar Republic received over a million refugees, about 500,000 to 700,000 of them from Poland, while by 1921 over 200,000 refugees had registered in Hungary (Stola, 1992). It is estimated that over nine million people had been victims of forced migration by the mid 1920s (Bade, 2003:200).

WW2 created an even larger number of refugees, whose estimate reaches 50 to 60 million (Bade, 2003:204). A large number of refugees, mainly from Poland but also from the Netherlands, Belgium, France, Denmark, and Norway, fled their homes to escape the advancing German armies. Some found refuge in Britain or Southern France, using whatever available means of transportation they had. Other refugees included people in the west Soviet Union who either fled the Germans or were relocated to the east, as part of the Hitler-Stalin pact of 1939, or were evacuated by the Soviets to the east or to Siberia on basis of their being accused of collaboration with the Germans. Equally, after the invasion of Yugoslavia by the Germans, many in the local population fled to more isolated parts of the country. At more localised levels, populations were displaced on a smaller scale across central Europe: Hungarians from Romania; Greeks from Thrace and Macedonia, following the Bulgarian occupation; the resettlement of Bulgarians and Romanians, following the Treaty of Craiova (1940); Italians expelled Slovenians from Slovenia; Serbs fled from Croatia. These are just a few examples.

A major feature during both WW1 and WW2 was increasing anti-Semitism in Europe, with the persecution of the Jews resulting in the exterminations in Nazi Germany. However, anti-Jewish feelings were not new in Europe, as Jews had been persecuted in many countries of Europe, for example, in Spain or in Tsarist Russia. Jews in major European cities were forced to live in separate areas, the ghettoes. What was different, especially during WW2, was the systematic and methodical manner of the persecution of Jewish people, who were collected from all German occupied areas and transported to concentration camps where the majority perished. Since Jewish persecutions had started from 1933 onwards, with the rise of Hitler, Jewish men and women had already begun to flee Germany. Neighbouring countries such as Belgium and the Netherlands attempted to stop their entry by legislative means, although by 1938 Jewish refugees were crossing the borders despite the restrictions. The terms 'illegal refugees' or 'illegal entry' were often use by public bodies, journalists, civil servants, or policemen with reference to Jewish refugees in the Netherlands (Van Eijl, 2009). Eventually, some entries were permitted; for example, Jews from Germany and Austria were eventually permitted to enter the UK (although equally many had been barred) while children arrived through the 'Kindertransport' initiative. Some Jewish refugees were resettled in the British colonies, such as in Hong Kong or Cyprus. Other receiving countries for Jews included the United States and Argentina. Responding to the large numbers of German and Austrian refugees escaping the Nazis, the Intergovernmental Committee for Refugees was established to help with the resettlement.

Refugees (Political)

Inter-European movements of population in the first half of the 20th century also included displaced people due to political changes or ideological conflicts (Marrus, 1985). The mobility of political thinkers, theoreticians, or activists was a feature of European cities throughout the 19th and 20th centuries, but the 20th century in particular created the circumstances for the politically related persecutions of individuals or groups of people. Migratory movements occurred in Russia during and immediately after the revolution but ended after restrictions were imposed in the 1920s, although people still crossed the borders illegally seeking asylum in the West until the collapse of the Soviet Union. Russian immigration at this stage consisted initially of members of the aristocracy or Tsarist ruling classes, but people from other social positions that opposed the state also migrated to the West and were accepted as refugees.

Another form of political migration includes political exiles from Germany, Austria, and the German-speaking Czechoslovakia in the period 1933 to 1945, from Italy after Mussolini took power in the period 1922 to 1937, from Spain after 1936, and from Greece after 1949. Most political exiles were intellectuals and activist opponents of the fascist regimes. They found refuge in many European countries but predominately in France and Britain. Most continued their political activities in the host country. Many of the Germans were university professors and scholars expelled from their posts in Germany and who then came to Britain where they took up teaching positions (Bramwell and Marrus, 1988). Others were artists who arrived and stayed for a short period or made cities like London their permanent home.

Finally, as a consequence of the outbreak of civil wars in Europe, a large mass of political refugees was created and there are two principal examples. First, millions of refugees during the Spanish Civil War (1936–1939) fled after Franco's troops, supported by the Nazi regime, began to advance towards the North of the country. Most refugees remained within Spain in the North but over half a million fled across the border to France; some immigrated to Latin America whereas others eventually returned to Spain. Second, the aftermath of the Greek Civil War of 1946–1949 also created around 100,000 political refugees to Eastern Europe following the defeat of the communists. It was not until the 1980s that these political refugees were repatriated.

EUROPEAN MIGRATION 1945–1976

After the end of the WW2, European economies began to grow again rapidly, and the demand for migrant labour to cover shortages increased accordingly. As a result, and in contrast to the migration restrictions imposed in the first half of the 20th century, the period between 1945 and 1976 is characterised by a boom in migration which manifested itself through three major events in European migration history (Castles and Miller, 2009).

First, inter-European migration was encouraged through a programme of guest workers that was introduced by some Western European states to encourage temporary migration at various stages to cover their labour needs after the war. The general idea behind the guest worker schemes was for migrants to come and work for a short period of time and eventually to return to their home country. In some cases countries imposed strict rules to keep migration on a temporary basis, whereas in other cases such rules were not as rigid. However guest worker schemes were aimed at recruiting migrant workers to the lowest skill (or lowest status) jobs and the lowest paid (King, 1995). The main recruitment areas included countries from Southern Europe such as Greece, Italy, Spain, and Portugal and two Northern countries, Ireland and Finland. In Britain, the European Voluntary Worker (EVW) scheme was introduced, again within the framework of strict migration controls, as workers did not have the right to family reunion. In terms of work, the system was inflexible, as migrants were recruited for specific jobs and were tied to these jobs for the duration of their stay. If they did not follow the rules, the penalty was deportation. Over 200,000 workers went to the UK under this scheme in the period 1946 to 1951 (Kay and Miles, 1992).

Germany recruited around four million workers to work in its rapidly expanding industries. The main areas of recruitment included Southern European countries as well as Turkey. The criteria for participation in the schemes included the particular skills of the workers and a successful medical test to prove that they were healthy. Germany imposed rules to keep migration on a temporary basis; however, the number of people recruited was large and in reality it was not possible to prevent family reunion. As a result, large communities became permanent residents. In contrast, France introduced a scheme for Southern Europe to cover labour needs but also to boost its population, as birth rates were particularly low. This meant that the overall purpose was to retain the migrant population by family settlements. Belgium also recruited workers until 1963 for its mining industry through similar schemes which were flexible and allowed workers to bring their families; after a certain period they could migrate without being part of the scheme.

Second, this period coincides with the end of the European colonial age (although, as noted above, the process had commenced before WW2). Migration for people from the ex-colonies became possible as quotas were provided, but many also acquired citizenship. This was most relevant in the case of Britain, France, and the Netherlands. During this period two types of migration took place as a result of decolonisation. First, the return (repatriation) of European descent employees who lived in the colonies as part of the colonial administration and military as well as people of non-European descent who had remained in the service of the colonial powers. It is estimated that around seven million came to Europe from the colonies during this period, from Kenya, Malaysia, and India for Britain; North Africa for France and Italy; the Congo for Belgium; and Indonesia for the Netherlands. The other main type of migration was of people from the colonies who migrated to cover labour shortages but stayed on as residents. In the UK, restrictions were imposed as a means of controlling the flow of these workers, for example, with the introduction of the Commonwealth Immigration Act of 1962. France also experienced migration from its former colonies as people came from Algeria, Morocco, and Tunisia. Like the UK, migration in France was also controlled through bilateral agreements for Algerians. Colonial migrations in France consisted mainly of males, but an increasing number of females also came. Integration between the host and migrant communities was limited, as the populations were segregated in terms of housing. Such divisions continue today.[4]

Third, international migration was encouraged to the US, Australia, Canada, and to a lesser degree to New Zealand to fulfil labour demands or as means to boost population shortages in the case of Australia. But in the later case migrant selection was made on racial grounds with a 'White Australia Policy' in force. Migrants were recruited from Europe, and the criteria for entry included that they had to be anti-communist and 'racially acceptable'. A second criterion was established to admit migrants from Southern Europe and the Baltic, as British migration proved to be on a smaller scale than anticipated (Castles and Mills, 2006). The US adopted a more open and non-discriminatory approach to migration in line with civil rights legislation in 1965 which led to large-scale migration from non-European countries. Similarly the adoption of a points system in Canada during the 1960s also attracted large numbers of non-European migrants (Castles and Mills, 2006:103).

EUROPEAN MIGRATION FROM 1976 ONWARDS

In 1974 a general recession after the oil crisis brought an end to the migration boom of the post-war years. During this period, migration fell sharply in all North European countries. For example, King looking at SOPEMI reports between 1974 and 1990 notes that in the Netherlands and West Germany, migration inflows were halved while outflows of returning migrants increased. In Sweden, the migration situation remained more stable, reflecting a more stable economic situation. In relation to country of origin, migration from Italy, Greece, and Spain decreased while migration from Turkey, non-European countries, and Central and Eastern European countries had started to show an increase in the period 1976 to 1985 (King, 1995). It can be argued that this is the beginning of a fourth phase of migration that starts from the 1980s and continues to today.

Although the conditions and circumstances are different, this migration phase shares certain similarities with past mass movements of population. First, Europe has once more become a main destination of migration while at the same time the issue of migration features high on the political agendas of European states. This is not surprising given historical experiences and concepts that have defined migration in the past. In all seven countries that participated in the UWT project (UWT, 2009), attitudes towards migration had been based on a contradiction: on the one hand additional labour was needed for the European economies due to the demographic changes and the ageing of the population; on the other hand the growth of xenophobia and racism is reflected in the policy of encouraging 'desired' migrants from within the EU while discouraging the entry of third-country nationals (although in the UK, for example, the debate is not usually about migration from Australia, New Zealand, or the US and Canada).

Second, once more there has been a rise in the refugee population, displaced by wars or political systems and thus seeking asylum in Europe. The main difference with the first half of the century is that today's refugees in Europe have mainly come from outside Europe. They have become the topic of policy making, and restrictions have been put in place to 'regulate' asylum. For example in the UK, asylum seekers are not allowed to work or claim benefits and they are forced to survive on very small amounts of welfare (Gentleman, 2010). The restrictions may have had the effect desired, as according to OECD International Migration Data, the number of people seeking asylum in EU countries almost halved in the ten-year period between 1999 and 2009.[5]

As well as similarities there are also some differences between the current period and previous migrations although they differ more on the focus than on the experience itself. First is the increase in the numbers of female migrants and second is the current emphasis placed by the state authorities on irregular migration.

Female Migration

Female migration is not solely a contemporary phenomenon and as we have already noted, women have always travelled as part of their family unit, as potential brides but also by themselves to search for a job. Yet, it was only recently that a gendered approach to migration became a subject of study within the social sciences:

> Only by the 1970s, feminist historians of migration were engaged not only in developing a critique of a scholarly literature that treated all immigrants as genderless men but were participating also in a number of interdisciplinary dialogues. Some were busy uncovering immigrant women's voices through oral historical methods consolidating their ties to the humanities, literature, and activist agendas for empowering women through consciousness raising. (Sinke, 2006:85)

During the 1950s and 1960s the majority of migrant workers who participated in guest worker schemes in Northern Europe were male. Female migrants followed later through family reunification programmes and usually they did not have the right to work. What is different in the current period is that female migration has reached more or less the same level as male migration (see Chapter 9). Moreover, a large number of female migrants initiate migration by themselves. OECD data for 2004 shows that the numbers of migrants by gender are almost equal if not slightly higher for women in two thirds of OECD countries (OECD, 2006).

We discuss female migration in Chapters 9 and 10 and suggest that the existing segregation of jobs by gender tends to favour women in terms of employment. What is not favourable is the work conditions and their low pay and defined low skills. Such jobs, for example in the domestic sector, tend to be more isolated and, together with the overall xenophobic attitudes in the receiving societies, may make women more vulnerable to social exclusion.

Despite this isolation, migrant women, both European and third-country nationals, have become active within unions or migrant associations to demand their rights and better working conditions. This is true also for women with irregular status who are more at risk when they start to become visible through their actions (Freedman, 2008). For example, in France when the sans-papiers started the occupation of the Saint-Ambroise church in 1996, women had a very large and visible presence among the occupants (Freedman, 2008).

Irregular Migration

Despite the emphasis placed by the authorities, irregularity is not a feature exclusive to our contemporary societies and, as this examination of the history of migration in Europe has demonstrated, migration status is very volatile. A migrant can become 'illegal' through changes in the law, introduced to satisfy political agendas with little or no consideration of their impact on individuals' lives.

Stateless refugees were exposed to the same vulnerabilities as today's undocumented migrants when mass refugee movements took place across Europe as a result of the 1939–1945 war or the racist persecutions by the Nazis in the case of Jews from 1933 onwards. The 'solution' was through the issuing of a stateless person's passport or, as it came to be known, 'the Nansen passports', named after the founder of the idea who was also a High Commissioner in the League of Nations in 1922.

"Illegality" has also been linked to racial notions of inferiority used in policy making. One example mentioned by Schrover, Van der Leun, Lucassen, and Quispel (2008) is that of Chinese workers who migrated to California during the Gold Rush and were resented by white workers who put a lot of pressure on the relevant authorities to exclude them from the labour market. As a result the America Chinese Exclusion Act of 1882 was introduced and until 1943 made it illegal for Chinese workers to immigrate unless they fulfilled certain criteria. And to this extent it has been argued that the concept of 'illegality' in Europe, which defines who should be included and who should be excluded, is also constructed around racialist assumptions. It has also, of course, been historically linked to the nation-building process of European states, mainly following WW1 and the interwar period but also the decolonisation period for European states with colonies.

It is easy to be mistaken and believe that the current mass migration movement, which has been linked to the processes of globalisation by many thinkers, is a unique phenomenon of our current society. The chapter has shown that this is far from true, as migratory movements have taken place throughout the centuries across Europe, in the forms of immigrations and emigrations. The main reasons for mass population movements have been identified as economic, religious, or political. Migratory movements have been also distinguished between voluntary, when individuals or groups of individuals decided to seek a better life elsewhere or to take advantage of opportunities on a short-term basis or forced through slavery, colonisation, persecution, and expulsion. European populations have experienced all of these in different periods.

CONCLUSION

The main purpose of the chapter has been to review the main historical moments of such migration movements in the history of Europe but also to link them to developments outside Europe. The chapter acts as an introduction to our account of undocumented migration in Europe, and for this reason there has been a focus on the way illegality has been constructed by states in historical terms. It has been argued that the concept of 'illegality' is relatively new and was advanced at particular moments of history as a means to exclude 'othernesses'. It has also been argued that there has never been a fixed policy on 'illegality' and that legislation prohibiting or limiting migration has been introduced whenever it was perceived as advantageous for any state. Nevertheless, following WW2 we can observe a common position wherein states adopt legislative and security systems to control their borders and limit the free movement of populations. Having provided a brief introduction to the history of migration in Europe we now move on to looking at theories of migration. In the next chapter we provide an overview of the dominant theories in migration studies before going on to look at our own theory of status transition.

3 Theories of Migration

A common feature of the theories that social science elaborate to apprehend reality is that they become widely accepted at a time when the phenomena which they explain have evolved beyond their grasp.

(Portes and Borocz, 1989:606)

Portes and Borocz (1989), in their review of contemporary migration theoretical perspectives, make it clear that theoretical developments never stand still. We draw positively from this standpoint, particularly in this chapter where we present an outline of our own theory of status transition, an attempt to understand better the status trajectories of migrants. Portes and Borocz thus remind us that the task of theorising migration is no easy one and that attempts to provide a theory of migration are unlikely to grasp the realities and lived experiences of migrants, precisely because they are part of a continually revolving and changing scene. We thus recognise that no single, coherent theory of international migration exists to date that can explain the multifaceted nature of the migration phenomenon. Rather, there is a set of theories, developed largely in isolation from one another and sometimes divided by disciplinary boundaries. The authors thus acknowledge the need of a complex migration theory that integrates the perspectives and assumptions of a variety of models to fully understand current migration processes. At the same time it is useful for us to reflect on some widely accepted theories of migration and to try to put them in context, before moving on to discuss our own theoretical developments and the reasons why we have chosen to focus this work on the issue of status and status transition, a key theoretical advancement in our own thinking, as a result of our work on the UWT project and the work of others, most notably Anderson (2010), Gordon (2007), and Ruhs and Anderson (2008). But to arrive at where we are now, it is useful to go back and to provide a brief account of some of the major theoretical positions on migration that have, either positively or negatively, influenced our own theoretical developments.

Undocumented workers are usually conceptualised as individuals who have crossed borders illegally, have been smuggled or trafficked into the country, and who are living in the shadows, working in the semi-legal and sometimes illegal economies. But in reality undocumented status is more complex. Individuals may begin their migration journey as documented workers and may fall into undocumented status, for example, when work permits expire. Or they may be pushed into undocumented status because the immigration rules are so restrictive as to not allow them to work sufficient hours to maintain themselves and/or their families.

They may also start their migration as undocumented workers, but due to changes in state legislation, may acquire documented status through a regularisation programme, through marriage, or in some other way. For these reasons it is important to conceptualise undocumented working (often inappropriately described as 'illegal' working) as the outcome of a combination of state legislative actions and individual decisions, rather than as a consequence of the individual's conscious approval of undocumented status. Migrants do not set out with the desire to be undocumented; it is the legal regimes that they find that place them in this category and also that oblige them to negotiate pathways into work, by whatever possible means.

The first thing to state is of course that migration is much older than any of the theoretical works that we will make reference to (Moses, 2006). As we have argued in the previous chapter, migration is a fundamental part of the human condition, so that the movements of people across the world throughout our history represent those significant moments when human beings developed new skills or understandings of the world that we inhabit. From the initial journeys of *Homo sapiens*, spreading across Europe, Australia, and Asia to later migrations from India, Greece, and Northern Europe and to the Americas, our collective histories embrace migration. For the authors, therefore, it represents a positive human experience. However, the first thing that we note, when looking at migration theory, is how much of it is located within an attempt to understand why it happens and usually to reflect on how it could be limited—either by moderating the conditions that are said to make people migrate or by worsening the conditions where they migrate to, so as to make the option of leaving less attractive and that of staying more acceptable. Practically no attention is paid to the equally important 'why not'; in other words, given the situation that many of the world's peoples find themselves in—hunger, poverty, unemployment—why is it that more people do not migrate in the hope of a better life? The prevailing discourse is based on a view that people are geographically locked (or ought to be locked) within spaces defined by constructed notions of nationality and that their rights as citizens are limited to the exercise of them within the national space. We in contrast wish to take account of what Bourdieu (1998: 17) asks us to do:

> Rethink the question of the status of the foreigner in modern democracies, in other words of the frontiers which can legitimately be imposed on the movement of persons in worlds which, like our own, derive so much advantage from the circulation of persons and goods.

THEORISING THE 'WHYS' OF MIGRATION

Although the first humans are thought to have migrated more than 70,000 years ago, it was not until the late 19th century that we see attempts to build a theory around migration, with Ravenstein's (1889) 'laws' an attempt to explain migration through 'push' and 'pull' processes, whereby a combination of disadvantages experienced in the origin country and presumed advantages present in the host country encouraged individuals to migrate. Thus the push factors are those life situations that give one reasons to be dissatisfied with one's present locale; the pull factors are those attributes of distant places that make them appear appealing (Dorigo and Tobler, 2005). Writing more than 100 years ago, Ravenstein's construction of migration identified as barriers to migration, principally distances and the difficulty of travel and the restrictions imposed by gender, although later studies of migration have demonstrated that in relation to gender, women have their own rich histories of migration (Kofman et al., 2000; Phizacklea, 1983; Sandell, 1977; Vecchio, 2006).

Whereas for Ravenstein, distance was an important factor in deterring migration, for today's transnational theorists (Collins, 2009; Horst, 2006; Morokvasic, 2004; Portes, 1997; Ryan et al., 2009; Turner, 2008) it is the collapse of distance, through easier travel routes and better communications, that sets the scene for migration. However, we would suggest that it is not in fact the case that at one stage travel was difficult and now it is easy. Even while Ravenstein was formulating his theory, a large body of evidence refuted the notion that distance was an effective barrier to migration. The movement of more than 30 million Europeans to North and South America between the 1820s and 1920s, representing one of the world's largest migrations to date and one where people crossed practically half the world to move from their old locations to their new destinations, shows that distance was never by itself a bar to migration. Indeed between 1880 and 1920, four million people emigrated from Italy alone, while similar numbers (but a much larger proportion of its population, left Ireland heading for the Americas) (Diner, 2001; Massey, 1990). In the early years of the 20th century around three million people a year migrated in search of work and a new life. Furthermore, the consequences of the settlement at the end of the 1939–1945 World War led to the resettlement of around 20 million people. However, these migrations have generally not been contained within the conceptualised notions of migration emanating from most scholars in the West, whose fundamental focus is on arrival points rather than on departures. These previous large migrations are therefore conceptualised as adventurous or as colonising expeditions and importantly are rarely represented as threats to the pre-existing order in the host countries. Why these differences are expressed is also a consequence of who is expressing them. As many migration theories have emerged as a response to conceived disruptions to established order, they inevitably start from a notion that the cultural or other social norms within the host society, defined by its own constructed borders, have the right to be guaranteed. Theories therefore have often focused on the 'why' of migration, with a particular focus on its economic rationale, rather than on the experiences of migration and on the effect of state constructions on those experiences.

Theories of push and pull continue to have resonance; in part this is because they highlight situations that are clearly real—at the simplest level, unemployment at home, employment in the host country. Writing many years after Ravenstein, Lee (1966) still retained the validity of the theory, although highlighting what he described as 'intervening obstacles' perceived by intended migrants, which prevented their migration, including distance, gender, and age. However, the stories we have collected in the UWT study show that neither distance (nor gender) is sufficient to impede undocumented migration. Furthermore we would argue that for many undocumented migrants, travel is no less problematic today than it was 100 years ago and indeed may be more dangerous for those travelling without documents, given the nature of security regimes at state borders, compared to a time when many countries had few checks or requirements for entry. One story from our study is that of a Chinese origin undocumented worker who was smuggled to the UK in a journey that took her almost a year, crossing through Siberia and Turkey, often on foot. We also were told of the experiences of two Algerian men who had arrived in the UK through Barcelona, but only after having previously been hidden in the container of a passenger ship from Algeria to Spain. One described the journey as 'very dark and cold' forcing him to wear three double jackets and jeans to keep alive. From Spain there were similar stories. A Moroccan undocumented migrant had begun his journey by travelling on a small, un-seaworthy boat first to reach the Canneries, from where he could make his journey onwards to Barcelona. A Bangladeshi had travelled to Greece on a permit. He had then been moved to Italy, carried for two days in a car inside a container stored on a ship. These experiences were not limited to migrants who had reached the industrially developed countries of the former EU15 states. Our Bulgarian partners had interviewed a woman who had been smuggled from Ghana through Libya to Morocco, travelling through the desert, then by ship to Spain, which she had expected to be her final destination. However, the ship took off again and she was eventually disembarked in Bulgaria. Another respondent from Afghanistan had travelled for three months across Pakistan, Iran, and Turkey, entering Bulgaria on foot. An Iranian, in the course of his journey to Bulgaria, had walked for three days through Turkey. An undocumented migrant from Burkina Faso had journeyed for five months to reach Bulgaria. We provide these examples to illustrate that travel for those without papers does not automatically assume a convenient journey by plane from departure to arrival point.

Market Theories and Migration

Because, as we have argued, the theorising of migration has focused to a great extent on the labour market, it is inevitable that economic theorists would come to occupy a major role, with economic rationalism leading to theories of global supply and demand. For those such as Sjaastad (1962),

Todaro (1969), and Todaro and Maruszko (1987), migration simply represents a method of redistributing human resources from areas (generally rural) where they are surplus to requirements to areas (generally urban) where they are in short supply, but based on an assumption that expected wages in urban areas are the drivers for migration. Individuals decide to legalise according to their utility maximisation. International migration is thus conceptualised as a human capital investment. The theory assumes that undocumented migrants will approach the registration offices when their expected benefits exceed, to some extent, the costs involved. Under this model normally a migrant can register to minimise risks of being caught by the authorities, penalised, and expelled from the country, thus securing a longer and safer stay together with free travel to the home country, as well as to ensure social security coverage for him and his family (in cases where a family joins him in the host country). The migrant is willing to legalise to attain access to public services (education, etc.), to widen her or his opportunities for human capital investment that might lead to professional advancement, and to improve her or his social status. This analysis posits migration as a rational choice made on the basis of informed decisions, where the potential migrant is aware of the situation in the host country and of the conditions that will apply. For Ghosh (1998), only opportunity-seeking migrants can act rationally with their migration being more a matter of choice than of compulsion, with a greater tendency to sensitivity to economic opportunities. We suggest that economic rational modes offer an incomplete picture of migration decisions. Migrants often gain information about conditions in host countries by those who have already migrated, but those accounts may be moderated by a desire to present their migration positively, as a success and not a failure. Furthermore for undocumented migrants, knowledge of what conditions they will find in the host country is less predictable, as situations may change as a consequence of the position taken by the host state in relation to undocumented migration.

Some of these theories have focused their attention on the extent to which the process of regularisation affects the decisions of undocumented migrants, a subject we address in more detail in Chapter 7. Central to these theories are what are described as 'survival migrants' (Papademetriou and Martin, 1991). For them, the search for basic economic security becomes a decisive factor in shaping their migration decisions. As they leave the home country, forced by dire economic circumstances, they are less likely to possess valid residence and work permits. They often hold irregular jobs in the underground economy of the receiving country, operating on the periphery of the formalised sector, making it difficult to reach them effectively through regular labour market mechanisms and measures. 'Survival migrants' represent a major objective of government regularisation programmes although they might be more hesitant and reluctant when there are opportunities to legalise.

The new economics of migration theory underlines family strategies to diversify sources of income, minimise risks to the household, and overcome barriers to credit and capital. Thus here the migrant is not necessarily the decision-making entity responsible for her or his migration (Stark, 1991). Possible legalisation of the stay and work of a family member can significantly reduce the costs and increase the returns to migration. An important component of the direct returns to the non-migrating family from the migration of a family member is her or his remittances. Thus, regularisation programmes safeguard legal channels for remitting. Moreover, they turn out to be the steady ground for family strategies to diversify sources of income and minimise risk. The decision to regularise can also be a family decision and the regularisation—a family strategy. Within this broad theoretical framework, institutional theory attempts to explain the organization and management of the regularisation program. The theory points to a variety of legal and illegal entities that provide transport, housing, and other services, which are often difficult for governments to register and regulate (Russel, 1997). Such institutions may facilitate migrants' participation in the regularisation programme by offering legal and other services as, for example, the filling of the application forms. Network theory also supplements new economics of migration theory. Stark (1991) proposes that assistance from prior emigrants in the host country is important to explain patterns of international migration. Migrant networks are conceptualised as playing a significant role in reducing the costs and risks of migration, including participation in regularisation programmes. Their role in publicising such programmes among the undocumented migrant communities is decisive. Network connections are thus said to constitute a form of social capital that people can draw upon to gain access to accommodation, employment, and regularisation routes. The networks are presented as operating on the basis of primary kinship ties, but the relationship can be widened to include all friendship patterns that exist in the communities of the sending country (King, 1996; McDonald and McDonald, 1964). Government policies of the host country often facilitate the development of such networks, thus providing better management of the regularisation programme.

Dual labour market theory, which we return to in greater detail in Chapter 7, also attempts to identify the critical factors shaping migrants' decisions whether or not to take part in any regularisation process. Under the traditional dual market approach, employers seek low-wage migrant workers to maintain labour as a variable factor of production. In the presence of a flourishing underground economy, migrant flows are mainly demand determined. The existence of 'willing-to-emigrate workers' becomes a necessary condition for emigration but not a sufficient one. Straubhaar (1988) suggests that the existence of 'willing-to-employ-undocumented-immigrants employers' forms the demand side in the destination country and can be specified as a necessary and sufficient condition for migration to take place.

THE CONSEQUENCES OF MIGRATION

Piore's seminal work (1979) is also an attempt to develop a theory of migration and to address policy issues, particularly in relation to undocumented migrants in the US context. In this he moves away from a theory of why people migrate to focus on the jobs that migrants do, arguing that they occupy particular posts that local labour rejects. He refutes the view that income is the determining factor in migration and instead states that it is the job characteristics. This leads him to conclude that even 'if the income differential between the United States and Mexico were somehow to disappear, the American economy would simply seek elsewhere for other workers'. Piore rejects restrictions on immigration as an 'ineffective policy instrument' as it fails to curtail the secondary labour market.

Piore's argument is that by restricting entry, the state forces migrants to stay longer and then to form permanent attachments extending periods of undocumented migration. He thus opposes sanctions against employers, arguing, consequent on protecting their profits, they encourage even higher levels of exploitation of undocumented migrants. Also 'to the extent that these restrictions actually set limits upon employment in that sector [secondary], the sector will then begin to expand beyond its present limits'.

Transnational Theories

For some, the development of transnational communities as a result of migration has been a major focus of theoretical development. Portes (1997: 3) provides the following definition of transnational communities:

> Communities that sit astride political borders and that in a very real sense are 'neither here nor there' . . . Dense networks across space and by an increasing number of people who lead dual lives. Members are at least bilingual, move easily between cultures and frequently maintain homes in both countries. But not everyone is transnational; the term is reserved for 'activities of an economic, political and cultural sort that require the involvement of participants on a regular basis as a major part of their occupation'.

Bourne (1916) is credited with the first attempt to theorise the impact of new communities and cultures that emerged as a consequence of migration. He defines America as coming to be not a nation, 'but a transnationality, a weaving back and forth, with other lands, of many threads of all sizes and colours. Any movement that attempts to thwart this weaving or to dye the fabric any one colour, or to disentangle the threads of the strands, is false to this cosmopolitan vision (at p. 95), and Bourne usefully reminds us that assimilation was not part of the original history of America and that early settlers not only brought their cultural traditions with them, but 'brought over bodily the old ways to which they had been accustomed' (Bourne, 1916:87). Bourne's theories on transnationality have been reviewed through the work of transnational theorists who emphasise the continuing bonds, which migrants maintain with origin societies.

Transnational theory constructs distance as no longer a factor when travel is cheap, reflecting an argument that the contemporary world is structured in a way that permits (certain) individuals to engage simultaneously in more than one locale (Collins, 2009), and when communication technologies bring distant families into the restricted corners of the living space of many migrants in their host countries (Horst, 2006). However, at the same time, Collins notes that access to communication technologies work 'to bring "home" closer to "here" extending both the opportunities offered by home and the constraints'. In short, he argues that while migrants have the continued possibility of engaging in the lives of their friends and family members who remained at home, the corollary is that these parties can also engage in migrants lives 'which in some cases can include attempts to discipline the bodies and actions' of the individuals who have left home. For this reason he concludes that 'national identities and related social formations remain highly salient in transnational lives' (Collins, 2009:856).

Ryan et al. (2009) recount that their participants' stories 'illustrate the importance of transnational family networks as on-going sources of practical and emotional support, facilitated through the availability of phone calls, e-mails and texts'. But they also note that migration may empower migrants to leave unhappy family situations. Others suggest that transnationalism is not so much about relying on transnational networking for improving their condition in the country of their settlement, but rather that new communication technologies allow migrants to settle within mobility, staying mobile as long as they can in order to improve or maintain the quality of life at home. 'Their experience of migration thus becomes their lifestyle, their *leaving home* and going away, paradoxically, a strategy of *staying at home*, and, thus, an alternative to what migration is usually considered to be' (Morokvasic, 2004:7). There are voices that question the usefulness of the theory. Indeed Portes (1997:2) suggests it may be 'one of those passing fads that grip social scientists' attention for a while only to fade into oblivion'. He argues that the emergence of transnational communities is tied to the logic of capitalism itself and that interests and needs of investors and employers in the advanced countries bring them into play. For him such communities represent a distinct phenomenon, at variance with traditional patterns of immigrant adaptation. At the same time, 'because the phenomenon is fuelled by the dynamics of globalisation itself, it has greater growth potential and offers a broader field for autonomous popular initiatives than alternative ways to deal with the depredations of world-roaming capital' (Portes, 1997:4). Ahmad (2008a:133) also suggests some limits in the theory noting: 'Sociologists of migration who focus on transnationalism and global networks, then frequently ignore the question of individual migrant motivation, treating the primacy of collective material betterment of the household as a given.'

A bigger though unresolved question is whether migration, in a situation where family and home country ties can be sustained, creates a new identity which itself is transnational, allowing migrants to straddle both their home and host countries. Turner (2008) argues that while transnational engagements span territories and transcend spatial fixation, they might also provide stabilised identities for those involved. Butcher (2009), however, could find no evidence of the existence of such an identity, arguing that it is not possible to feel about the world in the same way as one feels about home and that an attachment to being a 'global citizen' does not override the need to ascribe to a national identity. For her, there is still an impulse to belong to a place that is marked by characteristics of familiarity and comfort, including elements of the national imagination. This is supported by the maintenance of particular relationships which confirm that this identity and its associated practices and values are shared and therefore of value. Mandaville (2009), looking at Muslim communities, argues that the variegated experience of Muslims in Europe, who seek to make common cause across state boundaries, often bring the baggage of their unique national (or even local) experiences with them, making it difficult to unite around a shared sense of European Muslimness. However, others refer to migrant communities becoming culturally transnationalised, where migrants incorporate from both their origin and host cultures to create a 'culture of migration' distinct from both the origin and host nation (Massey et al., 1994). Given that national borders have not dissolved through the process of globalisation, in our view it is problematic to argue for the existence of a genuine new transnational identity although we draw from the theories, and in particular from Massey, to suggest that the process of migration creates a new identity built on both origin and host countries and which in the process expands beyond the confines of either of these two fixed identities.

In discussing migration theories it is important not just to focus on theories that attempt to understand why individuals migrate. One area of particular interest to us has been over the terms that are used to describe or explain undocumented migration and how this language itself can shape the debates around migration. While the term 'illegal' has largely been removed from academic discourse on migration, Schrover et al. (2008) have argued for the recuperation of the term.

STATUS TRANSITIONS

Although the UWT project utilised the term 'undocumented' to describe those who were resident or working in breach of the relevant legal rules, conceptually we drew on the work of Ruhs and Anderson (2008) in their identification of three types of status: the compliant—those with the legal right to reside and to work, principally migrants who are not subject to any controls or who have permits that cover both residence and employment; the non-compliant—those who have no residency rights and who therefore have no legal permission to stay, although this would include those who have had residency rights in the past (for example, overstayers); and the semi-compliant—those who are 'legally resident but working in violation of the employment restrictions attached to their immigration status'. These categories assist us in identifying the real pathways of migrants as not being fixed but as part of a changing process, affected by their own decisions as well as those of the host state. The impact of status is felt most acutely in the employment conditions faced. Anderson (2010) reflects carefully on the impact of migration controls, not only in creating undocumented migrants, but in forcing them into work in particularly exploitative conditions. Using the term 'precarious' to describe such workers, she argues that the notion of precariousness 'captures both atypical and insecure employment and has implications beyond employment pointing to an associated weakening of social relations' (at p.203). For this reason she also suggests that 'workers who are subject to immigration controls may be more desirable to employers than those migrants and citizens who are not' and that 'the construction of a category of people who are residing illegally is in part an inevitable function of any form of immigration control and nation state organised citizenship' (p.310). Precarious work therefore for those working illegally 'is not simply at the whim of individual employers, but structurally produced by the interaction of employment and immigration legislation'. This further leads to her asserting that close attention has to be paid to the relation between labour markets and immigration controls, which not only illegalise some groups but legalise others in very particular ways. Anderson (2010:314) further argues:

> Concerns about the impact of immigration on British workers may ultimately be a conjuring trick, a masterpiece of public misdirection, when what merits attention are issues of job quality, job security and low pay. Immigration restriction and enforcement are not only insufficient to reduce migrant precarity, but actively produce and reinforce it.

For the UWT project our main theoretical focus was on understanding the circumstances that resulted in individuals being undocumented. In particular we wanted to explore whether status was fixed or transitional, in other words whether the attribution of particular characteristics to migrants, dependent on whether or not they were documented, failed to take account of a reality where, for possibly a majority, their status changes. In our study, transition from regular to irregular status was more common that the reverse. This transition was sometimes a consequence of the expiry of a work permit or other form of visa. However, in addition, we observed cases, in many of the seven countries, of workers being thrown into irregularity simply because the state itself had decided to change the entry and work conditions. We found that the majority of the migrants we interviewed had indeed experienced changes in their migration status and that few had started their migration journey with one status (be it documented or undocumented or even semi-documented) and maintained this status consistently. Of the 211 interviews conducted with migrant workers, a very large proportion (71 per cent) had experienced at least one status transition, with one in five having had documented status and then losing it. The data illustrates that the status an individual holds is not fixed, in a sense that someone is consistently either documented or undocumented. In Table 3.1 we provide an example from the UK interviews that shows the status of the respondents and their status transitions where these had occurred. The most likely transition was from documented or semi-documented to undocumented status. Whereas only four of the 22 individuals started as undocumented,[2] 11 of the 22 were currently undocumented (Table 3.1).

Table 3.1   Status Transitions of UK Migrant Interviewees

Interviewee 1: Asylum application in Germany→Failed→Tourist visa to UK→Applied for refugee status→After 9 years given Indefinite Leave to Remain

Interviewee 2: Tourist visa (forged Greek passport)→Return to Bulgaria→Tourist Visa→Asylum Seeker→Refugee Status→Indefinite Leave to Remain

Interviewee 3: Asylum seeker→Undocumented (rejected asylum application)→ Discretional Leave to Remain→(now awaiting) Indefinite Leave to Remain

Interviewee 4: Visitor (A2 EU citizen)→Semi-documented (registered for National Insurance Number & Tax Number but without a permit for self-employment)→now awaits Home Office decision on an application for a self-employment status for an A2 EU citizen

Interviewee 5: Work permit holder→Work in violation of the conditions of the work permit (work for an employer different than the one specified in the permit)→Work permit holder→'Blue Card' of an EU citizen (unrestricted labour market access)

Interviewee 6: Tourist visa→Undocumented –awaits decision on wife's application for a self-employment status; if granted, will have a Dependent status (unrestricted labour market access)

Interviewee 7: Student visa→Undocumented –awaiting appeal for Post-Grad work permit

Interviewee 8: Illegal entry into France→Undocumented residence and work in France→Work permit and residence in France through marriage to a French national→French citizenship

Interviewee 9: Illegal entry into Spain→Illegal entry into France & Undocumented in France→Illegal entry into UK via Belgium & Undocumented in the UK

Interviewee 10: Tourist Visa→High Skilled Migration Programme

Interviewee 11: Work Permit holder, working for employer different than specified in work permit

Interviewee 12: Tourist visa (Germany)→Undocumented in Italy→Regularised in Italy→Tourist visa in the UK→Undocumented in the UK

Interviewee 13: Transit visa for the UK→Undocumented in the UK

Interviewee 14: Illegal entry into Spain→Entry into France on a forged French passport→Entry into the UK on a forged French passport→Residence and Work in the UK on a forged French passport

Continued

Table 3.1   Continued

Interviewee 15: Student Visa (three-week one, without the right to work)→Student Visa (1 year duration, with a right for a part-time work)
Interviewee 16: Smuggled into the UK & Undocumented
Interviewee 17: Smuggled into the UK & Undocumented
Interviewee 18: Smuggled into the UK & Undocumented
Interviewee 19: Smuggled into the UK→Asylum Seeker→Undocumented
Interviewee 20: Smuggled into the UK→Undocumented
Interviewee 21: Tourist Visa→Student Visa→awaiting appeal for HSMP Work Permit
Interviewee 22: Work Permit→Undocumented
Interviewee 23: Work Permit→Further Leave to Remain
Interviewee 24: Tourist Visa→Undocumented
Interviewee 25: Asylum seeker→Refugee Status→Indefinite Leave to Remain→British citizenship
Interviewee 26: Asylum seeker→Refugee Status→Indefinite Leave to Remain→British citizenship
Interviewee 27: Asylum seeker (child)→Refugee Status (child)→Indefinite Leave to Remain→British citizenship
Interviewee 28: Asylum seeker→Refugee Status→Indefinite Leave to Remain→British citizenship
Interviewee 29: Asylum seeker→Refugee Status→Indefinite Leave to Remain→British citizenship
Interviewee 30: Smuggled into the UK & Asylum seeker→Undocumented

Source: UWT, UK Field survey, 2007–2008.

A similar picture emerged from the 30 Spanish interviews, as Table 3.2 shows.

Of the 30 migrants interviewed in Austria, only 10 still had the same status as they had when they had arrived. Of those whose status had changed, two had had documented status but were now undocumented; nine had

Table 3.2   Pathways of Respondents Living in Spain

Types of transitions	
Legal entry→undocumented stage→currently in a legal situation	16
Legal entry as a regrouped relative→stage with a residence permit→currently in a legal situation	7
Legal entry→currently with a residence permit	1
Legal entry→currently in an illegal situation	2
Illegal entry→undocumented stage→currently in a legal situation	1
Illegal entry→currently in an illegal situation	3
Total	30

Source: UWT Spain, Field survey, 2007–2008.

been documented through their country's accession to the EU; one had applied for asylum, one had been granted refugee status, and one male from West Africa (who had arrived without documents in 2000) had been granted citizenship. Among those who had documents on first arrival was a woman from Poland who had originally obtained a visa to work in Germany. When that expired she was expelled but then returned irregularly three times, before moving to Switzerland and then to Austria where she acquired residency but was working without documents. This case was not unusual, in that individuals might have documents that gave residency rights but not a right to work (what Ruhs and Anderson, 2006, define as 'semi-compliant'). That did not mean that they were not working or seeking work. Indeed six individuals in our sample, with residency rights in Austria, had no right to work but were working. One was a student from Bulgaria who had arrived in 2002 and had always worked while studying even though she had no right to do so. Of the 31 respondents in Belgium, 24 had experienced status changes. A woman migrant had left Rwanda to join her children who were already in Belgium. She applied for asylum, but in the year before that was granted she had worked without documents. With respect to the interviews in Bulgaria, 23 of the 30 had changed status. In Italy it was 28 of the 30. Denmark was the only country in our study where it was a minority (10 of the 30) that had experienced a status change. These examples affirm our conclusion that status is rarely the outcome of a conscious decision on the part of the individual migrant but is determined by factors usually out of the control of the individual, although the passage of certain events or a fortunate combination of factors may open up opportunities to those in a position to exercise choices. Indeed in relation to the Austrian interviews it was the accession of the EU10 states in 2004 and of the EU2 states in 2007 that was the biggest factor in status transition. In relation to gender there were no differences, with women being as likely as men to have experienced status changes. Of the 149 respondents in that category, 72 (48 per cent) were women. There was also some evidence of time as a decisive element in transition from undocumented to documented status, with the Spanish interviews showing that, of those who were still undocumented, all but one had been in Spain for less than six years.

Our research has led us to a typology of undocumented migration as primarily a process of

- The unwillingness of the state to offer legitimate entry routes for migrants;
  - Strong economic growth; and either
  - The existence of a substantial informal sector or
- The existence of networks that can provide access to work.

In effect migrants are more likely to move to those countries which are seen as providing the best economic opportunities for work and for remuneration.

The status that they may have ascribed to them in the host country is likely to be a much less significant factor in determining where they choose to migrate to, in those cases where they are able to exercise a choice.

We found that in all seven countries there were means by which migrants, who arrived without documents or without a right to work, could acquire them. Some of the methods available were found, to a greater or lesser degree, in all seven countries, whereas others were unique to the particular legal or other arrangements in the host country. In such cases they were primarily dependent on the legislative system and on the availability or otherwise of regularisation programmes or amnesties. One means of acquiring legal status was through marriage. In Austria in an interview with a student from Turkey, members of the research team were told that he had worked without papers and on finishing his studies he had married, in the knowledge that this was a route to obtaining a residency and work permit. Similarly, another respondent had arrived with a tourist visa in 2004 but had subsequently married an EU citizen. A Croatian respondent had arrived in Italy in 1996 after having separated from her husband. After six years of working without documents, she re-married in 2002 and eventually became an Italian citizen. However, we also observed a tightening of rights to legal status through marriage in almost all of the seven Member States. Marriage, which had traditionally been viewed as a route towards greater integration within the host community, was no longer identified as such in those countries where the host community also consisted of individuals who shared a common ethnic identity with the newly arrived. It is clear to us that the concept of marriage as an integrative experience is being refuted because the state perceives elements of its *own* population as being outside its construct of its own ethnic identity. This suggests that as migration increases and as the size of the undocumented migrant population within a country is sufficiently established, particularly as a second generation emerges, bars on marriage as a route to regularisation and settlement are likely to increase. An example of where this has already occurred is in Denmark, where the state has tightened the rules on who can marry and in Austria where the state requires that the application of intention to marry must be presented while the migrant is outside the host country.

A second form of regularisation identified in our research was through exit and re-entry. Migrants in some cases had chosen strategically to leave their destination country and return to their country of origin with the specific aim of re-entering with the required documents. In other words, a period of irregular residency was exchanged for regular residency, as knowledge was acquired of how a particular state's migration policies operated and this gave individuals a route towards transition from irregular to regular status.

Spain and Italy were the two countries where mass regularisation has occurred through state intervention. These had been important routes to regular status for migrants in both countries, where there had been more than one million regularisations over the last few years. However, these were not the only two countries where the state had acted to regularise large numbers of previously irregular migrants. We argue, for example, that both the UK and Austria, which formally maintain a strong opposition to mass regularisation programmes, had presided over large-scale regularisations as a consequence of the accession of the new Member States in 2004.

Transition from regular to irregular status was more common among those interviewed during the project. Sometimes this was as a consequence of the expiry of a work permit or other form of visa. However, in addition, in some of the seven countries, workers became irregular simply because the state itself had decided to change the entry and work conditions. This had occurred in Austria in 2006 and in the UK in 2008. The restrictive nature of entry regulations could also have the effect of driving individuals into irregularity; this had occurred particularly in Spain, where rules that provided temporary entry only, created the conditions for overstaying, thus throwing workers into irregularity. At the same time, the impact of the economic crisis was encouraging short-term temporary employment forcing greater numbers into irregular work, as their opportunities to obtain work in their countries of origin also became more restrictive. This was particularly noted in Italy and in Bulgaria.

Those who are undocumented are utilised as a reserve army of labour with few or no rights, whether in relation to work, access to health, education, or other forms of welfare provision (Mottura and Rinaldini, 2009). Silverman (2005) suggests that the lack of rights is the consequence of a dynamic process where the lives of migrants are valued less and seen as culturally inferior and poorer.

Many of those interviewed in the UWT project described situations of employer complicity in undocumented working, echoing Bacon's description of undocumented labour in the US where he notes 'workers have paid the price for the enforcement of employer sanctions, not employers' (Bacon, 2008:6). In the UK, employer sanctions (including penal sanctions) were increased in 2008. However, not all employers were equally affected. UK Border Control authority raids focused primarily on small and visible minority ethnic businesses (Evans, 2008). A similar process of state control is noted in the US, where immigration law is described as 'a tool of the employers. Companies use it as a weapon to keep workers unorganized and the INS [Immigration and Naturalization Services] helps them' (Bacon, 2008:147). In the UK, increased sanctions on employers had changed behaviours, with some employers, particularly those employing workers in highly visible occupations such as construction and hospitality, moving to dismiss those whom they believed were undocumented, even where they had been working for the employers for many months, and in some cases years. One respondent stated that in the past none of the employers he had worked for were concerned about the conditions attached to his visa. All they wanted to know was that he had a permit; even if it was not for the work they were employing him to do. But the new immigration regime changed all this. In his last job he was suddenly 'asked to resign'. Another respondent also spoke of his employer suddenly starting to press for documents, shortly before the change in the law, and eventually being told to leave. In this case, a similar experience had occurred in France where he had lived prior to moving to the UK. In France, increased police raids had forced him to leave a job that he was enjoying and which the employer trusted him to do. A 21-year-old Algerian worker, working with a forged French passport, told of how his employer had stopped paying him because he was 'illegal'. The new sanctions also meant that the 'window' within which undocumented workers could work had narrowed considerably. As one respondent noted, while previously it might have taken 18 months for an employer to get round to demanding documents proving a right to work, this period had narrowed to less than two months. Undocumented workers thus had to be continually changing employers to stay ahead of potential raids.

Five of the six Chinese migrants we interviewed in the UK had become much more vulnerable as a result of changes to immigration laws. There had been widespread dismissals within the Chinese owned restaurant sector, which was targeted for police raids and which therefore had reacted by dismissing workers without documents. One 31-year-old married woman had not had a full-time job in the three months since being asked to leave her place of work because there was the risk of police raids. She said that she was now 'lucky' if she got one or two days work a week, covering for staff on leave. Work was sourced through Chinese friends. A 37-year-old male working in construction had been earning £60 a day for 10 hours' work. After two years and just before the increased employer sanctions came into force, the employer asked him for his papers. Because he did not have any, he stopped going to work. He described being frightened of going out in case the police stopped him. At most he now gets a day or two's work on construction sites. Another 32-year-old male, who had worked as a second chef, also lost his job because the employers did not want problems with the police. A woman lost her job after having worked in the same Chinese restaurant for several years. Again it was the increased number of police raids that forced her to leave her job. For these workers the outcome was not that undocumented work had ended, but rather that they had been forced into even more exploitative forms of casual labour.

For some workers in the UK, the government enforcement campaign and increased penalties for employers of undocumented labour had additional negative consequences, as they were unable to return to their countries of origin. The large amounts that they had borrowed to pay the gangmasters who had arranged their journey to the UK had not been paid off, and indeed it is difficult to conceive how they could ever be paid off, given that the average debt was in excess of €20,000 and their average rate of pay was under €6 an hour. Most workers, even when they were able to make payments towards the debt were merely covering the interest charges. The debt itself rarely reduced. In one case, the respondent reported that having already been late with a couple of payments, debt collectors in China began to harass his family which had borrowed more than €30,000 to pay for his journey to the UK. These realities of living as an undocumented worker in the new era of immigration controls are ignored by the government.

These changes to the immigration rules and greater enforcement, when previously irregularity had been widely ignored, had a devastating effect on peoples' working lives. For example one young woman respondent, who had established herself in a job related to her qualifications with no complaints about her working conditions, was suddenly thrown into uncertainty when a technical difficulty in her application form for a renewal of her work permit threw her into an undocumented status and caused her to lose her job. A male Algerian respondent had been working in a pub making pizzas, but once the new sanctions came into force he was asked to leave. Getting new work was proving difficult. These difficulties were not confined to those seeking low-skilled work. Even for the highly skilled, which states claim they want to attract, the continually changing and punitive immigration rules caused difficulties. One female doctor spoke of finding herself in a permanent dilemma as each time she adopted a new strategy to cope with a change to the immigration rules, no sooner had she overcome the existing obstacles when the rules changed again. After five years of trying to have her Colombian qualifications as a doctor recognised, the rules concerning training positions for non-EU doctors under the Highly-Skilled Migrant Programme changed and her view was that she would never be able to work in her profession in the UK. The 'goal posts' shifted too often.

The changes to the rules on work permits for senior care workers, which the UK government introduced in 2008, had also thrown mainly Filipino workers into undocumented status. This happened to one male respondent, who lost his job when the rules changed and who was unable to get a new job offer at the rate set by the government that would allow him to stay in the UK.[3] This had other consequences, as workers who had already built up years of UK residence would be unable to use these towards claiming their rights to permanent residence, which otherwise would have been available after five years working in the UK. One Filipino male nurse realised that his work permit was coming up for renewal and was assured by his employers that the renewal application was in hand. On the day before its expiry, he was called into the manager's office and his contract was terminated. This occurred just months before he would have reached his five years of temporary residency and could have applied for permanent residency. Another respondent had lost his work as a care worker in December 2007. If he had been able to work until June 2008, he would have gained his permanent residency rights. The effects of his loss of work was to push his wife into irregular work to support them; she had previously been working legally due to her dependant status attached to his work permit, but could not continue that job once her husband lost his employment. The couple felt it was safer for her to work in private households with less chance of detection by the authorities. Again this demonstrates that the tightening of controls has the potential to *increase* undocumented work. Workers in these situations relied heavily on compatriots providing them with moral and economic support, speaking of housemates and friends giving support during the months when individuals had been unable to access work.

CONCLUSION

In this chapter we have sought to set out some of the key theories that shape the discourse on migration. Our view is that the theories focus too much on questions related to why individuals migrate and that the theories thus can be used to provide arguments that policymakers rely on to justify tightening controls on migration. We have argued instead that theoretical debates need to begin from a standpoint that sees migration as a positive experience for migrants and also for citizens in the countries to which they migrate and that the focus needs to be on what happens as a consequence of migration to the key actors—the migrants themselves. Our second aim has been to show that the conceptualisation of migrants as either 'legal' or 'illegal' fails to take account of the transitions in status which many migrants experience. In Chapter 5 we return to these arguments by looking at the role of EU regulation on the shaping of national immigration regimes. But before we do this we wanted to set out, in more detail, the research methods that we used in our study and in particular to set out the particular challenges faced in conducting comparative trans-European research.

4 What Works and What Does Not
Methodologies and Migration Research

> What we can do is to create, not a counter-programme, but a structure
> for collective research, interdisciplinary and international, bringing
> together social scientists, activists, representatives of activists, etc.,
> with the social scientists being placed in a quite definite role; they
> can participate in a particularly effective way, because it's their job in
> working parties and seminars, in association with people who are in
> the movement. . . . [S]ocial scientists are not fellow travellers.
>
> (Bourdieu, 1998:56)

Acts of Resistance is one of Bourdieu's most directly 'political' works, but
it is also one where he asks us to consider a new approach to collaborative
research. This is also a focus of our discussion in this chapter, where we use
the experiences of the UWT project to reflect the challenges and the benefits of working collaboratively. While there is a considerable literature that
reflects on the methodological and ethical challenges in researching migration, and in particular in conducting interviews with migrants (Bloch, 2007;
Castles, 2007; McKay and Snyder, 2009; Mestheneos, 2006; Temple and
Moran, 2006), there is little literature that deals with migration methodologies in the context of comparative and cross-national research, particularly
in the context of researching undocumented migrants. It is this gap that
this chapter addresses. In this chapter we reflect on specific challenges in
conducting research across countries that potentially have differing traditions and understandings, both in relation to the conduct of research itself
and more specifically in the conduct of research with migrant workers.
What we aim to explore therefore is how methodologies are utilised when
researching beyond national borders. The chapter does not look specifically
at the choice of methods and what advantages they bring in researching
migration issues. For this discussion we refer to the authors' previous work
(Markova, 2009; McKay and Snyder, 2009). Instead we discuss the specific
issues that arose in our own research and which we hope will be of interest
to researchers conducting similar research in cross-national partnerships.

LEARNING FROM EACH OTHER IN RESEARCH PARTNERSHIPS

When submitting research proposals in response to tender calls, such as FP6
(the Sixth Framework Programme for Research and Technological Development), it is almost always the co-ordinating organisation that will perform

a crucial role, constructing the research consortium, submitting the first proposal suggestions to the other members of the consortium, and usually preparing the final proposal for submission. This inevitably means that initially the relationship between members of the consortium is not necessarily one of equality. Particularly where the timescale for delivery of the proposal is tight, the lead member of the consortium plays a pivotal role in its formulation. Although other members of course have an input, the speed at which many bids need to be put together often means that there is insufficient time to flesh out the different perspectives of different consortium partners, prior to submission of the proposal. In the UWT preparation, in practice, as the lead member of the consortium, those of us based at the Working Lives Research Institute (WLRI)[1] made the initial suggestions as to the proposed methodology. Consortium members could and did comment, but there was only a limited opportunity for in-depth discussion due to the impending deadline. In addition although some consortium members may be particularly engaged in the preparation of the bid, whether on the basis of their capacity or experience or indeed level of interest, particularly at a stage when the outcome is unknown, organisations may not have the capacity to put aside the significant resources required. This is compounded by the fact that the time taken to prepare bids is 'unpaid time', and researchers working in those universities and institutions that increasingly require of them that they effectively fund their own posts are not in an ideal position to devote a large amount of their time to a proposal whose outcome is always uncertain, bearing in mind that even in a institution relatively experienced in the preparation of bids, such as WLRI, only half of our submitted bids is successful.

The fact that not all partners are positioned to have an equal input into the proposed methodology makes it even more central to a successful research project that there is an opportunity for a detailed discussion on methods once the proposal has been accepted. For this reason we choose to make it clear in the bid submission itself that the methodology proposed would be the subject of in-depth discussion, and potentially to review, prior to the commencement of any fieldwork. Knowing and agreeing on the methodologies to be utilised is crucial to the successful working of a consortium. In our project it was inevitable that partners would be more experienced in the use of some methodologies over others, and because the partnership had brought together teams that had previously worked together successfully using qualitative methods, it was essential that we gave attention to the provision of training in the quantitative elements that the project would engage with. Increasingly, funders—whether research councils; national, local, or regional governments; European level bodies; or charitable or private funders—favour the use of a combination of qualitative and quantitative methods, using one method as confirmatory of the results gathered by the other. Working across two methodologies places a dependence on different skill sets. For the bulk of the data collection we were to rely on face-to-face in-depth interviews, both with stakeholders and, in the second year of the project, with undocumented migrants. All of our partners had substantial experience in the use of the qualitative methods. But we also had to be able to develop an appropriate statistical methodology that would allow us to produce estimates, no matter how tentative, of the size of the undocumented migrant population in the seven countries. The quantitative statistical data that we wished to explore was dependent on a level of statistical knowledge that not all of the members of the consortium possessed. It was our task to see how we could develop tools sufficiently advanced that would both provide a comparable method of data collection in the seven countries and at the same time would take note of the differing data availability throughout the project countries, a point which we return to in Chapter 7. A way to overcome this was first to look at the methods that had been used in the collection and analysis of available statistical data in each country. The preparation of a literature review by each team in the consortium was an important first step towards developing a common understanding of the problems the project was likely to face. The second step involved training in data analysis; the primary method for imparting this information was through a methodology workshop. The workshop provided an opportunity for each partner to present a short résumé of the existing available data and its method of collection and analysis. The process of research was thus transformed into a learning experience for all participants and this of itself was a valuable project outcome. In this way research is not only conducted to find answers to key research questions, it is also a process whereby researchers learn from one another, broadening their skills and focusing outwards rather than solely inwards.

In the UWT project, after a first meeting, essentially to enable all the partners to get together and to know each other better, the second meeting—a three-day session held in Vienna, hosted by the Austrian partner—was devoted to a discussion of methodologies. The meeting represented a key stage in the process of developing the partnership into a well-functioning team. It allowed partners to discuss the methods that they had used in the past and to come to a collective view as to what was likely to work best for the project, given its constraints in terms of time, budget, and geography. Among the key issues that emerged during the three days of the meeting was the question of how we defined and selected stakeholders in each of the consortium countries. Some consortium teams already had well-established contacts with relevant stakeholders, through their work on previous projects, or more generally through their political or social activities. However, for other members of the partnership, knowledge of who the best contacts might be was less well-developed, a factor that became more challenging when inevitable changes occurred within national teams, as individuals left their employment and the project and new people were recruited to replace them.

Thus time had to be spent in discussing who we might define as the key stakeholders and we eventually agreed that the following fell into the category: representatives of migrant organisations, individuals working within migrant support groups, academics working in the field of migration research, local activists who had good links within migrant communities, anti-racist and anti-fascist groups, government spokespersons, and regional and local administrations. Generally there was common agreement on these. However, the different experiences of migration in the seven countries meant that not all of the stakeholder communities were in existence, and we had to address this issue and to agree the best way forward taking account of the specific country situation.

The methodology workshop was also a good starting point for a discussion on the research instruments, and the opportunity was taken not only to discuss who would be interviewed but also to start to formulate the contents of the various interview schedules. Interview schedules are not necessarily an unproblematic research instrument. In our estimation, at least in relation to semi-structured, qualitative interviews of the type that we were using, it is rare that the subsequent interviews follow, to the letter, the interview script. The schedule is a requirement, so as to ensure that all of the interviews deal with similar issues and, conducting research across different countries, made it possibly even more important to ensure that there was a standard interview schedule, otherwise when it came to the eventual analysis of the data, we might have ended up with entirely different sets of information, making it well-neigh impossible to synthesise the data. However, that does not mean that on the day of the interview the interviewer will pose each of the questions laboriously and in turn. Good interviews aim to allow the interviewee to explain the story at her or his own pace, and areas to be covered in the interview schedule may be anticipated by the interviewee before they can by presented by the interviewer. The challenge of conducting a good interview is based on putting the interviewees at the centre of the interview; to allow the conversation to develop as naturally as possible; to give the interviewees the space to provide responses in a way that seems most comfortable to them; whilst at the same time making sure that all of the questions, set out in the interview schedule, are addressed. The extent to which we managed to achieve this is difficult to access. Certainly there was some variation in the interview transcripts, reflecting a combination of interviewer experience together with the cultural sensitivities of both interviewer and respondent.

Research partnerships obviously work more effectively where there exists a shared understanding of each of the country-specific contexts. For this the preparation of national State of the Art reports was invaluable in our project. Within the first two months each partner had to produce a country report. The reports had to provide a summary of migration and employment law, a historical and current account of migration, a résumé of any known data on the size and function of the undocumented migrant population, and information on the sectors where undocumented migrants worked and on the kind of jobs that they did.[2] Having these accounts early on ensured that all partners had the tools to understand the contexts within which the other would operate, and the reports themselves were useful when it came to analysing all of the data collected in the course of the project.

ONE LANGUAGE, MANY MEANINGS

We also found that although we were using a common language (English) in our partner meetings, and had used English when constructing the research instruments, this did not mean that we shared common understandings about the meanings of the words we were using in English. Terms like 'refugee', 'black', 'immigrant', 'forced migration', 'trafficking', and 'smuggled' all carried different connotations in different understandings of English. For example, in the UK, the term 'black' is considered the correct and appropriate term to use when referring to minority ethnic workers and is a political definition, implying power relationships and a past of struggle against the British colonial power. In Belgium, in contrast, the term was regarded as deeply offensive and would be used neither in its French/Flemish translation nor in English. In contrast the term 'black economy' was commonly used in a number of partner countries to describe the informal sector, whereas in the UK that term is generally avoided, usually replaced with other terms such as the 'grey economy' or the informal economy. And at the heart of the discussion was the term 'undocumented' itself. Terms like 'illegal', which the UWT project was committed from the start not to use, were commonly used in some of the partner countries and, in truth, despite months of discussion about the meanings attached to terms and their negative consequences, some of the partners never completely moved away from its usage, because it was so dominant a term in their own country context.

Indeed it was the issue of what we mean by what we say that led to the decision to produce a glossary[3] that would be our way of exploring the terms that we commonly used and of trying to come to a definition which each of the partners could sign up to. The aims of the glossary were to develop definitions that could be *analytically* applicable in different contexts, recognising that both the definitions and the institutional and practical consequences of words are

- Contextual: they are specific to the national and other contexts in which they are used and understood.
- Situational: they refer to the experiences of those people who are subject to those definitional and operational categories, specifically undocumented migrants themselves.
- Gradual: words have different meanings and consequences depending on many factors such as migrants' length of residency, year of entry, etc.

As the glossary notes, 'The research team's common understanding has been that words and terms are political, social, historical and cognitive constructions, serving the needs of different countries and times and are subject to ongoing conceptual development and redefinition'. Did we succeed in conveying the same message through speaking the same language? It is hard to judge. Deeply rooted understandings are difficult to set aside, and it is not the case that we came out of the project all 'singing from the same tune book'. But focusing on what we said, and consequently on what we wrote and how we conveyed messages and ideas, ensured that we were more careful in our choice of language, realising that how we conveyed a message, through the vocabulary we used, was an important element in the research, reflecting on Bourdieu's (1991) work on language and symbolic power.

Bacon too, in his work on the undocumented in the US, has questioned the use of the term 'illegal', asking 'What accounts then, for the almost universal use of "illegal"? Without doubt this has been a victory for a small but vocal nativist movement with deep racist roots' (Bacon, 2008:v). Furthermore, as we have already noted in Chapter 2, historical connotations of 'illegality' in the context of migration are closely associated with the stigmatisation of the Jews during the period of German fascism. We were further encouraged in this direction by the work of Ruhs and Anderson (2008), who had challenged the function and use of the term 'illegality' in relation to the discourse on migration. Their work, which argues for the abandonment of pejorative terms like 'illegal', substituting them with terms like 'compliant', 'semi-compliant', and 'non-compliant' (at p.1), reflected better the realities we found in the UWT research, where status was something that was not fixed and often moved between semi-compliance towards either non-compliance or compliance. Their analysis also fitted very much with our own attempts to posit that undocumented migration could not be linked with concepts of illegal actions per se, but that undocumented status was a consequence of state action and was a status of fluidity, with the so-called undocumented in fact often weaving in and out of different statuses. As our project statement made clear: 'The UWT project rejects the use of this term [illegal] to describe individuals, believing, along with many migrant organisations, that it has a connotation with criminality, and that most undocumented migrants are not criminals.'

In the glossary, too, the term 'illegal immigrants' was discussed and is rejected as a suitable term for the following reasons:

> 'Illegal immigrants' is a term used in public and political debate referring to those 'illegally resident' or those 'illegally working'. However, the term 'illegal' in connection with migrants has political and/or societal consequences, which lead to denying humanity or basic human rights for a person or a group of people not from a specific country. The term 'illegal migrant' also suggests a close linkage to, and maintains

a connotation of, criminality. Furthermore, labelling asylum seekers who find themselves in an irregular situation as 'illegal' may further jeopardize their asylum claims as it encourages a political climate of intolerance towards those seeking asylum.

Schrover et al. (2008:10) take a different position, arguing that alternative terms, such as 'undocumented', are ambiguous 'since sometimes it is used to denote migrants who have not been documented and sometimes to describe migrants without documents . . . [and that] neither situation applies to all illegal migrants'. For them the term 'illegal' 'has the advantage that it refers to the way in which migrants relate to the construction of what is legal'. We take a different position believing that the language that we use conveys particular messages and that it is insufficient merely to replicate the labels imposed, even if those on whom the imposition is made 'accept' the label. The fact that those who are vulnerable express their vulnerability (for example, by referring to their own status as 'illegal') is of itself not a reason for us to adopt it.[4] We have the duty as researchers not just to present the data we collect; we have to go beyond this to contextualise the data, so as to provide a clearer understanding of the world in which we conduct our research. We also have a duty not to contribute to the stigmatisation of research subjects, even if the very consequence of their vulnerability encourages their own self-stigmatisation.

Of course it should be stated that the issue is not resolved merely by being more careful in our choice of language. Issues of border controls and restrictions on entry to migrants, particularly because they usually are racially determined, are not simply a response to the terms that are used. We echo the observations of researchers like Wihtol de Wendon (2007), who argues that a new perspective on migration demands acceptance of a right to mobility as a fundamental human right and of Gordon (2007), who argues for a fundamental change in migration policies towards the construction of what she calls 'transnational labour citizenship' where migration is constructed around a model of demonstrated citizenship in the country of origin.

We need not only to understand what we are saying when we communicate with one another in research but we also need the more practical tools of communication. How do we ensure that all partners are included in all correspondence, that all documents are equally available, and that any discussion draws in all of the players, regardless of where they are geographically situated? In the UWT project this required the use of an open text management system[5] on which all documents were logged and where all email correspondence took place. There are many systems available, which allow for the effective exchange of documents. Furthermore, although we did not use e-conferencing systems such as Skype in the UWT project, we have since found them a useful means of sharing and communicating with partners in the course of our work on other European projects.

ETHICAL ISSUES IN RESEARCHING
UNDOCUMENTED MIGRANTS ACROSS EUROPE

In researching the lives of undocumented migrants, the need to work within clearly agreed ethical guidelines is always important but becomes even more significant whenever research teams come from different countries, possibly working under their own national ethical guidelines. In the UWT project it was clear from the beginning that we needed to have a set of guidelines that protected both the research subjects the undocumented migrants (whom we intended to interview) and the researchers themselves. The research had to be carried out observing standards that were transparent and which made it clear that the research was not compromised by unethical behaviours or methods. At the onset all consortium partners signed an agreement. This set out what each would do and what partners expected of one another. Importantly it laid down a mechanism for the resolution of disagreements between partners and provided that, in an extreme case, a partner could be asked to leave the consortium. Included within the consortium agreement was the RESPECT Code of Practice for Socio-economic Research, which is intended to form the basis of a voluntary code of practice for research in Europe. Having a well-recognised set of guidelines is essential and the fact that all of the partner organisations were familiar with RESPECT was useful. However, once we had begun our research it became clear that we needed a set of ethical guidelines and procedures that were specific to the project and which addressed both the research topic and the specifics of researching within an international partnership. At our second partner meeting we presented the UWT Project Ethical Guidelines and Procedures, which were drawn up by Tessa Wright, a member of the UK team. The guidelines begin with the following statement:

> The ethical issues involved in this research on undocumented migrant workers are considerable, both in terms of the duty of care towards the interviewees and interviewers, and the responsibility of the project to minimise the potential for misuse of the data provided for political ends that could stimulate a xenophobic or racist reaction.

The guidelines covered three areas of activity: avoidance of social and personal harm; data collection and storage; and publication and dissemination of research findings. While all three areas are also covered in the RESPECT guidelines, we sought to tailor them specifically to our project. By doing this we believed that partners would be more likely to apply the guidelines, given that they had emerged through a discussion based on an understanding of the particular issues related to our research. Our ethical guidelines called attention to their role within the partnership through their initial statement that 'ethical issues and their implications will be considered at all stages of the project, and discussed at twice-yearly project meetings'. This meant that there was a specific requirement to review our ethics throughout the lifetime of the project.

The issue of risks and their assessment was also important within the research. We were interviewing individuals who could risk deportation (and, in some cases, imprisonment and then deportation) should their identity or whereabouts be revealed to the state authorities. The important issue was that all partners should assess the risks to the individuals concerned before conducting any interview. We also needed to be absolutely sure that those being approached for an interview understood what we were doing in the project and what the research would be used for. It was for this reason that we required of all interviewees that they completed an 'informed consent' form prior to any interview. We agreed that if there were cases where the research might put an individual at particular risk, we would not go ahead with the interviews or with any further formal contact. This alone was a major issue to address but was magnified through our acknowledgement of vulnerability of those being interviewed and that they might conceptualise the research project itself as a support mechanism, valuable to them precisely because it was outside the networks which they had access to. Our guidelines made it clear that all interviewees would remain anonymous. No identification by name/address/or any other data, would be stored within our data collection material. The agreed project guidelines specified the following:

> The duty of care towards the interviewees, who may be non-compliant, semi-compliant or trafficked workers, must be paramount, and for this reason we will guarantee absolute anonymity to our respondents, in terms of both their participation in the project and published output. They will be informed that they do not have to give their name (or may provide a false name). Where names are given, these will not be recorded on any electronic documents, including lists, transcripts or notes, but will instead be replaced by a code. Other information that might identify the respondent may also be anonymised in published outputs, such as the workplace name.

These requirements were applied not only by the research team but also by any community fieldworkers appointed. The guidelines also made particular reference to the obligation on translators and interpreters to maintain confidentiality. Partners agreed that specific training on ethical issues would be given to anyone undertaking interviews.

The Ethics of Compensation

A major ethical issue arose at initiation of the research over whether to offer monetary compensation to the migrants whom we interviewed. As far as the funder was concerned, there was no budget for such payments and if members of the consortium wanted to make such offers they would have to provide for them out of their own funds. Some of the consortium members did not favour providing incentives and had never done so in any previous research. Others, including the authors, favoured the offer of small monetary incentives (usually by way of store vouchers) based on the view that 'the payment of an incentive represents, on the part of the researchers, a clear recognition of the value of the interviewee's time to the project' (McKay, 2009:47). A third position did not in principle disapprove of the giving of incentives but in these cases the partners did not have the available material resources, in the absence of provision from the funder. This meant that we had to come to a common understanding of the practices that we would adopt in the different countries. We did this by including within our ethical guidelines provision that acknowledged that although this was an issue that was contested, we commonly agreed that it was important to compensate individuals in whatever way was appropriate, to make it clear that we acknowledged the valuable contribution of the interviewee to the research. Compensation could range from the offer of vouchers to phone cards or even to the offer of a cup of coffee or something to eat during the interview.

Whether or not to offer monetary compensation is an issue where there are conflicts of opinion within the research community. Some contend that offering incentives can potentially distort research findings, as it may result in individuals offering themselves for interview solely because a payment is anticipated. But as one of the authors has argued previously (McKay and Snyder, 2009), there is no reason why an individual's story would be any more or less honest simply because a small incentive is available. Lammers (2005) similarly holds that incentives are no more likely to skew results than the non-offer. But what incentives may do is to facilitate access into communities and networks where otherwise there might be insurmountable hurdles. That remains our view, based not only on the UWT project but also in all of the projects that we have been engaged in, either separately or together, where we have found that offering incentives appears to increase the opportunities for access. But even if this was not the case, we would still favour their use because they provide for an element of reciprocity between researcher and interviewee.

CONDUCTING RESEARCH SAFELY

Research is not usually considered as a risk profession. We think of risks at work in relation to sectors like construction, security, or agriculture. The confines of a university or research institute are not normally associated with risk and risk assessment. Yet aspects of research can compromise safety, and we have been aware of the need to institute risk assessments related to the specific research being undertaken. Researching undocumented workers is not per se more risky than researching other groups of workers, but as in any research using qualitative methodologies, researchers will encounter situations where interviews are arranged in localities unfamiliar to them and possibly at times of the day where there are few others around. The consequences of workers being undocumented, as this book demonstrates, are that they are less likely to be available for interview during 'normal' working hours. The accommodation that they are able to access/afford is more likely to be in areas where poverty creates situations where violent behaviours are more on the surface. It is for these reasons that we favour having systems in place that help ensure that researchers in the field are not put in danger. This can include keeping a record of where interviews are taking place, using discrete mobile phone numbers for the research project, and phoning colleagues to provide whereabouts when interviewing either late at night, in the early morning, or at an address offered by the interviewee.

COLLECTING DATA IN CROSS-NATIONAL RESEARCH

How data is collected is important in any research but becomes even more central when it is being collected in very different country contexts. In the UWT project, partners included those researching in countries with long histories of inward migration (like Austria, Belgium, Denmark, and the UK); those in countries which had traditionally been exporters of labour and whose cultural heritage was still dominated by the notion of departure rather than arrival (Italy and Spain); and one country, Bulgaria, where there was some history of inward migration but within the closed confines of the previous Soviet system.

Each partner agreed to conduct 10 interviews with stakeholders and 30 interviews with migrant workers. But at this point we had to decide what common elements we would include within the selection of migrant interviewees. It may appear desirable to construct a sample that can be exactly mirrored in each country. This would have required that we each conduct the same number of interviews with each potential group within the sample—whether defined by their gender, ethnicity, period of time since migration, age, sector of employment, formal or informal economies, for example. However, in discussing the demographic composition of undocumented migration in the different countries, it became clear that it would not be possible to construct a sample which replicated conditions dominant in one country, given that they might to a greater part be absent in another. Imposing such a tight control on the sample risked skewing it as much as any other method, as researchers would be forced to seek out exact matches to the sample, at the expense of looking at wider experiences that could be brought into the research, by focusing on the dominant features within each country, as revealed through the country reports. Of course there were a number of similarities in terms of the eventual samples selected. Some sectors were more prevalent than others: domestic and caring work, primarily in private homes (predominantly female); construction (predominantly male); and catering and cleaning (both male and female). In the end we decided that interviewees were to be chosen through snowballing, gatekeepers, and any contacts that the researchers had already established. Some of the partner teams included individuals who had a shared country of origin with recently arrived migrants. This obviously advantaged the teams in their access to those groups of migrants, but, as Markova (2009) and Mestheneos (2006) show, this could also trap them within specific national groups and there is certainly the risk of less variation of country of origin in such cases. We all agreed that it was important that the interviews reflected the experiences of women undocumented migrants, as well as of men, and we agreed that at least 40 per cent of the interviewees would be female. In the end almost half of them were, demonstrating that the voices of women can be articulated where there is a commitment to do so.

Those researching migration often point to the difficulties that language barriers present and there is a body of literature on the issue (for example, Alcoff, 1991; Temple, 2002; Temple and Edwards, 2006) and on the use of interpreters, with some arguing that conducting interviews in the language of origin contributes to the situation of trust (Dahinden and Efionayi-Mäder, 2009). But in researching migrants in different countries, language is an additional problem. For it is not only that there may be a language barrier between researchers and researched, but there will equally be a language constraint between researchers themselves. Working across national boundaries requires agreement to use a common language, and this advantages those researchers whose first language it is and disadvantages those whose it is not. More importantly, the testimony of migrants themselves is potentially filtered many times. From individual through interpreter to national researcher, through a further translation to the research team responsible for compiling the final analysis leading to a publication. Not only is there a greater risk of loss of meaning, but also the process becomes very labour intensive, if interviews are to be transcribed from language of origin to language of destination country and from that to the common language of the research team, to enable the analysis of the data. Inevitably, given the time and budgetary constraints of most research projects, this is rarely permissible. In the UWT project, the method chosen to reduce the difficulties was for interviews to be conducted, where possible, in the language of the destination country or in a language otherwise common to researcher and interviewee. This avoided the intermediation of an interpreter but of course it was not possible in every case and interpreters were used where there was no common language. Interviews were recorded and although there were a few cases where individuals refused to be recorded, they proved to be in a minority, given that the research ethics in relation to confidentiality had been clearly explained. At this stage of the research process, we therefore had recordings of most of the interviews or at least a lengthy note of the interview. All partner teams were then asked to provide an interview note in the common research language (English). The note, generally around six pages in length for each interview, explored it through an agreed series of themes—status transitions, gender, social and human capital, and informal economies. Using this method has allowed all of the partners access to the data from the more than 300 interviews carried out in the course of the project. They can use this to produce their own research publications and articles for additional dissemination, and we are pleased that this has led to publications in different languages, all based on the UWT data.

CONCLUSION

In this chapter we have reflected on the particular methodological issues related to projects that involve working with partners in different countries. We have shown that working collaboratively means developing methods that take account of how we communicate with one another and agreeing on common ethical codes that are shaped to the needs of the project. Furthermore we have stressed that, in relation to researching undocumented workers, the methodological issues become entwined with issues of ethics that go beyond how the research is conducted to take note of the specific duties that we owe to those whom we are researching. Having now set out the overall context for the research, in the next chapter we turn to look at the European political context and at the measures that EU states have put in place in attempts to limit or prevent migration.

5   Controlling Undocumented Migration at EU Level

> In practice, as well as a tap regulating the flow of workers to a state, immigration controls might be more usefully conceived as a mould constructing certain types of workers through selection of legal entrants, the requiring and enforcing of certain types of employment relations, and the creation of institutional uncertainty.
>
> (Anderson, 2010:312)

We have begun this chapter with a statement taken from a recent article by Bridget Anderson, a UK academic who has written and researched on migration for more than a decade. Anderson's comment is useful because it reminds us that immigration controls do more than just determine state policies in relation to entry and border controls, they affect the employment conditions under which the undocumented work. States are bound by international obligations that protect fundamental human rights[1] and thus accept some restrictions on their powers in relation to migration policies. This is the case with regard to protections afforded to asylum seekers and refugees, but there is also a large body of international law that recognises the fundamental rights of migrants (Cholewinski et al., 2007; European Union, 2006). The focus of this chapter is not, however, on international law but on how the European Union and its Member States manage their immigration policies, with regard to undocumented migrants, including unsuccessful asylum seekers. We begin by looking at the context of EU migration policies from the 1970s onwards, emphasising the contradictions that have always been present, between, on the one hand, the need to encourage migration as a response to skill shortages, demographic changes, and competitiveness, and on the other hand, the seeming imperative to tighten borders and to reject those who have entered without state authority. This is further complicated by the principle of 'subsidiarity', defined in Article 5 of the Treaty establishing the European Community, which requires that decisions are taken as closely as possible to the citizen and that constant checks are made as to whether action at Community level is justified, where equivalent actions could have been taken at Member State level. This has restrained the development of Community law in the area of migration, although as the UWT study found, the legislative frameworks at national state level have become more unified in recent years. In this context both individual Member State policies and those at EU level are converging in a co-ordinated attempt to prevent undocumented migration, although differences remain over how this should be achieved. Furthermore, we note that

EU policies have moved towards an increased focus on security and one that links undocumented migration with a threat to security.

The chapter then turns to institutional frameworks and to the rules that guide immigration policies in the EU, as they impact on undocumented migrants. Finally we look at the range of the different (mainly punitive) strategies adopted in response to undocumented migration, principally, security and visa requirements; policies on detention, deportation, and return (the Return Directive); employer sanctions; carrier penalties; and readmission agreements. Although the latter are presented as positive forms of engagement with sending countries, we argue that they are under-scored by policies related to either the access or the withdrawal of aid.

In October 2005 the Global Commission on International Migration published a major report *Migration in an interconnected world: new directions for action* (Global Comission, 2005). The Commission had been established in 2003 on the encouragement of then UN Secretary-General Kofi Annan, with a mandate to provide the framework for the formulation of a coherent, comprehensive, and global response to the issue of international migration. The report pays particular attention to addressing irregular migration:

> States, exercising their sovereign right to determine who enters and remains on their territory should fulfil their responsibility and obligations to protect the rights of migrants and to re-admit those citizens who wish or are obliged to return to their country of origin. In stemming irregular migration, states should actively cooperate with one another, ensuring that their efforts do not jeopardise human rights, including the right of refugees to seek asylum. Governments should consult with employers, trade unions and civil society on this issue. (Global Commission on International Migration, 2005:4)

The Global Commission report argued that irregular migration challenged the exercise of state sovereignty; that it could become a threat to public security where corruption and organised crime were involved; and that it also could result in competition for jobs, while generating xenophobic sentiments. The Commission pointed to the fact that 'a large but unknown number of people die each year' (Global Commission, 2005:34) in trying to migrate without being detected by the state authorities, and it called on states to address the conditions that promote irregular migration, by providing additional opportunities for regular migration and by taking action against employers who engage migrants with irregular status.

How has the European Union responded to the Global Commission? It has certainly taken action against employers who hire undocumented migrants (see "Migration Policies at EU Level" below). However, rather than providing additional opportunities for regular migration, Member States, the European Commission, and the European Parliament have supported measures that limit the numbers of third-country nationals with regular status, a consequence of which, in our view, can only result in more undocumented migration, either in the short or the long term. At the same time, the European Commission has stood against those Member States (principally Italy, Spain, and Greece) that have introduced regularisation schemes with the aim of improving the position of undocumented migrants (see Chapter 7) by providing some opportunities for their regularisation. In its most recent annual report the European Commission calls on Member States to pursue return policies and to reject large-scale regularisation (European Commission, 2009). In April 2010 Cecilia Malmström, EU Commissioner for Home Affairs, criticised the Spanish state system, which allows all to register at their municipality of residence, regardless of their legal status, and which in turn gives access to essential welfare rights, such as health care and education. Malmström argues that registration should immediately result in the initiation of the 'return' procedures to remove undocumented migrants.

In his major contribution on migration, Piore points out that policies aimed at preventing people from entering result in those who do enter unlawfully not risking leaving, for fear of being unable to return (Piore, 1979:180). Engbersen (2001), in his study on irregular migrants in the Netherlands, demonstrates how strategies to enter and reside in the country are related to restrictive migration policy. He finds four residence strategies of irregular migrants: the mobilisation of social capital, marriages, manipulation of one's own identity and nationality, and operating strategically in the public sphere. European governments try to influence these residence strategies through immigration and also the criminal law. Engbersen states that 'panopticion Europe' evokes unanticipated effects with its restrictive policy towards immigrants: 'First, it generates its own crimes to subsequently combat these with advanced identification systems'. This results in a growing informal economy where irregular migrants work, as well as in a rising delinquency of irregular migrants in order to survive. 'Secondly the restrictive policy has a negative effect on the self-regulating capacity of ethnic groups in order to support illegal immigrants. . . .Third, the strengthening of the internal border control . . .has the effect that some illegal immigrants do not exercise the rights they—or their children—actually do have' (Engbersen, 2001:242–243).

Rejecting such well-established interpretations, the European Commission asserts that controls on migration are essential to ensure its effective management and to guarantee the integration of legally resident migrants. Such policies, however, rarely consider their impact on the numbers or the living conditions of undocumented migrants. While the Commission has recently pointed to evidence suggesting a fall in the number of undocumented migrants (attributing this in part to its policies in relation to tighter immigration controls), the Global Commission (2005) reminds us that '[t]he growth of irregular migration is also linked to a lack of regular migration opportunities'.

At the outset we have to point out that although we reject terms that associate undocumented migrants with illegality (see Chapter 4), we have been obliged to use such terms in this chapter, as any review of EU regulations in relation to migration cannot fail to note that, unlike the Global Commission on Migration—which acknowledged 'the controversy surrounding the adequacy of concepts' to describe those who have no authorisation either in relation to residence or work and, as such, concurred with the assertion 'that an individual person cannot be irregular or illegal'—the EU does not reject such descriptions. The Commission uses the term 'illegal migration' to describe a 'variety of phenomena', including those entering illegally (by whatever means, including by use of false documents), those entering legally either with or without a valid visa who then overstay or change their purpose of stay without approval, and those who are unsuccessful asylum seekers (Communication dated 19 July 2006).

EU policy in relation to undocumented migration is strongly associated with its identification of it with illegality, leading the Commission to make frequent reference to security with reference to undocumented migration.[2] There is a heavy reliance on measures favouring 'security' including in relation to border and return policies which Meng-Hsuan Chou (2006:15–16) suggests is linked to the requirement for unanimous voting in the Parliament that increases the likelihood that security-orientated measures will be adopted so that '[t]he overwhelming presence of the security rationale and the absence of a foundation for a common EU migration policy are two factors preventing a coherent comprehensive approach from being established and practiced.'

MIGRATION POLICIES AT EU LEVEL

Triandafyllidou and Ilies (2010) in their review of EU irregular migration polices, locate 1976 as the first time that irregular migration came into discussion at EU level, when the Commission presented a proposal for a directive on the harmonisation of Member State legislation on migration. They trace the second significant development to the 1985 Schengen Agreement, which eliminated border controls within a group of Member States, so that entry into one allowed free movement within all others. By providing for free internal movement between the states this allowed for a focus on a concept of a single border control and thus strengthened the role of the EU in its management.

An examination of EU migration polices from the late 1990s onwards shows that while there appear to be a raft of policies, one following on from the other, more or less every one or two years, they all focus on the same areas of activity, around expulsions and other forms of sanction. In 1998, the Justice and Home Affairs Council adopted the Vienna Action Plan (European Commission, 1998) of the Council and the Commission, on how best to implement the provisions of the Treaty of Amsterdam (European Commission, 1997) on an area of freedom, security, and justice. This underlined the effective combating of what the Commission, in its documents, has continued to refer to

as 'illegal migration'. The Amsterdam Treaty created the Community competences in the field, setting out the legal basis for regulations relating to border
controls and visa policies, together with measures on illegal immigration and
illegal residence, including the repatriation of illegal residents. Indeed, in its
Communication of July 2006 (COM, 2006:402), the Commission noted that
'addressing illegal migration has been a central part of the EU's common immigration policy since its inception in 1999'. In that year the European Council
in Tampere (Finland) agreed to coordinate national measures in the field of
migration, aiming at a common migration policy across the EU. This led to
adoption, in 2002, by the EU Council of Ministers of an *Action plan on illegal
migration to combat illegal migration and trafficking of human beings in the
European Union* (European Commission, 2002).

This common policy on illegal migration, based on a return action programme which suggested developing a number of short-, medium-, and
long-term measures, including common EU-wide minimum standards or
guidelines, in relation to the return of undocumented residents. This provided for greater exchange of information and statistics between Member
States and supported further co-operation with countries of origin on
readmission and return. It additionally proposed, as a condition of future
admission to the EU, that potential candidate countries incorporate the
relevant body of EU law into their domestic legislation and practices. At
the same time cooperation agreements were to be developed with transit
countries 'to help them tackle the problem of gaps at border controls'. The
stage was set for implementation of the Hague programme (European Commission, 2005) commencing from 2005, supporting a common policy on
illegal migration and 'return' procedures that was to apply in all Member
States. Although the programme called for a policy against illegal migration that was 'both firm yet respectful of the rights and dignity of third
country nationals', its key focus was on measures either to bar entry or
to enforce returns. The programme explained the need for such policies
as follows: 'In the absence of common criteria for the admission of legal
migrants, the number of third country citizens entering the EU illegally and
without any guarantee of a declared job—and thus of integrating in our
societies—will grow.'

The Hague programme was premised on the conclusion of 'readmission
agreements' between countries of origin and Member States. These agreements continue to be a key part of the EU's migration strategy and they
have been concluded with six third countries, with around another five
countries where discussions are continuing. However, they are not without
their critics who suggest that there is the potential for their close association with aid packages, with claims that aid will only go to those countries
that agree to the return arrangements (Adepoju et al., 2010).

Two years further on and the Commission had another set of proposals
on migration. In July 2006 it adopted a Communication on *Policy priorities in the fight against illegal immigration of third-country nationals*

(COM, 2006:402). For the first time this included formal cooperation with third countries (joint patrols, surveillances, and reinforced response capacity), the further strengthening of external borders (creation of a generalised and automated entry-exit system for registration, "e-borders" system), a position on regularisation, and a review of its returns policy based on further readmission agreements and enhanced use of joint return flights. It also called for improved information exchange systems through ICONet and Europol (see "Creating a Single Border and Transferring Information Data across Member States" below).

The concept of readmission agreements between sending and receiving states was advanced through the Rabat Action Plan (Euro-African Partnership for Migration and Development, 2006) when representatives from European states met with officials from African states to acknowledge the importance of addressing the root causes of irregular migration, within a declared focus on promoting circular and temporary migration, taking account of the needs of the labour market. They declared the following:

> We commit to creating and developing a close partnership between our respective countries so as to work together, following a comprehensive, balanced, pragmatic and operational approach, and respecting the rights and dignity of migrants and refugees, as regards the phenomenon of migratory routes that affect our peoples.

This partnership between the countries of origin, transit, and destination was aimed at offering a 'concrete and appropriate response to the fundamental issue of controlling migratory flows' and was based on a strong conviction that the 'management of migration between Africa and Europe must be carried out within the context of a partnership to combat poverty and promote sustainable development and co-development'.

In June 2008 a further Communication from the Commission on *A common immigration policy for Europe: principles, actions and tools* (COM/2008/0359 Final) noted that immigration was 'an opportunity and a challenge for the EU' but that there was the need for Member States and the EU to act 'on the basis of a common vision' as a prerequisite both for managing legal migration and for 'fighting illegal migration, whilst upholding universal values such as [the] protection of refugees, respect for human dignity and tolerance' (*Press release*, 17 June 2008). The Communication noted that there were no reasons to believe that immigration flows into the EU would decrease and for this reason:

> Managing immigration effectively means addressing also different issues linked to the security of our societies and of immigrants themselves. This requires fighting illegal immigration and criminal activities related to it, striking the right balance between individual integrity and collective security concerns.

The Communication forcefully linked undocumented migration with criminality, arguing that societal security was premised on excluding undocumented migrants and that '[i]llegal employment needs to be tackled as it creates situations of abuse and violation of fundamental rights and freedoms. It also undermines legal immigration and has negative implications with regard to cohesion and fair competition'.

The Stockholm programme (European Commission, 2009), which will cover the period 2010 to 2014, replaces the Hague programme. It represents no change in the EU's priorities regarding undocumented migration and indeed continues to focus on the same issues: return, border control, and readmission agreements noting:

> In order to maintain credible and sustainable immigration and asylum systems in the EU, it is necessary to prevent, control and combat illegal migration as the EU faces an increasing pressure from illegal migration flows and particularly the Member States at its external borders, including at its Southern borders.

The context of the Hague and Stockholm programmes is of interest in relation to its continued emphasis on the need to respond to undocumented migration. Whereas its claim is that the EU is facing increased pressure from illegal migration, in other contexts the EU has also claimed a dramatic revision downwards in its estimates of undocumented migrants, from 8 million to 3.8 million (European Commission, 2010). Clearly, either there are many fewer undocumented migrants in the EU and therefore the need for controls should be lessening and not increasing, or the numbers are still large and there is a policy imperative to imply that policies based on returns and bilateral agreements are effective.

In other areas, there have also been further developments. The European Parliament and the Council adopted Directive 2008/115/EC on *Common standards and procedures for returning illegally staying third-country nationals*. A year later it adopted the Sanctions Directive (see "Employer Sanctions" below).

At the same time the Commission Work Programme 2010 *Time to act* (COM (2010) 135 Final), while demonstrating a focus on 'integrating the immigrant population' again emphasises the need to ensure both an open and a secure Europe, the latter achieved through 'addressing illegal immigration' (para. 3.2).

CREATING A SINGLE BORDER AND TRANSFERRING INFORMATION DATA ACROSS MEMBER STATES

The principal body concerned with the management of the EU's external borders is FRONTEX. Established in 2004, with its head office in

Poland, the agency is charged with assisting Member States in the control and surveillance of their external borders. It now operates, along with the Member States located in the Southern Mediterranean, a Coastal Patrols Network. FRONTEX has organised naval patrols in the Aegean Sea and in the sea between Libya, Malta, and the Island of Lampedusa, aimed at deterring 'boatloads of migrants from entering European waters' (Bowcott, 2010). It is also heavily involved in return activities. FRONTEX has a particular focus on the control of the Schengen border, where the existence of a common Member State border highlights the requirement for competences beyond the Member State.

The FRONTEX 2009 report notes that in that year Member States and Schengen associated countries reported 106,200 detections of illegal border crossings at the sea and land borders of the EU, a 33 per cent decrease from the previous year. This fall was attributed to the economic downturn lessening the 'pull' factor and the 'strong deterrent effect' of reinforced navel patrols (PICUM, 2010:11). In terms of nationality, the largest single detections were of Albanians (around 40 per cent), followed by Afghans (15 per cent) and Somalis (10 per cent).

The system of funding for FRONTEX activities is one that has been strongly criticised by the Southern receiving countries of Malta, Cyprus, Greece, and Italy, who in 2010, constructed as the 'Quadro Group', called for the costs of patrolling the Southern borders to be shared by all Member States, rather than falling on them. A change to FRONTEX guidelines in 2010, which requires that migrants picked up in search and rescue operations must be taken to the mission's host country rather than to the nearest port, resulted in Malta withdrawing from hosting FRONTEX missions. At a meeting of EU Council of Justice and Interior ministers on 3 June 2010,[14] it was noted that Greece was the country with the largest influx of irregular migrants coming from Turkey, with a call for the Turkish government to cooperate with the EU FRONTEX.

In 2010, following an impact assessment on the role of FRONTEX, the European Commission amended Council Regulation 2007/2004/EC which established the agency, to provide for compulsory contributions, both financial and in terms of human resources, from all Member States, while giving the agency a co-leading role in the implementation of joint operations against undocumented migration. FRONTEX and the Fundamental Rights Agency have also recently signed a cooperation agreement, aimed, in part, at assisting FRONTEX in integrating a fundamental rights approach into its activities, suggesting, at the very least, that this was recognised as an area where FRONTEX was weak.

The development of this common agenda for combating undocumented migration has resulted in new forms of sharing of data across Member States, challenging the concept of Member State sovereignty as well as potentially impacting on civil rights. There are a number of different institutions which we argue have contributed to this reduction in civic liberties. ICONet (a web-based network for the exchange between Member States of strategic, tactical, and operational information concerning the movement of undocumented migrants), established by a Decision of the European Commission in 2006 (2005/267/EC), (Europa Press Release, 20 January 2006) consists of networks of immigration liaison officers of Member States posted in countries of origin which, in its 2010 report on migration (SEC(2010) 535 final), the European Commission indicated might be taken over by FRONTEX making it potentially more powerful. Indeed it is notable that within a relatively short space of time proposals to share information more widely have been accepted and adopted. For example, in September 2009 the European Commission presented a proposal to give police officers of Europol (the European Law Enforcement Agency) access to EURODAC, the European database holding the fingerprints of asylum seekers and persons who entered the EU irregularly. Europol itself was established to improve the effectiveness of Member States in dealing with preventing and combating terrorism, unlawful drug trafficking, and other serious forms of organised crime. The identification of undocumented migrants and asylum seekers with such forms of serious criminality is another demonstration of how the European Commission understands migration.

The impact of all of these new measures of control has meant a withdrawal of fundamental rights, as a report from the nongovernmental organisation PICUM (Platform for International Cooperation on Undocumented Migrants) has argued. In many Member States, undocumented migrants no longer have access to health care, despite the fact that this is recognised as a fundamental right (Cholewinski, 2006).

SECURITY AND VISA REQUIREMENTS

While EU policies are stated as 'providing a balance between rights and security' in practice, their emphasis is on security (Chou, 2006:1; Triandafyllidou and Ilies, 2010:26) and it is clear that the future direction of these policies is premised on an even greater focus on security. The Commission is open to policies that go far beyond those currently in place. Already, in 2002, in its proposals regarding the combating of illegal immigration, it noted that a visa policy could 'significantly contribute to the prevention of illegal immigration' and that a future harmonised visa policy in this area would make it possible to prevent the entry of non-authorised persons into the territory of the Member States. The aim is for

- Uniform visa standards to improve security through visa and resident permits, using new technologies including biometric data;
- The creation of a common administrative structure to strengthen co-operation between EU consulates and third countries; and
- Development of a European Visa Identification System.

Furthermore its 2006 Communication envisaged the extension of border controls through the registration of the entry and exit of all third-country nationals, noting, 'In the future biometric technology, such as fingerprints and digital photographs, will have a significant impact on border control systems and should be exploited to enhance the effectiveness of border control operations'. Two years later, a 2008 Communication supported a visa policy that would apply throughout the EU.

THE RETURN DIRECTIVE

Return is now a key feature of the EU's policies in relation to undocumented migration. It is conceptualised as a necessary part of migration policy, with an assumption that return is a requirement for public acquiescence to migration. The stated aim is that all undocumented migrants who are apprehended should be returned either to their country of origin or to a transit country. As the 2006 Communication notes, 'Return remains a cornerstone of EU migration policy. An effective return policy is key in ensuring public support for elements such as legal migration and asylum.'

'Return' is the preferred term rather than 'expulsion' or 'deportation'. It implies that the process is voluntary, whereas the reality is that, even if undocumented migrants leave without the state having to exercise force, return is not voluntarily chosen by those who are captured. In order to fully implement this policy a *Return Action Programme* was agreed in 2002, and in September 2005 the Commission took this further with a proposal for a directive. The declared objectives were to provide for 'clear, transparent and fair common rules concerning return, removal, use of coercive measures, temporary custody and re-entry, while taking into full account the respect for human rights and fundamental freedoms of the persons concerned'. In December 2008 a directive (2008/115/EC) on *Common standards and procedures for returning illegally staying third country nationals* (the Return Directive) was adopted and had to be transposed by Member States into their national laws by October 2010. Its stated aims are to favour a voluntary system over a forced system of return:

> Where there are no reasons to believe that this would undermine the purpose of a return procedure, voluntary return should be preferred over forced return and a period for voluntary departure should be granted. An extension of the period for voluntary departure should be provided for when considered necessary because of the specific circumstances of an individual case. In order to promote voluntary return, Member States should provide for enhanced return assistance and counselling and make best use of the relevant funding possibilities offered under the European Return Fund.

However, in practice, despite these stated aims, the forced elements of the returns' policy dominate. The Commission's 2009 Annual Report notes that although voluntary departure appears to have become the preferred option of return, 'several Member States also adopt a more stringent policy on forced return, pointing to the deterrent effect'. This suggests that the return policy is used as a form of punishment to create a climate of fear. Article 7 of the Return Directive provides 'an appropriate period' of between seven and 30 days for an individual's voluntary departure. During this period, to avoid the risk of absconding, Member States can set requirements such as regular reporting to the authorities, deposit of an adequate financial guarantee, submission of documents, or the obligation to stay at a certain place. If by the end of the period the person does not leave, a repatriation order can be issued and this can lead to coercive measures, including imprisonment (detention) for six months that can be extended by another 12 months (Art. 15). Those subject to an expulsion can also be barred from any application to re-enter for up to five years or for longer 'if the third-country national represents a serious threat to public policy, public security or national security' (Art. 11). There is a right to appeal, under Article 13. Article 5 of the directive sets out the principle of non-refoulement[3] in relation to returns. This says that implementing the directive, Member States shall take due account of

(a) The best interests of the child;
(b) Family life; and
(c) The state of health of the third-country national concerned.

A Return Fund was established under the Hague programme in 2005, with €759m set aside for the period 2007 to 2013. The Return Directive stipulates that the fund can be utilised to assist in return procedures.

The Return Directive supports the organisation of 'joint return' flights. These are organised by FRONTEX and in 2009 flights were organised to Nigeria, Ecuador and Columbia, Georgia, Mongolia, Cameroon, Kosovo, Albania, Ivory Coast, Togo, Vietnam, and Gambia. One campaigning organisation newsletter (*Frontexplosion*) estimates that in 2009 more than 30 such flights took off, carrying more than 1,600 individuals. An issue that has arisen is to whether EU legislation requires that Member States return all undocumented migrants apprehended. This is important in the context of the provisions of the directive, in cases where the Member State is aware of the presence of undocumented migrants in the state territory. The European Court of Justice, in a ruling delivered in late 2009,[4] held that under EU law, where a person does not fulfil the requirements for lawful residence, a Member State *may* adopt a decision to expel that person but is not obliged to do so. This welcome decision makes it clear that there is no absolute requirement to implement the directions contained in the directive.

The Return Directive is one of the most contested areas of current EU policy. Undocumented migrants are now being returned, either to countries of origin or of transit, with seemingly little regard for their human rights, leading the Council of Europe's Committee for the Prevention of Torture and Inhuman or Degrading Treatment or Punishment to report, of its visit to Italy in 2009, that 'in its present form, Italy's policies of intercepting migrants at sea[5] and obliging them to return to Libya or other non-European countries, violates the principle of non-refoulement'. This is not a lone voice of opposition or concern. In September 2009 the Council of Europe's own Commissioner for Human Rights, in a speech entitled 'Europe must respect the rights of migrants', deplored the trend across Europe 'to repel, at any cost, irregular migrant flows, thus putting human lives at serious risk' arguing that the methods employed often violated international law principles (*PICUM newsletter*, October 2009). The Association for Human Rights in Andalusia, in a 2009 report, also found that 'peoples' rights are systematically violated in migration via Europe's Southern borders' (PICUM, 2009).

Readmission Agreements

A key part of the return policies are the readmission agreements concluded between Member States and third countries, the legal basis for which was originally in the Treaty of Amsterdam. As the First Annual Report on Immigration and Asylum (SEC(2010)535) notes, 'cooperation with countries of origin and transit is essential for policies on illegal immigration' and that 'further efforts should be made to negotiate and conclude readmission agreements'. Agreements have been concluded with Hong Kong, Sri Lanka, Macao, Albania, Russia, and Pakistan, with talks occurring with Libya, Morocco, Turkey, Georgia, and Cape Verde.

On 10 March 2004 the European Parliament and the Council adopted a regulation establishing a programme for financial and technical assistance to third countries in the area of migration and closely tied to readmission agreements is the issue of financial and technical assistance. Some Member States clearly link their aid programmes to their cooperation on readmission particularly through the AENEAS programme, which provides financial support to third countries in 'their efforts to deal with the problems arising from legal, illegal or forced migration'.

There has been criticism of the use of readmission agreements. As noted, from the list of countries where agreements have been concluded, this includes countries whose human rights record is poor. Furthermore, as Bouteillet-Paquet (2003) notes (cited in Chou, 2006:21), these partnerships are 'a euphemism for a policy that has so far produced little more than extended the control-driven policy' with little progress on economic development in countries of origin.

EMPLOYER SANCTIONS

As a measure aimed at tackling illegal employment, on 18 June 2009, the European Parliament adopted Directive 2009/52/EC *Providing for minimum standards on sanctions and measures against employers of illegally staying third-country nationals* (hereafter referred to as the Sanctions Directive). The directive will mainly have the effect of harmonising existing Member State arrangements rather than introducing new requirements, as the Commission has noted that at least 26 of the 27 Member States, at the date when the directive was passed, already had sanctions in place. The directive imposes financial sanctions on employers (including sub-contractors) who knowingly or recklessly employ undocumented migrants. The size of financial sanction can also include the costs of return, where return procedures are carried out (Art. 5(b)).

The preamble to the directive suggests that 'action against illegal immigration and illegal stay should therefore include measures to counter the pull factor' of employment. Jacques Barrot, EU Commissioner responsible for Justice, Freedom and Security welcoming the adoption of the directive, stated:

> The ease of finding illegal work in EU Member States is a main driving force behind illegal migration from third countries. The employment of illegally staying migrants is not a trivial matter, as it is harmful in many respects. Because of their dependency on the employer, such persons run a high risk of ending up in the harsh reality of exploitation and even sometimes slavery-like conditions. (*Press Release*, 19 February 2009)

The directive applies only with respect to those without a right of residence. It is not intended to apply to migrants with residency rights but without a right to work. However, it does cover all forms of employment including activities that are or ought to be remunerated, undertaken for or under the direction and/or supervision of an employer, irrespective of the legal relationship where work is undertaken. Under the terms of the directive, employers have to check residence papers before individuals start work, although they are not liable if papers subsequently are found to be false. They also have to inform the relevant authorities where they hire or terminate the employment of a third-country national. A simplified procedure for notification applies where employers 'are natural persons where the employment is for their private purposes' (work in a domestic household).

The Sanctions Directive contains three elements that could be considered as beneficial to workers. The first is that where it is found that an employer is employing undocumented workers, there is a requirement to pay any wages due and at least at the minimum rate of pay and that with respect to any outstanding remuneration to the illegally employed third-country national:

> The agreed level of remuneration shall be presumed to have been at least as high as the wage provided for by the applicable laws on minimum wages, by collective agreements or in accordance with established practice in the relevant occupational branches, unless either the employer or the employee can prove otherwise, while respecting, where appropriate, the mandatory national provisions on wages. (Art. 6)

This means that if employers are found to be employing undocumented migrants, they lose any economic advantage that they had in paying lower wages than the 'going rate'. However, there is nothing in the directive that requires the employer to make back payments for any wages that were less than the going rate, if the employee has already been paid. If the employer fails to make the payment, there is no obligation on the state to make it. Unless evidence to the contrary is provided, there is an assumption that the employment relationship has lasted at least three months (para. 17).

The second beneficial element is with respect to workers who have been 'subjected to particularly exploitative working conditions', defined as the following:

> Working conditions, including those resulting from gender based or other discrimination, where there is a striking disproportion compared with the terms of employment of legally employed workers which, for example, affects workers' health and safety, and which offends against human dignity; or who were illegally employed minors and who cooperate in criminal proceedings against the employer. (Art. 2(i))

In these cases the directive encourages the granting of residence permits of limited duration, linked to the length of the relevant national proceedings, to affected third-country nationals. Although this will only affect a minority of undocumented migrants, it provides at least a limited right to residence and might even encourage undocumented migrants to make complaints in relation to employer abuse.

The third positive element is in relation to taking complaints. Third parties designated by Member States, such as trade unions or other associations or a competent authority of the Member State, can lodge complaints against employers. This means that they can take such action without risking being taken to court for having assisted someone to stay in the country illegally (*Europa Press Release*, 22 January 2009).

The Sanctions Directive does not lay down the specific nature of sanctions, which can be administrative or criminal, as these are left to the Member State. However, Article 7 allows for states to do the following:

- Exclude employers from entitlement to aid or subsidies, including EU funding managed by Member States, for up to five years;
- Exclude participation in public contracts;

- Recover some or all of public benefits, aid, or subsidies, including EU funding managed by Member States, granted to the employer for up to 12 months preceding the detection of illegal employment; and
- Temporarily or permanently close any establishments that have been used to commit the infringement, or temporarily or permanently withdraw a license to conduct the business activity in question, if justified by the gravity of the infringement.

In serious cases the directive obliges Member States to provide for criminal penalties (Art. 9). These are cases defined as representing

- Persistently repeated infringements;
- The illegal employment of a significant number of third-country nationals;
- Particularly exploitative working conditions;
- The employer knowing that the worker is a victim of trafficking in human beings; and
- The illegal employment of a minor.

The Sanctions Directive also requires of Member States that they set an annual target number of inspections (raids) in workplaces 'where there is a particular risk of exploitation of illegally staying workers'. In our view this can only serve to encourage inspection authorities to go for 'easy' targets, principally ethnic enclave employment, as a quick route to meeting targets. The experience of immigration raids in the UK is that more than 80 per cent of them have been against minority ethnic employers (Evans, 2008). The Commission emphasises that the sanctions envisaged are against employers and not the workers themselves, but a major criticism of the use of sanctions is that they worsen conditions for undocumented migrants in two ways. First, employers faced with the threat of fines do not necessarily ensure that they only employ those who are documented. Instead they may pass on the possible costs of being caught, by providing even worse terms and conditions to those who are undocumented. An example taken from the UWT research is of a Chinese origin worker whose employment conditions had become substantially worse as a result of the threat of heavier sanctions on her employer if caught. She still was employed but was no longer offered regular employment, while her hourly rate of pay was reduced. The employer explained that because he was taking the risk in employing her, she had to pay for this risk with lower pay. Employers may also use the use of raids to weed out workers who have been fighting for better terms and conditions. Fear of deportation makes workers frightened of challenging employer malpractice, and deportation becomes a way for employers to deal with militancy at work. Immigration raids therefore can be spontaneously organised by the state authorities or may be the result of an employer approach to the authorities. Of course employers who do this also escape prosecution. There are a number of examples where this has happened. In 2009 cleaners working at London Underground won their claim for a living wage (a wage higher than the national minimum), but then came what their trade union representative described as 'the backlash'. Document and immigration checks were initiated, creating a fear among workers who 'disappeared from the job and disappeared from the union' (Labour Research Department, 2010). In another case, migrant cleaners working in a London university had been organising for around two years and had built up a strong union membership, leading to a successful union recognition claim. Shortly after their victory, their management called workers to a meeting where 40 immigration officers greeted them. A number of workers were then detained and immediately deported. The trade union had no doubt that the raid was a response to their organising imitative. These are not just recent developments. Writing more than 30 years ago, surveying the US situation, Piore (1979:173) pointed out that US border agents (the INS) strategically targeted the undocumented: 'when school lets out in June, various restaurant and hotel jobs are raided in order to open them for youth; when school resumes in the fall, such enforcement activities are relaxed. Enforcement activity also varies cyclically in some industries'. He also noted cases 'in which the INS has responded to employer requests to remove workers who appear to be distinguished from the many others not apprehended, chiefly by a tendency to assert themselves' (Piore, 1979:175). More recently Bacon (2008:81) confirms that employers have continued to use INS raids to rid themselves of migrant workers: 'These draconian exclusions are intended to make life unpleasant for undocumented immigrants, who presumably are encouraged to leave the country. But by making them more vulnerable and socially isolated, the exclusions make their labor cheaper'.

The Carrier Directive

Council Directive 2001/51/EC of 28 June 2001 (the Carrier Directive) is the last of the main EU instruments that we highlight in relation to undocumented migrants. As a supplement to the Schengen provisions, the Carrier Directive lays down the obligations of carriers transporting foreign nationals into the territory of the Member States and supports the harmonisation of financial penalties for cases where carriers fail to meet their control obligations. The directive imposes penalties of between €3,000 and €5,000 for each person carried, to a maximum of €500,000. Carriers have the obligation to return any persons refused entry to a Member State either to their country of origin or to another country and to meet the costs of this return. There is no exact data on the numbers of persons refused access to airlines each year, but one study suggests around 5,000 a year for each major carrier, suggesting that many thousands of individuals have had their right to travel denied as a result of the Carrier Directive (Guiraudon, 2006).

CONCLUSION

In this chapter we have highlighted the main aspects of the EU regulation of migrants, demonstrating how European policies have sought to make links between undocumented migrants and criminality. This means that the focus has essentially been on security-related measures, rather than on any attempts to provide a migration regime that would respond to the needs of the market for labour and that might offer a wider range of migrants the opportunity to work lawfully, whether under temporary arrangements or otherwise. The main conclusions that we can draw are that the European policy agenda is a narrow one, with the same range of policy measures repeated time and again. Seemingly new initiatives turn out to be based on the same old imperatives, of denial of entry and expulsion, while never admitting that whatever the size of the undocumented migrant population in Europe—with estimates varying as widely as three or eight million—there is no way that a return policy could ever meet the EU's stated objectives for the expulsion of all who are caught, as this would require a state whose level of authoritativeness was such as to amount to a police state.

In this chapter we have focused on two key directives—the Sanctions and Return directives. Both envisage a range of punitive measures, but neither deals with the circumstances that cause people to cross borders illegally in search of work. Until this issue is addressed, and this means looking beyond attempts to secure readmission agreements, undocumented migrants will continue to work under the harshest conditions, with each new piece of sanctioning legislation merely worsening their situation.

One area where EU Member States have not come together in a co-ordinated way is in relation to regularisation programmes. This represents the weak point in EU policy and one which the Commission is keen to bring under control. In the next chapter we therefore look at the regularisations that have occurred, setting out what they have achieved, but also looking at the positive and negative consequences of regularisation.

6 Immigration Policies and Regularisation

> Regularisation is the least bad strategy. It is not a long-term solution but creates pockets of hope and opportunities for some people.
>
> (Interview with Baldwin-Edwards, 2008)

Martin Baldwin-Edwards highlights the paradox of utilising migrant regularisation as a short-term policy measure. In this chapter we investigate how regularisation has been used by some countries and what its limits and advantages have been. The Member States agreed on a common migration policy at the European Summit in Tampere over a decade ago. This was regarded as a great EU success at the time, as it was an official recognition of the increased presence of undocumented migration in Europe and a collective commitment to manage it. As we showed in the last chapter, the outcome to date has been rather disappointing. Not much has been done at EU level, except for the vigorous installation of sophisticated systems for guarding Europe's external borders and the establishment of a web-based system, coordinated by the Commission for the exchange of intelligence and other information related to issues of asylum and immigration.[1] At the same time, countries have continued to respond to increased numbers of irregular migrants in their territories individually, reflecting the reality of the sovereign nature of immigration policy, demonstrating that regularisation is also a prerogative of the state.

This chapter will attempt to provide a better understanding of the regularisation issue, recognising it as a highly contested policy tool for managing undocumented migration. It will draw on past experiences of regularisation programmes in a number of EU countries and the US, utilising data—interviews with social actors on national and European levels as well as expert input via stakeholders' meetings—collated mainly in the life of the UWT project.

THE REGULARISATION DEBATE

Of all the measures to tackle irregular migration, regularisation has been most controversial and politically loaded. It is still poorly understood by policymakers even though more than 40 regularisation programmes have been implemented in Europe and the US so far. The regularisation of undocumented migrants has long been recognised as a measure of last resort. 'When all else fails, governments may have to resort to amnesty measures to remove the threat of expulsion that hangs like the sword of Damocles over the heads of foreigners', warned Bohning (1996:82) from the International Labour Organisation. This is particularly the case for long-term undocumented migrants, who have been economically active in the host country, contributing to its welfare and tax systems, possibly being joined by other family members or married. Most governments adopt regularisation programmes in the hope of 'setting the meter to zero' before the implementation of major amendments to their migration legislations.

For some experts and policymakers, regularisation is an admission on the part of the government that it has lost control of the situation and that it does not have either the resources or the will to manage migration (Telephone interview with migration expert, 28 February 2008). For others, it is the existence of transnational labour markets, and regularisations just recognise this and provide greater rights to workers who are already part of the national economy. 'By implementing regularisation programmes, states recognise that there exists demand and supply for labour; employers and labourers will find each other and they will do this illegally if they have to' (Telephone interview with OECD migration expert, 28 February 2008).

Many politicians and the public are sceptical, however, that it is feasible for these programmes to 'clean the slate' and eradicate irregular migration. Past regularisation experiences are a testimony of this scepticism. However, it is not so much scepticism but rather fear of the pull effects of the programmes that would attract more irregular migrants, raising hopes for new regularisations. Some support for this argument comes from the US experience. Several studies have shown that the US mass amnesty of 1986 had not reduced but rather increased undocumented migration, because it triggered new immigration flows due to networks and family ties (Orrenius and Zavodny, 2004). The European evidence is mainly incomplete or anecdotal. For Greece, there were claims that the 1998 regularisation programme had served as a 'magnet' for another 500,000 undocumented migrants by 2001 when a new regularisation was implemented. In Portugal, the Service of Foreigners and Borders, responsible for carrying out the 2007 regularisation programme, argued that immigrants were arriving from other parts of Europe lured by the prospect of regularisation (European Council on Refugees and Exiles, 2007). In Europe, however, there is a general consensus that amnesties or regularisations are only a modest factor in producing new undocumented migration (Papademetriou and Sommerville, 2008; Council of Europe Assembly, 2007). In Southern Europe, in particular, other factors appear more significant in causing irregular migration. These include geographical location, colonial and linguistic ties (Spain and Portugal), increased demand for low-skilled labour, relatively tolerant authorities, very few legal migration routes, and a thriving irregular economy. Another argument opposing large-scale, one-off regularisations advances the idea that these programmes are rewarding those who have come and/or stayed in the country in breach of its legal rules and that this sends erroneous messages to the public. This opposing argument then goes on to suggest possible post–regularisation effects, including the imposition of additional burdens on the welfare benefits system and public services, while depressing the wages of low-skilled native workers.

And, finally, a new fear has emerged in the debate against the use of regularisation programmes—the fear of terrorism.

As a counter-argument, regularisation proponents use the 'societal case' for regularisation. 'Regularisation makes us safer', claim Papademetriou and Sommerville (2008:16) in their arguments for an 'earned' regularisation in the UK. By reducing the number of the 'unknown' population, the security services can focus their efforts and resources on those that constitute a real threat to national security. They develop the argument further by suggesting that useful intelligence can be gathered by newly regularised migrants who were previously not in touch with the authorities due to fears of deportation. Protecting national security by reducing the number of people 'unknown' to the authorities is a favourable argument with increasing significance for Europe. The Council of Europe also puts forward the improvement of the human rights and dignity of migrants as an argument in support of regularisations (Council of Europe Assembly, 2007) while interest groups campaign for migrant regularisations to reduce their exploitative work conditions and the appalling social environments they propagate.

A very practical argument for the implementation of regularisations is in its cost, compared to those incurred in the removal of undocumented migrants. The 1986 regularisation in the US was decided on a comparative cost-benefit analysis of the two alternative methods: locating and deporting between three and 12 million undocumented migrants or establishing procedures to enable certain members of this population to become legal residents. Deportation appeared to be both prohibitively costly and unworkable (Smith et al., 1996).

Increasing the amounts collected in tax and social security contributions is another argument in support of regularisations.[2] It was used at the beginning of the regularisation debate in the UK in 2006 but with no significant effect. The Institute for Public Policy Research (ippr, 2006:12) presented calculations, according to which a regularisation could bring an additional tax contribution of £1bn per year into state coffers. This argument is particularly valid for the Southern European countries of Italy, Spain, and Greece, where an expanding irregular sector absorbs large numbers of migrants and locals in equal measure. A regularisation programme can only achieve its goal of increasing labour market transparency and reducing the size of the unregistered economy if implemented in concert with labour enforcement measures.

DEFINING AND CATEGORISING REGULARISATION

Regularisation in Europe (and 'legalization' in the Americas) refers to one potential state response to rising numbers of undocumented migrants in their territories. The Odysseus study of 2000 (Apap et al. 2000; De Bruycker, 2000) remains the most comprehensive comparative legal work on the legislative and administrative procedures applied in regularisation practices across Europe. Its definition of regularisation pertains to residence and covers "the granting, on the part of the State, of a residence permit to a person of foreign nationality residing illegally within its territory" (Apap et al., 2000:263). It refers to any state procedure of offering third-country nationals who are in a country illegally the opportunity to regularise or normalise[3] their status on a temporary or permanent basis.[4] The latter has been more of an exceptional practice in Europe even though some programmes open the way for a more permanent residence and eventually citizenship. The REGINE project[5] distinguishes between regularisation programmes and regularisation mechanisms. The former indicates a time-limited procedure, which does not form part of the regular migration policy framework (usually involving a large number of applicants), and the latter specifies a more-open ended policy that typically involves individual applications (made by virtue of long-term residence or on humanitarian grounds) and, in most cases, involves a smaller number of applicants (Baldwin-Edwards and Kraler, 2009:8–9). A broader definition of regularisation does not specify the dimensions of the regularisation programme, that is, whether it targets residence or employment or both.

'One-off' (or one-shot) regularisation programmes are most common in Europe. They are time-specific both in terms of the submission date of applications and the entry date of the applicants into the country. They are normally economically driven and provide temporary residence and work permits. The countries of southern Europe have tended to carry out 'one-off' regularisations. Permanent or continuous regularisation programmes are more often found in the migration legislation of the northern European countries. They are implemented on an individual or case-by-case basis, and the length of residence is a determining factor.[6] For example, in the UK irregular migrants are eligible for permanent residency if they can prove they have been in the country continuously for 14 years. Short-term permits are granted via exceptional regularisation programmes (i.e., on humanitarian grounds or for family reunification purposes). Exceptional humanitarian programmes provide residence permits to asylum seekers or irregular foreigners with extraordinary health conditions that will not allow them to travel (in cases when there is an intention of voluntary return or of removal). Similarly, family reunification programmes allow family members to either reunite with their spouses or children living in the host country or to legally remain in the country together if not all family members have residence permits. France has frequently applied exceptional regularisation programmes (on humanitarian grounds, including personal or family ties or after 10 years of continuous residence) since the adoption of the legal provisions in 1998. Such exceptional regularisations have gained particular importance in recent years in relation to overall annual admissions of third-country nationals in France (Sohler, 2009). The REGINE study points to the important role of family-based regularisations as routes to legality in several Member States, thus confirming deficiencies in national legislations in regard to the right of access to family reunification. The Parliamentary Assembly (Council of Europe Assembly, 2007) adds a new regularisation typology, 'earned regularisation'. It is the newest and least experimented-with form of programme. The term for it was developed in the US context (Papademetriou, 2005) and has recently found its way into the British regularisation debate (Papademetriou and Somerville, 2008). The main idea is to provide migrants with a temporary residence and work permit and for them to 'earn' afterwards their right to renew their permit or to be awarded a permanent residence through the fulfilment of different criteria, such as knowledge of the host country language and participation in community life.

With regard to the duration of the permit offered by the regularisation procedures, some countries are in favour of bestowing short-term, temporary residence permits (from six months to five years in Luxemburg, Greece, Italy, Spain, and Portugal), whereas others grant permanent residence as a 'generosity gesture' (France and the US) (Levinson, 2005).

THE CRITERIA FOR REGULARISATION

Although the management of irregular migration, including the implementation of regularisation programmes, has become a matter of common concern for Europe (COM (2006) 402, 19.7.2006), there are no European guidelines on the implementation of regularisation programmes or the eligibility criteria for them, and even more so on the criteria for renewal of a regularisation permit. It is precisely in the regularisation criteria that we find the distinction between selective programmes and mechanisms for regularisation and general amnesties applied to all migrants, with the latter granting legal status to irregular migrants in a general manner (Global Commission on International Migration, 2005:38). Clearly defined and straightforward eligibility criteria are the necessary condition for a successful regularisation programme, both at the regularisation stage and at the subsequent renewal stages. Regularisation criteria are dependent on the type of the programme, whether it is a 'one-off' or a permanent (continuous) regularisation. Most one-off programmes have required some proof of employment. This could be a job offer, certificate of employment, employment contract, or receipts of paid social security contributions. Employer-driven regularisation programmes, with the parallel involvement of the Labour Ministry through labour enforcement mechanisms—for example, the one in Spain in 2005 (Arango and Finotelli, 2009; Parliamentary Assembly, 2007) and in Italy in 2002 (Ruspini, 2009)—have been hailed as success stories as they have met the interests of irregular migrants, the trade unions, the employers, and wider society. A similar view was shared by the participants of the stakeholders meeting in Italy in 2008,[7] where a successful regularisation programme was defined as one that is implemented in concert with other labour regulation measures that can provide options for more secure and permanent work. The employment requirement is usually difficult to fulfil by irregular migrants whereas irregular status is often seen as an advantage by employers in pursuit of labour cost reductions, operating in a burgeoning irregular economy. In Italy, a trade union respondent spoke of employers who forced migrant workers to pay the whole amount of the required social security contributions, including the employer's share. Stakeholders also spoke of bogus firms that were issuing fraudulent contracts to migrants to enable them to qualify for regularisation. This almost guaranteed a slip-back into irregularity during the renewal stage. The Italian regularisation of 2002 was also believed to have produced other one-off regularised workers in the domestic and care sector, who had bought their regularisation while working in the construction sector,[8] as many permits did not record the actual employment of the holder. Similar incidents were reported in Greece (Monastiriotis and Markova, 2009), where it had been a normal practice for migrant workers employed in the hospitality sector to pay social security contributions to the Agricultural Insurance Fund (OGA), thus preserving their comparative advantage of cheap labour.

Time is a major requirement in general, one-off regularisations. Applicants are asked to provide proof of residence in the host country prior to a certain date. The latter requirement is normally introduced to avoid encouraging new immigrants into the country. Similar to the evidence of employment, this requirement has also encouraged fraud and triggered the involvement of organised criminal groups in Greece (Baldwin-Edwards, 2009).

Most regularisation mechanisms are a combination of different criteria, with varying degrees of significance. It is a common understanding that general regularisation programmes have simpler eligibility criteria than the permanent ones and exceptional regularisation measures. Clearly defined criteria for regularisation are only part of a successful procedure. Publicising them in languages understandable by the applicants and in formats accessible to them is also crucial. One of the major failures of the first regularisation programme in Greece, in 1998, was the lack of information on the programme criteria and application forms available in languages other than Greek. At the one end, bogus 'entrepreneurs' were quick to respond to this situation by even selling the otherwise free application packages and making profits off the unprepared government apparatus; organised crime was also involved at different stages of the process. At the other end, NGOs, trade unions, and newspapers were attempting to fill the gap by offering assistance to migrants in the process. Somewhere in the middle were the solicitors who benefited immensely from the government's approach (Baldwin-Edwards and Kraler, 2009; Markova, 2001).

One of the failings of the 2005 Spanish programmes with regard to regularisation was the lack of unified, common criteria among the government authorities in different provinces. Allegedly, in some provinces the process was harder than in others and this was not publicised in circulars, contributing to migrant uncertainty with regard to their legal status (stakeholders' meeting in Barcelona, October 2008).

POSITIONS ON REGULARISATION: THE EU, THE COUNCIL OF EUROPE, AND THE EUROPEAN TRADE UNION CONFEDERATION (ETUC)

Even though there is no official position of the European Union on regularisation programmes, several Commission Communications refer to the topic. The *Communication on the links between legal and illegal migration* (June 2004) (COM (2004) 412, 4.6.2004), studied, among other issues, the effectiveness of the regularisation programmes on the migrants concerned and the state. It concluded that the impacts were mixed for different countries and that more mutual information and transparency was needed in order to identify and compare different national practices and their impact on irregular migration. It envisaged that at a later stage common criteria could be drawn up that would lead to the development of a common approach to regularisation programmes so that large-scale regularisations were avoided or limited to exceptional circumstances. The last regularisation programme in Spain in 2005 served as a milestone in the future development of European common migration policy. Even though it was evaluated as successful and as something that other European countries could learn from, Spain was also severely criticised by some European leaders for failing to inform the rest of Europe of its intentions to carry out such a programme. This caused some misunderstandings as to the nature of the regularisation programme and also created a backlash against the use of such programmes in other countries across Europe. A year later, in 2006, it also led to the adoption by the Council of the EU of a *Decision establishing a mutual information mechanism* (Council Decision 2006/688/ EC). An Early Warning System was established to ensure better coordination between Member States in the process of the introduction of certain immigration measures at state level such as regularisation programmes. Finally, the Communication from the European Commission on *Policy priorities in the fight against illegal immigration of third country nationals* (COM (2006) 402) also addressed the issue of regularisation programmes. Subsequently, the International Centre for Migration Policy Development (ICMPD) was commissioned to undertake a study on practices in the area of regularisation of illegally staying third-country nationals in the Member States of the EU (the REGINE study).[9]

A stark contrast emerges between the EU's position and the Council of Europe's position on undocumented migration with the former clearly supporting an economic argument and the latter being more concerned with human rights protection. The Parliamentary Assembly of the Council of Europe is particularly concerned with protecting undocumented migrant rights and specifying the rights that they enjoy. As a result, the Assembly adopted Resolution 1509 in 2006 and Recommendation 1755 on irregular migrant rights in the same year, recognizing the benefits of regularization programmes in safeguarding the rights of migrants in an undocumented situation. The Council of Europe Assembly (2007) also supported irregular migrant regularisation on the grounds of international human rights' instruments that provide clear statements on migrants' rights, regardless of their status, particularly with regard to non-discrimination on the basis of national origin. Such international human rights' instruments include the Universal Declaration of Human Rights (UDHR), Articles 2 and 7; the International Covenant on Civil and Political Rights (ICCPR), Article 26; the International Covenant on Economic, Social and Cultural Rights (ICESCR), Article 2; the European Convention on Human Rights (ECHR), Article 14; and, the Protocol 12 of the ECHR. The most significant development in the protection of the rights of migrant workers is the UN Convention on the Rights of all Migrant Workers and their Families (ICMW), which came into force in April 2003. The ICMW has a broad range of purposes such as to improve the conditions of migrant workers and their families by expanding international law, emphasizing the hardship they face, and recognising the rights of irregular migrants. The fact that no EU country has ratified the convention is a cause of concern.

At European level, the ETUC has not had a clear position on regularisation. In the view of one commentator, this reflects opposing views among affiliates. The regularisation measures are seen as a 'crisis tool, to let off steam' rather than a properly managed system (Interview with trade union official, Brussels, 20 September 2007).

PAST REGULARISATION EXPERIENCES

Regularisation as a state response to increased numbers of undocumented migrants in its territory dates back to the 1970s in Europe, with some mini-regularisations in France in 1976, 1979, and 1980 (Garson, 2000) and in Belgium in 1974. France initiated its first one-shot programme in 1981–1982, followed by Italy and the US in 1986. Since 1980, the US and eight EU countries (France, Belgium, Greece, Italy, Luxemburg, Portugal, Spain, and the UK) have implemented 25 one-shot programmes. A study of regularisation programmes in the eight Member States calculated they took place in a cyclical manner, every 6.5 years on average (Apap et al.,

2000). Demetrios Papademetriou, Co-founder and President of the Migration Policy Institute in Washington commented on this frequency:

> The European Commission has opposed individual countries' efforts to regularise their immigrant populations because regularisation is just an expedient action and until the countries adopt coherent immigration policies, they will always end up with more irregular migrants. That opposition was manifested in the 2008 European Immigration Pact, which urged Member States to 'avoid' mass regularisations.

The inconsistent requirements posed by every new programme further exacerbate the problem. It is only the regularisation programmes in the US, in 1986–1988, in Canada in 1973 and in France in 1981–1982 that granted permanent residence to their applicants. In all other places, regularisation programmes gave people a very temporary legal status that could easily revert back into undocumented status (Telephone interview with migration expert, 28 February 2008).

The US's sole experience of a mass regularisation programme occurred in 1986 when the Immigration Reform and Control Act (IRCA) came into effect. It was the result of growing perceptions that undocumented migration in the US was out of control. The provisions of the IRCA included two significant programmes. The first legalised unauthorised migrants who could demonstrate they had resided in the country illegally prior to 1 January 1982 and who had filed their petitions for legalisation during a 12-month period beginning on 5 May 1987. The provisions were written to generally bar from amnesty foreign students who had been working in the US in violation of their student visas. The IRCA also established a separate Special Agricultural Worker (SAW) programme whereby undocumented foreigners who had worked in the US perishable crop agriculture sector for at least 90 days in the year ending in May 1986 could qualify for legal status. IRCA also provided for another category of foreign agricultural workers, referred to as Replenishment Agricultural Workers (RAWs). The scheme commenced in the fiscal year 1990 and lasted for three years, during which replenishment workers were admitted in cases of shortage of workers in the sector. Qualified foreigners were first given temporary legal status. After 18 months in this category, they entered a 12-month period during which they had to apply for permanent residence status. As a prerequisite for permanent residence, they had to demonstrate some knowledge of both the English language and the US government, and refrain from using federal assistance benefits for at least five years.[10] The IRCA granted temporary residence to about 2.6 million undocumented foreigners, and almost all of these applicants acquired permanent residence or US citizenship (Smith et al., 1996).

Similarly, Belgium has carried out only one large-scale, one-off regularisation programme in 2000, following the public outcry against the treatment of a Nigerian woman who died during an attempt to repatriate her. Apart from the mini-regularisation of 1974, previous years had allowed only case-by-case regularisations. The 2000 programme was predominantly social-humanitarian in nature, even though measures to reduce the size of undocumented migration and tackle problems to do with public order also featured in the public discourse (Kraler, 2009). Unlike similar (in magnitude) programmes in Southern Europe, which were motivated by economic reasons, this one did not have economic criteria as a requirement for regularisation. Instead, regularisation was permitted on the condition that an applicant had had an unresolved asylum petition pending for four years (three years for families with children), or that she or he was seriously ill or unable to return to her or his country of origin for humanitarian reasons, or had been in the country for longer than six years. Congolese and Moroccans were the main beneficiaries of the programme. Migrants from Rwanda, Burundi, Algeria, Tunisia, and Turkey were also strongly represented (Apap et al., 2000; Levinson, 2005; Council of Europe Assembly, 2007).

Despite a large population of undocumented migrants, there has never been an official mass regularisation in the UK. However, several small-scale programmes have been applied since 1974 to a similar effect. The first regularisation measures ran in the period 1974 to 1978. They were restricted to a limited number of citizens from the Commonwealth and the former colonies (Lenoel, 2009). The first exceptional one-shot programme in 1998 applied to a small number of overseas domestic workers, who had become illegal after leaving or changing an abusive and exploitative employer, at a time when the law did not permit this. The very small number of participants in the programme was most likely related to the application criteria that required workers to have a valid passport, to prove that they could support themselves, and to show they had entered the country legally and for the explicit purpose of employment as a domestic worker. Regularised migrants were mainly from Sri Lanka and the Philippines (Parliamentary Assembly, 2007). A backlog clearance exercise for outstanding asylum applications (1998 White Paper) took place between 1999 and 2000. Most people with outstanding claims going back at least to 1993 were granted indefinite leave to remain. Those with pending initial decisions on asylum applications made between 1993 and 1995 were considered on an individual basis against factors such as community ties, family connections, and employment records in the UK (Lenoel, 2009). The most significant measure was the 'family regularisation programme' of 2003 that granted settlement to asylum-seeking families who had been in the UK for four or more years. The basic criteria were that the applicant had to have applied for asylum before October 2000 and had at least one child under the age of 18 in the UK. Nonetheless, the most common regularisation measure is a case-by-case system that grants indefinite leave to remain to those who can prove that they had been in the country continuously for 14 years (seven years for families with children).

Spain has implemented the greatest number of large-scale regularisation programmes in Europe, followed by Italy. Since 1985, six programmes (in 1985, 1991, 1996, 2000, 2001, and 2005) have regularised the status of about 1.25 million undocumented migrants in Spain. Italy's first experience of mass regularisation occurred in 1986; since then the country has implemented five mass regularisations (in 1986, 1990, 1996, 1998, and 2002), granting legal status to over 1.4 million immigrants. The first regularisation measures in both countries formed an integral part of laws, which for the first time defined their immigration legislation. The 'French model' was used as the basis for the regularisations. However, France had a long tradition of immigration and mini-regularisations with a collective one in 1981, whereas the regularisation procedure was a novelty for Spain and Italy, which partly explained the difficulties encountered by the two countries in setting up their regularisation programmes (Garson, 2000). The two countries—motivated primarily by economic reasons and demanding from applicants some degree of labour market integration—have been implementing large-scale regularisation programmes, on average, every four years. Sizeable informal economies, a robust demand for cheap labour, limited routes for legal migration, geographical position, and costly and unworkable deportations are understood to have contributed to a growing size of their undocumented populations. The Odysseus study (Apap et al., 2000) explains the type and frequency of the regularisation practices in Spain and Italy with the countries' gradual transition from traditional emigration into immigration areas since the 1980s and the creation of a totally new situation. The regularisation programmes were perhaps attempts to reinstate order among the growing undocumented population. The 2005 Spanish regularisation programme was considered a success both as an institutional approach and in terms of numbers of applications submitted. The programme attracted 691,655 applications at an approval rate of 82 per cent (Arango and Finotelli, 2009). The programme had two categories of applications. In the first category, employers were allowed to file applications on behalf of the migrants and had to certify that they would continue to employ them for at least six months (three months for seasonal employment sectors). The second category permitted migrants who were employed part-time or working for several employers to apply themselves. The new element in the scheme included built-in mechanisms to reduce fraud and to ensure that the newly regularised were brought out of the shadow economy, thus contributing to social insurance registers. Italy has been less successful with its regularisation programmes. Even though all schemes were intended to 'set the meter to zero', in reality they were plagued by bureaucratic failure in processing applications on time, resistance from employers unwilling to sponsor migrants, weak public support, fraud, and large numbers of migrants falling out of legality after their permits expired. In the absence of pathways to a permanent residence status, regularisations remain the only policy tool for managing undocumented migration in the country (Papademetriou and Somerville, 2008; Council of Europe Assembly, 2007; Ruspini, 2009).

REGULARISATION CHALLENGES

Previous regulations that only provided temporary work and/or residence permits have encountered numerous challenges related to all stages of the process. Among them, the most common included reversion to undocumented status. Many programmes, especially in Greece and Italy, led a large percentage of migrants, previously regularised, to slip back into illegality; often regularised immigrants would fail to qualify for renewal of their permits because of unclear renewal criteria (Greece, 1998 regularisation programme) or employers unwilling to sponsor them, that is, pay their social security contributions (Italy, Greece). The OCED Secretariat reports persistent patterns of non-renewal of migrant permits in Italy in the 1990s. For instance, between 1991 and 1994, over 300,000 foreigners were unable to renew their permits and presumably fell back into illegality (OECD Secretariat, 2000:64). However, improved retention rates were reported for Italy in the mid-2005 survey. Some 98 per cent of the interviewed immigrants were estimated to have retained their legal status and 88.5 per cent had renewed their permits with an employer, even though loss of employment appeared as a significant risk. For Spain, Arango and Finotelli (2009) report that a year after the 2005 regularisation, some 80 per cent were still in the social security system and were able to renew their residence permits. High retention rates were reported of the 2000 regularisation in Belgium. The government claimed that almost 100 per cent of those granted regularisation managed to renew their documents (Baldwin-Edwards and Kraler, 2009).

The insufficient administrative support to handle the regularisation programmes led to backlogs and to the slow processing of applications in countries such as Italy, Greece, Spain, and Belgium. In Greece, lack of communication between the ministries involved in the regularisation of 1998, notably of Justice, Public Order, and Health created massive delays. Even bigger delays followed the 2001 regularisation programme, propelled by inadequate staffing levels, personnel training, and computerised systems and infrastructure. This resulted in automatic renewals of permits and overburden of public offices for more than three years.

Lack of publicity among migrant communities has resulted in low turnouts. This occurred in the regularisation programmes in Spain before 2005, Italy, and the UK—the domestic workers' regularisation of 1998. At the same time strong publicity and coordination with migrant organisations and the media have also led to success, for example, leading to high turnouts of migrants in the 1981–1982 programme in France and in the 2005 programme in Spain.

In some cases regularisation criteria can encourage fraud, for example, where there are eligibility criteria that require evidence of past behaviour (date of entry into the country) and which cannot be verified by public records. Employment criteria can also provide incentives for fraud, especially in countries with flourishing irregular economies and employers unwilling to sponsor migrants. Migrants' attempts to comply with the regularisation requirements boost the market for false documents. For instance, one of the negative outcomes of the IRCA programme of 1986 was the surge in the document fraud industry. Some of the programme criteria created a market for false documents to demonstrate residence and off-the-books employment (Papademetriou, 2005). Some studies have estimated fraudulent applications as high as 73 per cent in the general IRCA programme and 40 per cent in the agricultural one (Levinson, 2005). Fraudulent documents were also detected in the Belgium regularisation programme of 2000. A total of 786 dossiers were confiscated because of forms of fraud (Baldwin-Edwards and Kraler, 2009). During Italy's 2003–2004 regularisation, about 20 per cent of the inspected applications were found to contain false information regarding the job offer, and many migrants paid their own fines in the name of the employer (Papademetriou and Somerville, 2008:24). Naturally, application fraud contributes to unsustainable programme outcomes, which translate into endogenous reproduction of illegality.

The real problem is what states should do with respect to rejected regularisation applicants. One of the unwanted side effects of any regularisation procedure is the production of refusal decisions, and of course many rejected undocumented migrants will continue to live in the country. No regularisation has a 100 per cent acceptance rate. There are different reasons for it, including but not limited to difficult-to-fulfil eligibility criteria, inefficient management, or incompetence of the responsible authorities. There is no evidence on the fate of those migrants whose regularisation applications are rejected. There is only an aggregate figure of rejected applications. According to the authors of the Odysseus report, even though rejected applicants are technically required to leave the country, there is no evidence that they become a higher priority for the authorities to deport. As the authorities hold the identity and residence information (if not fraudulent) of the rejected applicants and realistically, they remain in the country following the failure of their applications, they become a phenomenon that the French Senate describes as the 'official illegal' (Apap et al., 2000:307).

REGULARISATION IMPACTS

Political Impact

Regardless of the country context, the decision to implement a regularisation programme is always highly controversial, polarising public opinion and evoking heated debates between state and civic actors.

In the past, various groups have defended migrants' rights and supported the adoption of regularisation programmes in Spain, Greece, and the UK. In the UK, the 'Strangers into Citizens'[11]—the largest civic alliance for regularisation of long-term undocumented migrants campaign—has been particularly active and in May 2007 organised a massive rally in London to support their demands; religious leaders and representatives of the Transport and General Workers' Union joined them (Hickley, 2007, cited in Dentler, 2008). In Spain, major trade unions (e.g. CCOO), Labour Commissions and UGT (General Workers' Union), professional associations, and NGOs like the SOS Racismo supported and campaigned for the 2005 regularisation programme. They even participated in the drafting of the regularisation legislation (CCOO & UGT, 2005, and SOS Racismo, 2004, cited in Dentler, 2008). In Greece, the General Confederation of Greek Workers-GSEE, (Greece's largest trade union) not only campaigned for the first regularisation programme of 1998 but also organised to prevent the adoption of earlier drafts of the legislation that would have excluded neighbouring country nationals (mainly Albanians and Bulgarians) from participation in the programme (Markova, 2001).

In France, the CGT union supported and coordinated a collective strike movement of several hundred *sans-papiers* for their regularisation; the union assisted with some 1,000 regularisation applications filed in the regional prefectures as part of France's ongoing exceptional regularisation schemes (Sohler, 2009). In Italy, trade union FILLEA-CGIL's campaign for migrant regularisation is also aimed at combating the informal economy. The union has petitioned the government for reasons of justice to grant residence permits to undocumented migrants who had reported their employers' failure to comply with the law and to pay taxes and social security contributions. The union supports workers in their making formal complaints to authorities in cases of employers' non-compliance (Interview with a FILLEA-CGIL respondent, Venice, Italy, 3 August 2007). In Portugal, the Catholic organisations have been at the forefront of the campaigns for mass regularisations (Peixoto et al., 2009).

There are various accounts of undocumented migrants' mobilised protests that have led to government decisions for regularisations. The actions of the migrant movement in the province of Brescia are credited with the Italian regularisation of 2002. It mobilised migrants from Rome, Caserta, Treviso, Venice, Florence, and Naples and was the impetus for the establishment of the Immigrants in Italy Committee (Interview with a FILLEA-CGIL respondent, Venice, Italy, 3 August 2007).

In Europe, the Platform for International Cooperation on Undocumented Migrants (PICUM) has not been a keen supporter of regularisation. NGOs and other interest groups have been putting pressure on PICUM to become a European campaigner for regularisation but the organisation's assessment of the likelihood of this happening is very remote. It is more important for PICUM to consolidate and become more strategic in getting the engagement of civil society in issues that affect migrant workers (e.g. how to move from trade unions making 'sympathetic noises' to running training programmes for their organisers and representatives on recruiting migrants and fighting for better conditions for migrant workers) (Interview with PICUM representative, London, 21 September 2007).

Fiscal Impact

Manolo Abella (2000) argues that it is difficult to establish an overall balance between state expenditures and fiscal revenues accrued as a result of regularisation. Even though it is feasible to expect that state revenues will increase as a result of regularisation, the evidence from most extensively studied IRCA programme is contradictory. The US Department of Labour claims that the 1986 legalisation enabled federal authorities to integrate millions of regularised foreigners into the federal, state, and local tax systems by also straightening out their social security accounts. Abella refutes this with evidence that two thirds of undocumented workers in the US had already been paying social security prior to regularisation to avoid detection (Abella, 2000:206). Another survey among Mexican migrants in the US showed that 66 per cent of undocumented migrants were paying taxes, and 87 per cent of those regularised under IRCA's provisions for agricultural workers and 97 per cent of those regularised under the law's general provisions had already paid taxes prior to regularisation (Papademetriou et al., 2004). Recent data from Spain indicates an increase in social security contributions by three per cent as a result of the country's 2005 regularisation. Fiscal impacts are country specific. Unlike previous regularisations, recent experience in Spain and Italy appears to have had an impact on reducing unregistered employment, thus contributing to states' revenue.

Regularisation Impact on Migrants' Employment Terms and Conditions

The UWT study discusses the extent to which regularisation could lead to improved terms and conditions. It suggests that immediate improvements may be experienced in terms of psychological welfare together with a right of access to state welfare and service provision. The study bears out previous research which suggests that regularisation may improve terms and conditions for workers, although there is likely to be a time lag between change in status and improvements and this may also require the worker to move from the sector of employment where she or he had been working when undocumented. Furthermore it is difficult to demonstrate that it is indeed not just time by itself that promotes improvements, as workers develop the locally specific skills needed to negotiate their routes into better jobs and may over time acquire documents, even if false, that allow them to access such jobs. Most robust empirical evidence comes from the US. A plethora of studies have been conducted in the period before and after the Immigration Reform and Control Act (IRCA), which was implemented in 1986 and granted amnesty to 1.7 million undocumented workers who could prove continuous residence in the US since 1982. Kossoudji and Cobb-Clark (2004) demonstrate that pre-legalisation mobility, either upward or downward, was principally driven by English language ability and job characteristics. Thus it is plausible to assume that knowing the host country language or having spent enough years in the host country simply gives the ability of the undocumented worker to move between jobs, possibly maximising his or her own opportunities in a limited labour market. It was demonstrated, however, that legal status itself creates a whole new set of opportunities and indeed legalised (Mexican) men were employed in occupations that were higher up the occupational ladder (ibid:347). Nonetheless, research demonstrates that the IRCA amnesty in the US had a differentiated impact on migrant women. Cobb-Clark and Kossoudji (1999) argue that migrant women managed to alter their migration status but did not manage to improve their labour market status, at least in the short term. The wage gap between them and similar regularised men continued to widen after legalisation, and there was little evidence to suggest that legalisation promoted mobility out of traditional migrant jobs, at the margins of the US labour market. The change in legal status for women did not change the determinants of their wages, 'leaving human capital unrewarded and the penalties associated with traditional migrant employment unchanged' (ibid:12). Conversely, previous results for legalised men showed that they benefitted from the amnesty through a narrowing of the wage and increased returns to their human capital promoting additional wage growth (Kossoudji and Cobb-Clark, 2004; Rivera-Batiz, 2004). The European experience is related mainly to occupational mobility. A recent study on post-regularisation trajectories of regularised immigrants in the Belgium 2000 regularisation programme reports a major exodus from construction and agriculture to manufacturing and, to a lesser degree, to services (Dzhengozova, 2009).

Similarly, for Spain, Arango and Finotelli report a trend for a change of employment sector of regularised migrants, from agriculture to construction (for men) and from domestic work to restaurants (for women), whereas, on the other hand, in the South of Italy, employment opportunities for regularised migrants were almost doubled in construction and agriculture (Arango and Finotelli, 2009).

There is still insufficient evidence to explain the exact mechanisms that operationalise these opportunities. Undoubtedly, some changes occur in workers' behaviours as a result of acquiring a legal status and not fearing deportation. Other changes occur in employers' attitudes towards legalised workers. In the context of Italy, Reyneri (2003) argues that legal status does not necessarily provide a legal job. It is a necessary condition but not a sufficient one. In fact, legalised migrants frequently move in and out of formal employment, which is seen as an "adaptive response" to the serious difficulties involved in retaining a legal permit and a formal job. It can also be seen as a maximising behaviour by the legalised migrant who intends to renew his residence permit (a registered job is a necessary condition for this). As shown earlier, employers, too, are faced with the option of employing legal migrants to carry out jobs which are conducted illegally. Research on legalised migrants in Greece has confirmed similar behaviour on the part of employers, who for labour cost savings (i.e., social insurance contributions) would declare fewer working hours than were actually worked (Monastiriotis and Markova, 2009). The enforcement of the legislative norms significantly alters such behaviour. The Italian trade union, CGIL, has succeeded in its campaign to include, within the 2006 national budget, measures targeting informal working, notably increased inspections, an obligation on employers to register contracts a day before the actual employment starts, in addition to the presentation of a document (DURC) regulating payment contributions. It is estimated that these policies have led to the 'recovery' of over 70,000 jobs in the underground economy, some 20,000 of which involved migrant workers (Interview with a representative of CGIL, Venice, 20 June 2007).

Thus it may be that it is a combination of time plus regularisation and post-regularisation labour enforcement measures that promote improvements, at least as far as male workers are concerned. Additionally, we suggest that this time lag is also influenced by other facts, including the following:

1. The industrial relations environment in the country and in particular the strength of trade unions and their ability to enforce legal conditions on employers;
2. The existence of collective bargaining and the general applicability of collective agreements;
3. The degree to which there are effective enforcement mechanisations to guarantee the application of employment rights and the strength of the legal remedies;
4. The extent to which regularisation provides opportunities for movement into new work;
5. The extent to which regularisation results in family reunion or re-grouping;
6. The size of the casual/temporary force and the extent to which casual labour is normalised; and
7. The existence of factors such as minority ethnic businesses as significant employers and/or the presence of a large informal sector.

Thus we argue neither that regularisation makes no difference nor that it automatically improves conditions for previously undocumented migrants. In the typology set out above, 1 to 5 correspond to situations that promote improvements in terms and conditions following regularisation, while 6 and 7 correspond to factors which may impede the opportunities for improvements following regularisation. Where an industrial relations system is weak, it is less able to guarantee equality even following regularisation. Thus the extent to which those whose position has been regularised may take advantage of this change is dependent on the overall strength of formal mechanisms for enforcing employment rights, and in particular on the existence of both a strong trade union movement and on one that can enforce the general application of collective agreements. It appears also to be associated with factors (like family reunion) which may act as an impetus to seek better jobs and may also be a stimulus towards greater integration and therefore towards the development of effective social networks. However, in the absence of these additional enforcement mechanisms, regularisation may be insufficient to guarantee equality of rights to migrant workers (McKay et al., 2009).

CONCLUSION

Of all the measures to tackle undocumented migration, regularisation appears to be most controversial and politically loaded. The decision to implement such a programme still divides Europe and polarises state and civic actors. Most of the heated debate stems from a poor understanding of the regularisation programmes by policymakers despite the fairly large number of regularisation programmes that have been implemented in Europe and the US. Governments still consider the implementation of regularisations as a shameful admission that they have lost both control of the situation and the will to manage migration. This may explain why there are still no European guidelines on the implementation of regularisation programmes or on the criteria for the renewal of regularisation permits. Clearly defined and straightforward eligibility criteria are the necessary condition for a successful regularisation programme, both at the regularisation stage and at the subsequent renewal stages.

Moreover, the issue is fraught by scepticism that it is feasible for these programmes to 'clean the slate' and eradicate irregular migration. Past regularisation experiences have been a testimony of this scepticism. Much of this scepticism has been intertwined with fear of the pull effects of the programmes to attract more irregular migrants, raising hopes for new regularisations. Past US experience partially supports this argument. Some studies have shown that the mass amnesty of 1986 had not reduced but rather increased undocumented migration, as it triggered new immigration flows due to networks and family ties. And, finally, a new fear has emerged in the debate against the use of regularisation programmes—the fear of terrorism.

As a counter-argument, regularisation proponents adopt a 'societal case' for regularisation. Their success in winning such arguments has been limited. In Europe, most common regularisations have been 'one-off' (or one-shot) programmes. They are normally economically driven and provide temporary residence and work permits. The countries of Southern Europe tend to carry out such regularisations. Permanent or continuous regularisation programmes are often found in the migration legislation of the Northern and Western European countries.

The retention of regularised status stood out as the most common challenge of previous regularisation programmes. Lack of clear renewal criteria and employers unwilling to support migrant applications were among the most important reasons for why many regularised migrants slipped back into irregularity.

It terms of the effects of the regularisation programmes on migrants, an immediate improvement may be experienced in terms of psychological welfare, together with a right of access to state welfare and service provision. Long-term effects are likely to be a combination of time plus regularisation and post-regularisation labour enforcement measures that promote improvements in the life and work of regularised migrants. The time lag is inevitably affected by other factors, among which are the industrial relations environment in the country and powers of the trade unions; the existence of collective bargaining; the degree to which there are effective enforcement mechanisations to guarantee the application of employment rights; and the strength of the legal remedies.

7 European Undocumented Migration

> Illegal (undocumented) migration expresses the will of the individual to move to a new land, settle down and work in the host country in order to improve one's living standards and socio-economic conditions.
>
> (Ennaji, 2003:1)

Moja Ennaji's words, even though reflecting on Moroccan migration to Europe, can easily be applied beyond any geographical context for as long as there are people who, sometimes without the necessary documents and at other times with them but only on a temporary basis, cross many lands to arrive in a new state in search of work and with the hope of a new, better life. This chapter uses the term 'undocumented migration' to first discuss measurement methods and estimates in Europe, and then, taking a profile of the undocumented migrant population in Europe, we proceed to a discussion on the elusive nature of migrant status and its impact on migrant work conditions and prospects, analysed through the prism of regularisation experiences. Our analysis utilises data collected through the UWT project.

MEASUREMENT OF UNDOCUMENTED MIGRATION

Measurement Problems

As undocumented migrants generally avoid being registered because of fears of deportation, any estimates on their total numbers in Europe can only be 'guesstimates' (Stalker, 2002:156). In addition, information that can lead to establishing a person's legal status is often dispersed between government departments, police, and employment offices, thus making access to migration data very difficult. Within the seven UWT countries, we found widespread variations. At one end of the spectrum the UK enforcement statistics are a good example of a coherent data set on undocumented migration figures, although still with its own limitations (Cangiano, 2010). In contrast, statistical information from Bulgarian government departments, police, and border agencies is an example of a system that still lacks integration and transparency and is characterised by a reluctance to share information and make it accessible to researchers.

The mere task of identifying data sources on undocumented migration is even more complex than trying to measure documented migration. Available data from primary sources, such as government data from detention centres, border points, and government departments granting legal status, or secondary sources from previous studies are often controversial and therefore present limitations for more reliable assessments. Despite the intentions of the member states, for a common approach on managing migration and reducing undocumented migration, different countries still have different migration measurements and different definitions of legality and illegality, which renders any attempts for constructing internationally comparable data on undocumented migration very difficult.

Population census is generally recognised as a credible source of undocumented migrant statistics. Subject to a post-census adjustment for under- and/or over-counting, refusals to participate or just missing off of respondents, this method provides an estimate of the population size at the moment of counting. Nevertheless, in some countries like the Netherlands, censuses do not take place. The Netherlands, however, has adopted a very successful scientific model for estimating the number of the illegally resident foreigners, mainly by utilising law enforcement data from the police and the labour inspectors (European Commission, 2009). Similarly, Austria uses administrative data (enforcement and crime statistics of the police and failed asylum statistics) for estimating the size of the country's undocumented foreign population. The most up-to-date information typically comes from the population registers of the local authorities (municipal registers, or the *Padron* in Spanish). They are typically maintained by the legal requirement that both nationals and foreigners must register with the local authorities. A key feature of the migration data derived from population registers is the fact that departures tend to be less well recorded than arrivals, often because registration gives certain rights to migrants (e.g., access to healthcare and education), whereas there is less incentive to inform authorities about departure. These have been used in Spain only. An increasing number of Spanish researchers argue that the *Padron* still represents the 'ground for achieving more clarity on such an opaque phenomenon as the extent of irregularity' (Arango and Finotelli, 2009:90). The local authority registers constitute a unique data source on undocumented foreigners, including children and people who are not employed. Undocumented migrant regularisations—both programmes[1] and mechanisms[2]—are another source of very credible figures. It is worth noting, however, that even migrants who apply for regularisation may provide inaccurate or false data because they fear deportation. Data obtained from such programmes is also fraught by the fact that not all undocumented foreigners are able or willing to take advantage of them. This is compatible with the notion that legalisation has its costs for undocumented immigrants and these costs must be balanced out against the expected benefits. According to the REGINE study (Baldwin-Edwards and Kraler, 2009) in the period between 1996 and 2008, the number of persons who applied for regulation of their status in the EU27 countries was about five million. Most of the applications for regularisation were received in regularisation programmes. Some 43 regularisation programmes were implemented in 17 EU Member States in this period, involving altogether 4.7 million applications, of which at least 3.2

million were awarded a legal status. Most applications for regularisation, just under 1.5 million, were submitted in Italy, followed by Spain with 1.3 million and Greece with just under 1.2 million; although the latter figure might be overstated by about 230,000 owing to a two-stage legalisation process in 1998 (ibid).

Migration Estimation Figures in Europe and in the Member States

For Europe as a whole, the total number of undocumented foreigners had been assumed to be between two and three million at the end of the 1990s, which constituted some 10 to 15 per cent of the total foreign-born population on the continent (International Organization for Migration (IOM), 2000). The CLANDESTINO study questioned the figures on undocumented migrants often quoted in European policy documents (between two and eight million) as vague and of unclear origin. It proposed instead to use a country-specific aggregation of estimates, based on a combination of methods and adjusted for approximate comparability, as the best way for calculating comprehensive European estimates on undocumented migration. Aggregate country estimates were calculated for three years, 2002, 2005, and 2008, showing a decline in the stock of the undocumented migrant population, when keeping the geographical or the political region constant. The assessments show that in 2002, an estimated 3.1 to 5.3 million undocumented foreign residents lived in the European Union. In the same region of the EU15, the corresponding aggregate figure for 2008 was only 1.8 to 3.3 million. The estimate for the EU27 countries is only slightly higher, 1.9 to 3.8 million, as most of the undocumented migrant population is estimated to reside in the old Member States. Arguably, these figures must be an underestimate, considering the regularisation figures mentioned earlier. It is for this reason that we continue to suggest that the regularisation programmes undoubtedly remain one of the most reliable sources of statistics on the undocumented migrant population. It should be acknowledged, however, that part of the decline in undocumented migrant figures may be due to methodological changes and differences in legal definitions (Kovacheva and Vogel, 2009). For instance, some countries classify asylum seekers as migrants whereas others do not. Data for Germany includes some asylum seekers but not all. If stocks of undocumented migrants are difficult to measure, it is even more difficult to estimate undocumented migrant flows.[3] The late Jonas Widgren, founder of the Vienna-based International Centre for Migration Policy Development (ICMPD), formulated in 1994 one of the most frequently quoted migration flow estimates in Europe. He started from a 1993 apprehension figure of 60,000 undocumented migrants at European borders. After talking to border control authorities, he estimated that approximately four to six times as many people were not caught. This meant that some 250,000 to 350,000 were getting through European borders each year (Widgren, 1994). Naturally, it appears that publications on undocumented migrant stock (foreign nationals residing without authorisation in the host country at any one point in time), both Europewide and in particular countries, have substantially outnumbered the publications on undocumented migrant flows (foreign nationals entering the country in an unauthorised fashion). In the UK, the first formal attempt to use government data to estimate the number of unauthorised migrants produced a figure in the range of 310,000 to 570,000 people, 0.5 per cent to 1 per cent of the total UK population respectively, with a midpoint of 430,000[4] (Woodbridge, 2005). The think-tank Migration Watch UK (2005) (which has a well-voiced opposition to migration into the UK) criticized government estimates for failing to include between five per cent and 15 per cent of undocumented migrants' children, as well as failed asylum seekers who had not been deported after 2001. Its overall estimate was in the range of 515,000 to 870,000, with a mean estimate of 670,000 at the end of March 2005. Arguably, failed asylum seekers form a considerable part of the undocumented migrant population in the UK, and the National Audit Office estimated their number to be between 155,000 and 283,500 in a 2005 report. Gordon et al. (2009) have recently revised and updated the government (Woodbridge, 2005) figure suggesting a central estimate of the undocumented population in the UK of 618,000, ranging between 417,000 and 863,000. The UWT team combined enforcement statistics and secondary events data (common crimes, marriages, issue of driving licences and national insurance (NI) numbers) to infer the size of the undocumented population in the UK. Data covered the period between 1997 and the first quarter of 2008. Home Office statistics and International Organization for Migration (IOM) newsletters were the main data sources. Data covered included Removals/Assisted Return data (asylum and non-asylum cases of removals and voluntary departures, and non-asylum cases of assisted return by the IOM and after-entry controls); and Refusals of Applications data (refusals of extensions of settlement; refusals of initial recognition of right to reside; refusals of recognition of permanent residence; number of people in detention; dismissed appeals determined by immigration judges; withdrawn applications; suspicious applications for NI numbers; suspicious applications for driving licences; sham marriages; refused asylum, ELR, HP, and DL). Nevertheless, even though we used the widest range of statistical data available, the assessed figure has still to be read with caution. First, it is mainly based on enforcement statistics and these, by definition, cover only migrants who have been subjected to immigration controls. Furthermore, the assessed figure can be an overestimate as the calculations assume zero undocumented migrant mortality and they are inevitably distorted by double counting. All voluntary returns are assumed to be actually captured by the enforcement statistics based on Home Office data. Removals/Assisted Return is denoted by RAR and Refusals of Applications as ROA. Therefore, the cumulative total of ROA–RAR for each year between 1997 and 2008 gives an indicative figure of the undocumented migrant stock for the 11-year period.

$$\Sigma(\text{ROA-RAR})[1997\text{–}2007]\text{—RAR}[2008] = [(30,630\text{—}$$
$$10,720)+(32,900\text{—}10,855) + (32,005\text{—}11,345) + (83,880\text{—}13,815)$$
$$+ (132,595\text{—}16,940) + (116,655\text{—}22,000) + (135,215\text{—}29,260)$$
$$+ (122,785\text{—}24,990) + (102,675\text{—}28,410) + (136,816\text{—}31,970) +$$
$$(168,416\text{—}68,410)]\text{—}3,025 = 825,857\text{—}3,025 = 822,832$$

In Spain, the available data is controversial. The *Padron* statistical information in 2006 indicates 1,145,641 undocumented migrants. However, different interpretations of the *Padron* suggest a figure of 1,640,000 (according to the Partido Popular[5]) or 440,000 (according to the government). As for Spain, there are also very different estimates of undocumented migrants in Belgium. The Flemish Federation of Small and Medium Sized Companies in Construction estimated that in 2001, between 80,000 and 130,000 undocumented migrants were working in the country. But based on data from inspection controls, the Ministry of Social Security has calculated a figure of only 1,669 people (UWT, 2009). In Italy, there are no primary sources on undocumented migrants. Data is produced from regularisations, and the statistical data for 2006 indicates the existence of around 760,000 undocumented migrants (Fondazione ISMU, 2007). Data from the Italian Ministry of the Interior suggests that the majority of undocumented migrants are those that have overstayed their permit or those who have entered Italy from other Schengen countries. Bulgaria is a relatively new immigration destination, and research on the undocumented migration phenomenon is still very rare. The UWT study assessed the size of the undocumented migrant population in Bulgaria using a formula that presents the size of undocumented migration as a share of the total working population in the 'shadow' (unregistered) economy. The calculated figure was at around 13 per cent (13,000 people) of the total migrant workforce. In Denmark, where there is a lack of systematic and official statistics on undocumented migration, experts' estimates—based on numbers of failed but remained in the country asylum seekers—suggest that in 2006 there were between 1,000 and 5,000 undocumented migrants. For the same year, the Danish Ministry of Integration indicated that about 1,400 Ukrainian students resided and worked without permission in the country (Rezai and Goli, 2007). With regard to Austria, a recent estimate, based on police crime statistics and the multiplier method, indicates that the number of persons with an irregular residence status in Austria had decreased significantly from an estimated 78,000 in 2001 to about 36,000 in 2008 (European Commission, 2009). There is, however, another estimate of 60,000 to 170,000 people working illegally in the domestic sector (Haidinger, 2006).

The Use of Migration Estimation Methods

Notwithstanding our emphasis on the difficulty in providing robust estimates, we recognise that the most successful estimation method that has
been used is that for the US. This is based on variants of the residual method,
which compares an analytic estimate of the legal foreign-born population
derived from administrative data with a survey-based estimate of the total
foreign-born population. The difference between the two is an estimate of
the total foreign-born undocumented population (Passel, 2007).

The use of the most appropriate estimation methods on the size of the
undocumented population is not only a scientific or methodological issue;
it also involves considerable ethical considerations. Calculations must be
based on a combination of credible data sources. And the interpretation of
undocumented migrant estimates should be done with great caution and
within a specific context. It is important to always flag the limitations of the
estimated numbers. First, there is an acute problem of reliable and coherent migration data in general and of data on undocumented migration in
particular. The methods of estimation are always dependent on the available data. Second, estimation methods usually rely on certain assumptions.
The use of these assumptions is unavoidable, due to the nature of the issue
of undocumented migration, and it is impossible to test these assumptions
beyond any empirical doubt. Therefore, by their very virtue, any estimates
on undocumented migration should be treated as indicative and useful for
informing policy—for information only rather than absolute numbers that
perfectly reflect the problem at hand. Data on undocumented migration
estimates also should be disseminated in a way that does not endanger any
particular individuals or communities. Dissemination of undocumented
migrants' data must prevent misuse for political campaigns or policies
targeting deportations. Triandafyllidou (2010) rightfully raises the alarm
of 'conflicting group interest' when disseminating undocumented migration data. It is this delicate balance that must be taken into consideration,
between the interests of undocumented migrants, lobby groups, society at
large, and statutory agencies.

PATHWAYS INTO THE EU COUNTRIES

In Chapter 3 we presented our theory of status transitions and used some
of the data collected in the course of our interviews with undocumented
migrants to illustrate the theory. Here we look in more detail at the data
from the 211 interviews, focusing on migrant demographics, covering methods of entry, personal characteristics, and work. Just under a quarter of the
interviewees in the UWT sample had previously worked in other EU countries. Italy and Germany were the most frequently mentioned transit countries. The inability to retain or obtain a legal status and the search for work
were identified as the main reasons for moving elsewhere in Europe. These

combined experiences did not necessarily bring improvements in work and living conditions. A quarter of the respondents in the UWT sample, 39 men and 15 women, had entered the host country clandestinely; most of them had entered Austria (n = 14), followed by Denmark (n = 11), Bulgaria (n = 10), the UK (n = 9), Spain (n = 4), Italy (n = 4), and Belgium (n = 2). Another five men had entered on forged passports; of them, two had entered the UK, two Denmark, and the remaining one Bulgaria. Others became illegally resident by overstaying a tourist, student, or a work visa; one had remained in the UK while on a transit visa to the Philippines. An Algerian man in his 30s had legally entered Turkey on a tourist visa; he continued his journey to Bulgaria illegally, buying a forged Dutch ID card in Turkey. Young North African men would buy forged French forged passports while in Spain. There was a practice whereby undocumented Brazilian men in Belgium had arrived on tourist visas but then remained in the country by purchasing a Portuguese passport.

Of those who had entered the host countries in the survey illegally, nearly two thirds remained undocumented while the remaining third managed to obtain legal status through either a successful participation in a regularisation programme, an asylum claim, or marriage to an EU national. For some interviewees, pathways into European countries were particularly challenging and could be very dangerous, where they were smuggled into Europe. In Chapter 3 we described the stories of some of those who were interviewed. They include those of North African men who had reached Spanish shores hidden in a container in a cruise ship and Chinese and African origin migrants who had undertaken journeys lasting weeks or even months, with long waiting periods, usually in Turkey, Hungary, or the Czech Republic. A former military Chinese man in his 50s recalled carrying a woman who could not walk across a snowy mountain in the Czech Republic: 'I was a very fit man so I carried her like a child in my arms. The "organiser" wanted to dump her there to die'.

Bulgaria is one entry point for undocumented migrants travelling on land from Asia Minor or by sea from Africa and crossing the 'green zone' between Turkey and Bulgaria, with the help of smugglers. There is a well-established smuggling route from Turkey to the nearest border villages in Bulgaria. Sometimes, no 'guides' are needed for migrants to cross the border. In our study some young men from Burkina Faso had entered Bulgaria through the 'green zone', relying only on information on the border landscape, which they had obtained from the Internet.

Payments to smugglers varied depending on the year of arrival and the country of destination. In the UK, the price from China ranged from €24,000 in 1998 to €30,000 in 2004. For Algerians and Moroccans in the UK, who were helped by friends and co-ethnics in Spain and France, the cost of the journey mainly included the purchase of a forged EU passport, which for one Algerian man was €250 in 2006. For North-East African men travelling to Bulgaria, the journey usually involved a tourist visa to

Turkey and the purchase of a forged EU ID card, which cost about €300 in 2007. A young family from Armenia, who had fled persecution because of the Azerbaijani origin of the woman, came to Austria with the assistance of a smuggler, which cost them some €2,000 in 2001.

Almost half of the interviewed undocumented migrants reported travelling alone while the rest had travelled with friends, acquaintances, or, in the case of smuggling, with people from their country they did not know. Figure 7.1 shows that most of the undocumented migrants in the sample had arrived in the period 2001 to 2005 (particularly in Belgium, Spain, and Denmark) whereas those in the UK had been in the country much longer. There was a significant increase in undocumented migration in Bulgaria after 2007 when the country joined the EU.

Most clandestine journeys were organised by smugglers. North African men were more likely to travel on the initial legs of their journey to Europe on their own and in the course of their journey were assisted by friends.

Almost none of the interviewees had crossed the border illegally accompanied by their families. A similar pattern was identified by apprehension data reported in the ICMPD 2006 *Statistical Yearbook on Undocumented*

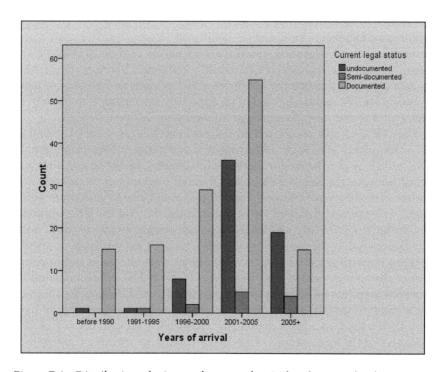

Figure 7.1   Distribution of migrants by year of arrival and current legal status.
Source: UWT, Field survey, 2007–2008.

Migration in Central and Eastern Europe (CEE) where it was very rare for whole families to be caught at borders. Those apprehended were typically single men, between 20 to 45 years of age, with completed secondary education. A slight increase in women among those illegally crossing the borders of the CEE countries was recorded, which was seen as a response to the growth in demand for female labour in the shadow economies of the Western countries. A similar profile of undocumented migration was outlined in the individual European countries in the CLANDESTINO study. In Austria, in 2008, the majority of persons apprehended (smuggled or staying/entering illegally) were male and over half were between 19 and 30 years of age (European Commission, 2009). Conversely, in the Netherlands, police apprehension data shows that considerably more men, under the age of 40, were found to be residing illegally in the country; women represented almost a quarter of all undocumented migrants, while the share was higher among the East Europeans and those from the former Soviet Union (ibid).

PROFILING UNDOCUMENTED MIGRATION IN EUROPE

Personal Characteristics

Profiling undocumented migrants is as difficult a task as providing estimates on undocumented migration, given the very nature of their undocumented status, which is not registered or statistically counted. This chapter will draw on data collected through the life of the UWT project, as well as post-regularisation studies and studies based on apprehension statistics, to attempt to construct a profile of undocumented migration in Europe today.

The UWT sample comprised 68 (32 per cent) migrants out of a total of 211 respondents who were undocumented at the time of the interviews in 2007–2008. A significant correlation (chi-square = 16.184, p < 0.001) was found between the number of undocumented migrants in the sample and the country they were currently residing in, with the largest share being found in Denmark, followed by Belgium, Bulgaria, and the UK, while the lowest share of currently undocumented respondents was surveyed in Italy. The figures reflect the availability of legal channels for residence and work in those countries. China and the Philippines were the main origin countries of the undocumented migrants surveyed in the UK, while most undocumented migrants in Belgium came from Brazil and Ecuador. As this was not a random sample, the choice of migrants to be interviewed may have been determined, to a great degree, by accessibility factors, but it was also indicative of the main groups of undocumented migrants in a country.

The majority of currently undocumented migrants in the UWT sample (n = 38, 66 per cent) were male, concentrated in the 25 to 49 age group (Table 7.1), and similar proportions of them were married with children or single; half of those with children were living with them in the host country while over half of those who were married were not living with their partners in the host country.

Table 7.1 shows that the currently undocumented migrants in the sample had a higher share of people with minimum education, compared to those who were documented (35.8 per cent and 10.4 per cent respectively) and a slightly lower share of secondary education graduates (45 per cent and 47 per cent respectively), whereas most university graduates and those with professional qualifications were currently documented (n = 53, 42.4 per cent). The corresponding figure for the undocumented migrants was 13 people (19.4 per cent).

In an earlier OECD (1994) review of the profiles of migrants regularised in 1991 in Spain, it was shown that those who had benefited from the regularisation programme were mostly young, unmarried, and male; had a good standard of education; and spoke Spanish well. More recent data on Spain shows that the profile of regularised immigrants has changed considerably since 1991; in particular, the share of female immigrants benefiting from regularisation has significantly increased, as has the number of family members. Suffice to say that the different profiles above all indicate significant changes of structural conditions and migration patterns

Table 7.1 Distribution of Migrants by Legal Status (at interview date), Gender, Age and Education

	Undocumented	Semi-documented*	Documented	Total
Age group:				
18–24	11 (16.2%)	2 (15.4%)	7 (5.4%)	20 (9.5%)
25–34	27 (39.7%)	4 (30.8%)	52 (40%)	83 (39.3%)
35–49	25 (36.8%)	6 (46.2%)	56 (43.1%)	87 (41.2%)
Over 50	5 (7.4%)	1 (7.7%)	15 (11.5%)	21 (10.0%)
Total:	68 (100%)	13 (100%)	130 (100%)	211 (100%)
Gender:				
Male	38 (55.9%)	12 (92.3%)	62 (47.7%)	112 (53.1%)
Female	30 (44.1%)	1 (7.7%)	68 (52.3%)	99 (46.9%)
Total:	68 (100%)	13 (100%)	130 (100%)	211 (100%)
Education:				
Minimum	24 (35.8%)	3 (23.1%)	13 (10.4%)	39 (19.5%)
Secondary	30 (44.8%)	6 (46.2%)	59 (47.2%)	95 (46.3%)
University/tertiary	10 (14.9%)	2 (15.4%)	35 (28.0%)	47 (23.0%)
Professional qualification	3 (4.5%)	2 (15.4%)	18 (14.4%)	23 (11.2%)
Total:	67 (100%)	13 (100%)	125 (100%)	205 (100%)

Source: UWT, Field survey, 2007-2008.

Note: Semi-documented migrants are defined as those who work in breach of their residency status (see chapter 3).

over time, reflecting an increase in female migration from Eastern Europe (Baldwin-Edwards and Kraler, 2009).

Work Location

The UWT study demonstrates relatively high levels of employment among the migrants in the sample, with just 20 per cent unemployed and in search of a job. Respondents interviewed in Copenhagen confirmed that migrants would always be more likely to have jobs because they would accept any job on offer as long as it pays. As one put it, 'usually you don't make any conditions for offering your labour; the only parameter is whether you get paid and how much you get paid'. Indeed, most of the undocumented migrants in the sample (78 per cent) were in low-skilled jobs in the 'shadow' economy, with just eight people reporting work in the primary sector (cleaning offices or working in restaurants and bars).

The UWT sample shows that three quarters of the currently undocumented and semi-documented migrants were employed on casual contracts, while the corresponding figure for the currently documented migrants was only 18 per cent (n = 22). Twelve currently undocumented migrants and two semi-documented interviewed in Austria and Belgium reported being on permanent contracts, doing low-skilled jobs in hospitality, cleaning, and elderly care. A Colombian woman in Barcelona explained that these sectors offered optimum stability of employment because tenure depended only on the trust established between employers/agencies and workers, regardless of legal status. She added that the instability came from the low pay and the lack of sufficient numbers of working hours needed to make ends meet.

Some jobs done by undocumented migrants were found in the 'periphery' or 'grey zone' of the formal economy. This is explained by the very nature of undocumented migrant employment. Whether it is done in the primary or the secondary sector of the economy or in the 'grey' area between the two, it refers to 'informal' employment in a segmented labour market. (In Chapter 8 we provide a more detailed analysis of the informal economy.) Informal employment is heterogeneous and ranges from 'organised' employment undertaken by employees for a business that conducts some or all of its activities informally or more 'individual' forms of informality (Williams and Windebank, 1998:30–32). Informal employment can be highly paid and autonomous work or low-paid and exploitative work (Vasta, 2004:4). Informal employment for 'organised' businesses was identified in the kitchens of ethnic restaurants and in English pubs in London, in a multinational fizzy drinks company in Sofia, and in restaurants in Vienna and Barcelona.

Wage levels for undocumented migrants varied between host country, sectors of employment, occupational status within a sector, employment experience in the host labour market, and knowledge of the host country language. Educational levels and training prior to migration were not significant determinants of migrant wages. Undocumented migrant women in domestic work in the UK and Belgium were earning similar hourly wages, €9 on average, while in Spain the corresponding figure was slightly lower, €8 an hour. Undocumented men in construction doing unskilled or semi-skilled jobs reported sporadic employment, which resulted in low monthly wages. The average hourly wages in construction differed considerably between countries. In the UK, undocumented migrant builders were earning €8 an hour while the corresponding figure in Bulgaria was €2.75 an hour and in Belgium it was €7.5 an hour.

A certain degree of deskilling was observed among Arab and Chinese undocumented migrants in the UK and Middle Eastern migrants in Bulgaria who held university diplomas and had worked in information technology and accounting in their countries of origin. Nevertheless, particularly in the UK, young Arabs saw the situation as a temporary opportunity for skills' acquisition and additional investment in their human capital, particularly for mastering their English language skills while working. Undocumented migrants in Bulgaria, on the other hand, interpreted their experience as only temporary and a necessary transition to a more economically and industrially developed country in Western Europe. No university graduates were included among the undocumented migrants interviewed in Spain and Belgium. For some educated East European women in Denmark, working as erotic dancers was a way to earn large amounts of money within a short time, using it for socio-economic advancement upon return in their home countries.

Concerning sectoral patterns, the undocumented migrants in the sample across all study countries were concentrated in four sectors: construction (men), cleaning (women), care (men and women), and (ethnic) restaurants (men and women). In Bulgaria, some interviewees were involved in prostitution as their main occupation. It was only in the UK where we interviewed men who were working in care. Undocumented status does not permit self-employment, and there was no reported incidence of it except in Austria where some migrants were working as street vendors. An analysis of the submitted applications for regularisation in Italy in 2002 showed a prevalence of services to families as the main sector of undocumented migrant employment, followed by trade and catering activities, manufacturing, and agriculture (Zanfrini, 2006). The OCED Secretariat (2000) review argues that the decline of these industries, rather than leading to their outright disappearance, leads companies to systematically resort to 'subcontracting, and in some cases, to cascading subcontracting', both of which are closely associated with illegal employment. In the UK, illegal working was found to be more of an issue for low-skilled jobs, particularly among smaller employers and those that use a number of sub-contractors or agencies, among hotels and catering, agriculture, and construction services (Dench et al., 2006). The OECD Secretariat (2000) review further notes that illegal work carried out by undocumented migrants is, in some sectors, an essential ingredient to the successful 'flexibilisation' of production processes, and regularisation potentially reduces the flexibility achieved by using irregular work. In other sectors, notably in personal services, and in particular in domestic services, other processes are at work and illegal migrant employment often goes along with a broader rise in employment in this sector. Thus, the argument is that many of the jobs created are a consequence of the availability of cheap and flexible migrant labour; were costs to increase (for example, by requiring employers to pay minimum wages, taxes, and social security contributions in the context of regularisation programmes), a certain share of jobs might be lost.

Only a third of the undocumented migrants interviewed were currently working for co-ethnic employers even though there was a view by some of the respondents that ethnic businesses were more 'accepting' of undocumented workers and there was not necessarily any difference in treatment from other workers. A young Algerian man in Brighton noted, 'it is more about trust than having the right documents'. It was believed that where employers trusted workers, they would pay them more, secure them regular work, and promote them in the business. Trust and a strong emotional relationship with the client appeared to be the necessary conditions for stable work arrangements in the care sector. Other workers had been the victims of 'co-ethnic solidarity'. For instance, undocumented Brazilian migrants interviewed in Belgium had been left with no pay by their sub-contractor employer, who had disappeared with their wages, claiming company liquidation. A Turkish woman in an ethnic business in Vienna suffered what could only be described as serious exploitation by compatriot owners.

DISCRIMINATION AGAINST UNDOCUMENTED MIGRANTS

One of the main issues surrounding undocumented migration is the degree to which migrants are exploited, or discriminated against, in the host labour markets by being paid less than what locals and legal migrants are paid and by being assigned jobs in dirty and dangerous conditions.

The UWT study noted that particularly for semi-documented workers (for example, those with a residency but not a work permit—asylum seekers would fall into this category), working conditions were more likely to mirror those of fully undocumented migrants. The heightened enforcement of immigration controls and high fines on employers of undocumented migrants in the UK are already changing the relationships in ethnic businesses discussed earlier.

The UWT study reveals a marked correlation between undocumented work and inferior working conditions, suggesting that in some cases employers exercise a positive choice in choosing to employ undocumented migrants. As a result of the increased enforcement against employers of undocumented migrants targeting ethnic businesses, we found cases where irregular migrants in Chinese restaurants in London could only find work at the absolute margins and under very low pay conditions, significantly below the minimum wage, and much lower than the London living wage (see also Chapter 3). Similarly, the current economic climate and tightened internal controls had served to exclude undocumented migrants from construction sites in London, Barcelona, and Vienna.

However, more importantly, there was a strong correlation between status and the other conditions under which work was performed. Status affected entitlement to rest breaks, social security, and sickness leave. In some cases, it even determined whether a worker would be paid at the end of the day or a month. There was high incidence of undocumented migrants in Barcelona, Brussels, and London doing heavy labour in construction for a month and then being refused payment at the end. Undocumented status also had an impact on physical and emotional health. For the undocumented migrants interviewed in Spain, working in 'hidden situations' and having to 'accept the jobs and wages that legal migrants reject' was very stressful.

Bullying, harassment, and discrimination at work by employers and supervisors, as well as co-workers, were the issues most frequently mentioned by the interviewees without documents in all the countries surveyed. Some of the workers in care homes in the UK referred to being bullied by employers, supervisors, and co-workers on the grounds of their undocumented status. In some cases, the harassment was triggered by poor English language skills; in others it was because of a perceived threat to local workers that migrants might be better qualified and could replace them. In an extreme case, a 40-year-old Filipino male worker working in construction was bullied by local co-workers who knew he was undocumented, so he eventually left the job. 'The English guys would shout "police" every time I was high up on the scaffolding and every time I was ready to jump', he recounted. Some interviewees working in catering in Austria reported incidents of employers applying 'tricks' to not pay them at times when there were not many customers. Employers would lie that they saw the police coming and ask the undocumented workers to disappear and to not come back. Undocumented women working in bars and restaurants reported sexual harassment and bullying by their employers. 'If you are working as a waitress, you are indirectly obliged to go to bed with your employer', one said. Similar experiences were shared by live-in carers, where exploitation was related to the informality of both the job and the status of the worker. Discrimination had a clearly defined economic character with migrants' country of origin being the 'reference point'.

> People I worked for (and also the employers of my friends), they look
> down on us. . . . These people treat us without respect . . .because we

are foreigners, because we have little money and therefore we have to work. They are proud of having a servant. (Ukrainian female working in Austria)

While many of those interviewed referred to unequal treatment against them on the grounds of their status as migrants, it was only those migrants who were visibly different who raised the issue of their different treatment, not just because they were migrants, but on the grounds of their ethnicity, and it was only black migrants who spoke of experiencing racism. In all seven countries in the UWT study, black migrants were more likely to raise the issue of racism, as experienced by them. For example, of those interviewed in Austria, just two had migrated from Central and West Africa but both, without any prompting, referred to racist treatment. A male from Benin, West Africa, reported how he had faced a lot of discrimination in the labour and housing market, even though he was now regularised. He had been discriminated against by a middle manager who had objected to his being employed at the supermarket where they both worked and he told the members of the UWT team that, without the intervention of a friend, he would have been dismissed.

> She said that she doesn't want any black people to work in this shop and that I have to be dismissed. Then the friend of my father who is my boss in the branch answered: If you want to dismiss this black worker you also have to dismiss me and then she denied it. Later my boss called a higher boss in the headquarters and made a complaint about her and from this moment on she left me alone. (Beninese male worker now documented in Austria)

This was not the only discrimination he had experienced. He had suffered a violent attack from skinheads that, in his view, the police had ignored, and he also referred more generally to discrimination by the Austrian police in their stop-and-search methods that appeared to target black migrants. One in four of the black migrants interviewed in Belgium also raised the issue of race discrimination. A migrant from Niger referred to labour market discrimination focusing on black migrants. A journalist from Bukino Faso, West Africa, expressed a conviction that he would never find a job commensurate with his qualifications, making the point that the Belgian national broadcasting society did not employ any black journalists. His experience had led him to conclude that 'Belgian society does not support the hiring of black people in regular employment'. Similarly one in four of the black migrants interviewed in Italy also specifically raised the issue of racism. A Bangladeshi male told of how his employers had behaved in a racist manner towards him and at the end of the season paid him just €7 an hour instead of the €10 that had been agreed upon. A male from the Cameroon spoke of 'often being treated in a racist manner'.

Individuals sometimes found it difficult to accept that they had been treated badly on the grounds of their ethnicity, as this interview demonstrates:

> It was the first job I had where I heard racist slurs from a colleague. That's where I heard the first racist slurs. He said a really ugly word to me that I can't repeat, I don't want to ... I keep this thing inside me. ... It's a disappointment I had, I didn't think that in a country like Italy. (Senegalese female working in Italy)

Discrimination on the grounds of ethnicity was also encountered even in countries with very recent migration histories like Bulgaria, with one in six black migrants interviewed having directly experienced race discrimination. A Guatemalan woman had experienced discrimination on several occasions when her colleagues would call her 'the yellow', an allusion to her skin colour. Even in the Northern European countries of Belgium and Denmark, race discrimination was an issue. A 24-year-old Nigerian woman, interviewed in Copenhagen, spoke of the 'disadvantages' of being of black in Northern Europe:

> When I get my papers, I want to go to the UK or USA so people cannot so easily see that I am African. It is very easy to identify people in Europe because everybody is white and black people are having a tough time.

A woman migrant from the Philippines working in the 'entertainment' industry in Denmark stated, 'Asian girls and African girls get less in tips from the management than European girls; even Russian girls get more in tips'. However, even though the comment from the Nigerian woman in Copenhagen (cited above) might suggest that the UK was a better destination for black migrants, there too the issue of discriminatory treatment was raised. A Nigerian male spoke of discrimination at work as based on colour. Black people on security sites were rarely made supervisors; white people were preferred for these posts. He had also experienced discrimination for racist reasons on another occasion when he had been interviewed and accepted for a job over the phone, but when he presented himself in person the company withdrew the job offer.

There were some signs that things had improved. A migrant from the Congo in Central Africa, working in Bulgaria, spoke of past discrimination in hiring practices, 'at the beginning there was, a bit, the mentality of not hiring Arabs, of not hiring Africans' but that things had improved significantly, while some migrants stressed that the racism they had experienced had also to be set against the good treatment they had also received from local workers and employers.

REGULARISATION AND THE RETENTION OF LEGAL STATUS

Among the study countries, opportunities for regularisation existed to any significant extent only in Spain, Italy, and Belgium. The highest number of interviewees who benefited from these programmes was in Italy, where over half had participated in a regularisation programme. In all study countries, most had arrived as tourists or visitors and subsequently participated in a regularisation programme in Italy, Spain, or Belgium; a few had claimed asylum in the UK, Austria, or Bulgaria. Others had initially arrived as visitors, students, or work permit holders and had subsequently become undocumented, failing to meet the necessary requirements for renewal of their permits. It is estimated that this affects some 400 to 600 foreigners annually in Austria (European Commission, 2009). As we have already noted, undocumented citizens from the A8 member states became regularised overnight in the UK, Ireland, and Sweden on 1 May 2004, when their countries joined the EU. Similarly, undocumented migrants from Bulgaria and Romania acquired legal residence status with the two countries' EU membership in 2007. For the undocumented migrants interviewed in Belgium, Italy, and Spain, participation in a regularisation programme was the main route to legality. Most of those benefiting from the programmes had arrived in the host countries on visitor visas while a few had been smuggled into Italy and Spain. In Italy, 13 of the 30 people interviewed had taken part in a regularisation programme and had managed to retain their legal status. Similarly, in Spain, six people in the sample managed to regularise their status through regularisation programmes and retain it. It was only in Belgium where some people in our sample who took part in a regularisation programme and gained only temporary legal status, had slipped back into irregularity. However, as already discussed in Chapter 6, we know from the literature that the possibility of losing regular status following regularisation is relatively high.

CONCLUSION

Profiling of undocumented migrants and providing estimates on their numbers are notoriously difficult tasks, given the unregistered nature of the migration status. Several estimation methods on the size of the undocumented population in Europe have been critically reviewed, acknowledging the fact that even the most appropriate of them is not scientifically or methodologically robust. It also involves a great deal of ethical consideration. For this reason, any data on estimates of undocumented migration should be used and interpreted with sensitivity, responsibility, and care, without endangering individuals or communities. Such data should be protected from misuse for political campaigns or policies targeting deportation.

The employment profile of the undocumented migrants surveyed was characterised by work not only in the informal economy but also in the periphery zones of the formal sector. Wage levels for undocumented migrants were determined by the sector of employment, the duration of experience in the host labour market, and the knowledge of the host country language. Overall, a significant correlation was found between undocumented status and inferior working conditions, an indication of a positive choice by employers to employ undocumented migrants. Status affects entitlement to rest breaks and has an impact on health and accidents. An alarming finding emerged that even though some migrants had managed to secure legal status, they remained trapped somewhere between the formal and informal labour market, working for employers who would not pay them their actual hours of work or would fail to pay the necessary social security contributions. Conversely, some legal migrants had chosen the 'freedom' of the informal contacts.

Undocumented migrant women were more likely in our sample to be working in private homes, restaurants, and bars and in these circumstances were more likely to be subjected to inferior treatment and to suffer serious psychological trauma as a result. Although international conventions against trafficking and against forced labour give an appearance of concern for the exploitation of women migrants, they ignore the vulnerable working conditions of the vast majority of women migrants who do not fall under the category of trafficked or forced labour but who cannot escape their difficult conditions of employment because they have no way of regularising their presence or enforcing employment rights (McKay et al., 2009). In the next chapter we look at informal economies and their relationship with undocumented migrants.

8 Informal Economies and Dual Labour Market Theories

> One can better understand migration by ignoring income differences and recognizing instead that people are rooted in a social context in ways that other commodities are not.
>
> (Piore, 1979:8)

Michael J. Piore remains one of the most prominent proponents of the theory that deliberately ignores income differences between countries in order to explain migration through the job characteristics that migrants do and the sectors where these jobs are to be found. Building on Piore's argument, this chapter will analyse migration through the jobs migrants are doing in the secondary niches of a segmented labour market.

Informal economies are not a new phenomenon. They have become a permanent element within capitalist economies, which nevertheless sometimes have been challenged in periods, such as after the end of World War 2, when capital could expand. While some countries have historically had large informal sectors—for example, Italy and Spain—expansion has also been observed in countries with, in the past, very limited labour force participation in the underground economy (McKay et al., 2009). For our purposes we have defined the 'underground economy' as 'constituted by irregular production and/or labour that is perfectly integrated into the formal economy and 'represents that ensemble of activities which contribute to the formation of the revenue and of the wealth of a nation without, however, being reported in the official statistics' (UWT, 2008:11–12). The term informal employment' is often more useful in describing the range of work situations of irregular migrants, and while the concept of an 'informal economy suggests that it is separate from the formal economy, many argue that they are closely related (UWT, 2008).

This chapter explores migration and informal economies through the lenses of theories of labour market dualism. It draws on evidence provided in interviews with migrants who had experience of working in the informal economies of seven EU member states that were the subject of our study as well as interviews with national, European, and international experts and stakeholders.

THE ESSENCE OF THE THEORY OF LABOUR MARKET DUALISM

Dual labour market theory was initially formulated by a group of economists in the US in the 1960s. It was based on observations of the labour market behaviour of the urban poor in Boston, Chicago, and Detroit. The conclusions were that the poor tended to be confined to the secondary labour market, characterised by low wages and unstable, dead-end jobs and that this market was different and completely separated from the primary labour market (Lowell, 1978). However, for Fields (2004), labour market dualism was discussed even earlier, in the 1950s, in Arthur Lewis's classic paper entitled 'Economic development with unlimited supplies of labour'. In the Lewis model, dualism is reflected in the wage differences depending on the sector of the economy where work was performed. Fundamentally the labour market was divided into two sectors. One sector was described as 'capitalist', 'formal', modern', 'industrial', or 'urban'. The other was described as 'subsistence', 'informal', 'traditional', 'agricultural', or 'rural' (Lewis, 1954).

Migration was first incorporated into the dualistic models as a way of explaining the intensified rural-urban migration in developing countries (Todaro, 1969). This introduced the concept of the segmented urban labour market with its urban traditional sector[1] and the urban 'modern' sector. The size and rate of the increased labour migration and the occupational distribution of the urban labour force were shown to be the product of the interdependence effects of industrial expansion, productivity growth, and the expected differential real earnings' capacity of urban versus rural activities. This was a microeconomic model of individual choice, based on a cost-benefit analysis and expectations for higher monetary returns. The labour market segmentation and its significance for immigrants was identified a decade later by Piore (1979). As one of the most passionate and forceful proponents of the dual labour market theory, setting sights away from the microeconomic migration theories (i.e., decisions made by individuals), he argued that international migration stemmed from the intrinsic labour demands of modern industrial societies. In his analytical framework, migration was not only a response to general labour shortages or shortages at the bottom of the social hierarchy; migration satisfied the requirements of the secondary sector within a dual labour market.

Almost 30 years later, the seeming relevance of Michael Piore's labour market dualism theory has increased, rather than diminished. This is particularly true for the Southern European countries of Italy, Spain, Greece, and Portugal where migrants, both undocumented and legal, tend to cluster in the informal niches of the market.

This is explained by the role of the secondary market, which traditionally has been used to deal with fluctuations in the product market demand (Piore, 1979). Dual labour market theory provides insights not only into segmented labour markets but also segmented business establishments (Doeringer and Piore, 1971). For Piore (1980) dual labour markets often arose within the same firm: the firm used a 'core' of primary workers along with a 'periphery' of secondary workers who were disposable in the face of reduced demand. Even where the two tiers did not formally coexist within the same firm, the same outcome could be achieved by using sub-contractors or agency workers. In Europe, collective bargaining had operated to prevent larger firms from utilising a two-tier labour force (Saint-Paul, 1996), whereas in small and medium-sized enterprises both sectors operated, more or less side by side, demonstrating a divided workforce. Migrant workers, especially newcomers with little or no knowledge of the host country language, were crowded into bottom-end jobs in such small establishments. Dualism is also claimed to arise exogenously in the labour market as a response to labour market regulations represented by the imposition of a minimum legal wage rate, high worker protection, and effective health and safety regimes. Firms that comply with minimum wage legislation are more likely to belong to the formal sector whereas those that ignore it tend to belong to the informal economy (Loyaza, 1994). The duality in the economy stems from, and is sustained by, differences in wages and capital costs between formal and informal sectors. Nevertheless, the informal sector can expand in output and employment, even when the formal sector contracts, regardless of the linkages that exist between the two (Chaudhuru, 1989). Warhurt et al. (2008) suggest that it is not the employers' compliance (or lack of compliance) with minimum wage legislation, but rather the management and employment practices centred on employer demand for flexibility that result in low pay. Hence dualism endogenously arises within firms as a response to demand fluctuations. Employers can fire and hire in correspondence to current demand (Entorf and Moebert, 2004). Similarly, they can modify pay rates to correspond to current demand.

Some experts talk of the advantages of informal employment as a 'buffer' to economic fluctuations. The informal sector is characterised by its flexibility and reduced labour costs, through withholding taxes and social insurances contributions.[2]

The secondary tier of the economy, along with 'grey' zones in between the two tiers, therefore, is characterised by high degrees of uncertainty and instability. Gills Saint-Paul (1996) further decomposes labour market dualism into 'good' and 'bad' jobs, existing both in the economy and within a firm. For him 'bad jobs' are increasingly perceived in Europe as the price that has to be paid for full employment. Many of the labour market reforms in the 1980s have increased flexibility at the 'margins' contributing to the creation of a two-tier labour market. The analogy between 'bad' jobs and irregular jobs has already been analysed in the informal economy literature (Boeri and Garibaldi, 2002; Cavalcanti, 2002) even though suggesting different interpretations of wages in the irregular sector, which can be higher (Boeri and Garibaldi, 2002) or lower than those in the regular sector (Cavalcanti, 2002). Although informal sectors of the labour market provide entry points for both undocumented and documented migrants, employment in the informal sector remains a more likely permanent location of work for those who remain or become undocumented. The relationship of undocumented migration with informal employment in Europe and the US is also identified as a significant factor in the growth of pre-existing informal sectors as well as the stimulation of undocumented migrant labour flows (Baldwin-Edwards and Arango, 1999; Reyneri, 2002).

THE UNDERGROUND ECONOMY AND ITS CHARACTERISTICS

'Structural Phenomenon'

Despite the intensification of immigration controls in all EU Member States, informal labour has nevertheless grown, becoming a 'historically significant phenomenon', what we describe as a 'structural phenomenon'. For example, in 2004 the underground economy in Italy produced an added value equal to 17.7 per cent of GDP with 2,794,000 undocumented workers, corresponding to a rate of irregularity of 11.5 per cent (Cillo and Perocco, 2007). In Austria, a study by Enste and Schneider (2006) estimated that by 2004 the number of people working informally had increased to 789,000 Austrians and 114,000 foreigners, compared to 575,000 and 75,000 respectively in 1995. Among migrants with legal permits for residence, some 50,000 to 70,000 had engaged in some form of work in the informal economy (Biffl, 2002). In Spain, for 2006, a combination of data from the LFS and social security records shows that in the same period around 777,826 workers were not registered and were likely to be part of the informal economy.

A continued falling rate of profit has resulted in the cyclical and structural worsening of living and working conditions, particularly for work carried out on the peripheries of national economies. In this situation, a role for migrant undocumented labour is established as labour that is marginalised, exceptionally vulnerable, and therefore cheap and flexible. The recent evolution of welfare systems in Europe and of migration policies continue to provide incentives for a private-enterprise solution to the growing demand for care-giving services. EU enlargement towards Central and Eastern Europe has made it possible to employ administratively documented workers without any employment contract, in the pursuit of low labour costs, because, in case of immigration controls, the risk of their deportation is sharply reduced. Thus the liberalisation of migration rules may actually encourage the growth of informal employment.

Similar patterns of working arrangements occur in many EU Member States, suggesting the existence of specific production processes that are reliant on undocumented labour. These include fixed processes that are difficult to programme for such as in construction; the outsourcing of welfare, as in elderly care; as well as the pre-existence of an informal sector within which local and migrant labour is absorbed. In some sectors, undocumented labour is sought out precisely because it is considered as flexible and disposable. However, it may also be required in those circumstances where working conditions are poor but where long-term employment relations are highly prized, particularly by employers. It can be argued that informal economies are not necessarily the product of particular national traits but are a consequence of specific changes in the labour market. These changes are identified as dependent on subcontracting and self-employment; third-party employment relationships, in particular through the use of labour providers; and the outsourcing of human resource functions.

Jeff Dayton-Johnson, an OECD economist, supports the view that there is a persistent geographical imbalance between the North and the South of Europe. The industrial structure of the Northern economies is focused on large manufacturing firms whereas in Southern Europe it is smaller, more service-oriented firms. Along with Piore's (1979) lines of enquiry, immigration appears more of a consequence than a cause of those labour market structures.[3] Baldwin-Edwards claims that 'it is the economic structures that are pushing for the illegality of the informal sector to continue'.[4] There is also a view that it is the availability of cheap labour for the informal economy that holds up innovation and restructuring in the entire economy.[5] It is also the case that the informal economy has an anti-inflationary effect, in the same way as immigration of unskilled workers may depress inflationary wage pressures. The availability of undocumented work brings gains to many actors. Sending countries receive remittances, agents run successful businesses, and the 'host country gains by having cheaper pizzas'.[6] The growth of the underground economy in Europe can be seen as a component of the increased casualisation of labour and is promoted as just another way for Europe retain it competitiveness in the global economy. This is one of the reasons for governments to not want to go any near it, Martin Baldwin-Edwards commented: 'They know that labour laws have been broken or violated but they don't want to do anything about it because that's how wages are kept under control'.[7]

The Informal Economy as a 'Pull' Factor for Migration

There is strong evidence from the interview data in the seven countries surveyed that the existence of an underground or shadow economy did not act as a pull factor for undocumented migrants. Most interviewees had no clear idea of the shape of the host countries' economies prior to arrival. Although many had anticipated being able to access work (mainly through co-ethnic channels), they had not conceptualised that work as part of an underground economy. Nevertheless, as Table 8.1 shows, it was the case that the majority were working in the underground economy. However, a small number (eight people) was indeed working in the declared economy but as undeclared workers. Some of them were working on fake documents (Brazilian men in Belgium using fake Portuguese passports to work in construction or Arab men in the UK using fake French passports for work in restaurants).

Legal status appeared to have a significant relationship with the sector of employment—declared, informal, or in the niches between the two (Table

8.1, chi-square = 77.937, p < 0.01%). There were no significant differences between the characteristics of migrant workers employed in the informal economy and the declared economy, respectively. Those employed in the informal economy appeared to be slightly older, with the highest concentration in the 35 to 49 years age group, compared to those in declared employment. Similar age distribution is observed in the two sectors, with a prevalence of men. Nevertheless, fewer women reported being employed in the informal economy than in the declared economy. There was a significant relationship between the levels of completed education and the sector of employment (chi-square = 19.61, p < 5%). The majority of workers in both sectors had secondary education whereas more workers with minimum or no education and fewer workers with professional qualifications or university degrees were found to be working in the informal economy (Table 8.1).

Table 8.1 Distribution of Migrants by Sector of Employment and Gender, Age, Education, Legal Status

Characteristics	Primary sector employment	Informal employment	Between primary and informal employment
Age:			
18–24	7 (7.1%)	9 (10.1%)	2 (16.7%)
25–34	43 (43.9%)	34 (38.2%)	5 (41.7%)
35–49	38 (38.8%)	35 (39.3%)	5 (41.7%)
50–64 (m),	10 (10.2%)	11 (12.4%)	0 (0.0%)
50–59 (f)	98 (100%)	89 (100%)	12 (100.0%)
Total			
Education*:			
No education or minimum	10 (10.5%)	26 (40.0%)	1 (8.3%)
Secondary	42 (44.2%)	41 (47.7%)	8 (66.7%)
University or tertiary	27 (28.5%)	13 (15.1%)	2 (16.7%)
Professional qualification	16 (16.8%)	6 (7.0%)	1 (8.3%)
Total:	95 (100%)	86 (100%)	12 (100%)
* chi-square=19.61, p<5%			
Gender:			
Male	52 (53.1%)	49 (55.1%)	5 (41.7%)
Female	46 (46.9%)	40 (44.9%)	7 (58.3%)
Total:	98 (100%)	89 (100%)	12 (100%)
Legal status*:			
Undocumented	8 (8.2%)	53 (59.6%)	2 (16.7%)
Semi-documented	2 (2.0%)	11 (12.2%)	0 (0.0%)
Documented	88 (89.9%)	25 (28.1%)	10 (83.3%)
Total:	98 (100%)	89 (100%)	12 (100%)
*chi-square=77.937, p<0.01%			

Source: UWT, Field survey, 2007–2008.

Some of the employers of those interviewed were operating in the declared economy although this did not mean that they were declaring all of their activities, and some interviewees made it clear that their employer was not declaring either all or part of their work to the authorities and this was the reason why they did not have tax or social insurance deducted. Across the seven EU countries surveyed, these exceptions were found in relation to the cleaning sector, both in private households and industrial cleaning, construction, and agriculture.

Night work also was more likely to be associated with undocumented or irregular work, as night work, at least psychologically, provided anonymity and was seen as less 'out in the open'. Among the Turkish-speaking interviewees in the UK, informal employment had primarily been in the textile sector and was categorised—a precise reflection of the dual labour market theory—as hard work, under poor conditions, and with a high degree of harassment and bullying. Two of the women of Turkish origin talked of ongoing health problems as a result of hard and repetitive work. 'We were a cheap and silenced group of unsafe migrants' (Turkish female, UK).

An Ecuadorian woman in Belgium spoke of malnutrition and of exhausting manual labour at the employer's house where she worked as a live-in carer; she had ended up seriously ill in hospital, as a result. A large number of interviewees across all of the surveyed countries talked about the psychological burden of being detected at work and deported. 'I had terrible stomach pains; went to hospital using my sister's yellow card (we look very similar) and was told it was stress', a Turkish woman in Denmark stated.

Employment in ethnic businesses—restaurants, bars, and in construction—was a more recognised entry route for workers without documents. Recruitment on the basis of country of origin also emerges in the concept of 'exploitative solidarity', when working for a 'compatriot boss' may mean long workdays, underpayment, and difficult work conditions (Erdemir and Vasta, 2007). Undocumented Chinese workers in the UK tended to work in ethnic enclave restaurants in the kitchens, late at night, whereas workers with documents were employed as 'front end' staff, according to a Chinese interviewee, who had worked in the restaurant sector. Similar experience was reported by Turkish migrants in Vienna working in ethnic businesses. Their jobs were characterised by long working hours, no holidays, no health insurance, and having no choice but to work, even when seriously ill. A 25-year-old Turkish man spoke of how he had to work two whole weeks with not a day off even though he had pneumonia and was secreting blood. The ethnic underground economy played a decisive role in the lives of many of the undocumented worker interviewees. The Turkish community in Vienna was described as one where 'social control is very high and information is floating quickly'. A young woman spoke of the high degree of dependency on the community, which forced her to accept an irregular job with working conditions more recognisable as being of the 19th century—working 12 hours a day, seven days a week, and working even when ill for a monthly wage of €400. 'My mind was totally occupied by surviving', she stated.

Employers in the Informal Economy

Many interviewees without documents spoke of a dependency on employers that never seemed to end, or at least it continued as long as their undocumented status lasted. Work conditions might improve over the years, but the dependency on employers remains. 'I needed to borrow money from him to pay for a fictitious marriage', a young woman declared. For some respondents, the nationality of their employer was an important determinant of their working conditions. Table 8.2 reveals that over half of the interviewees in informal employment were working either for a person from their community or another migrant employer. Unsurprisingly, most of the migrant employers (66.3 per cent) in the declared economy were local.

For migrant women working in bars and restaurants, native employers in the informal sector were preferred as they 'pay more and you have to work less'.

> In Turkish [owned] bars we began working earlier and longer; the daily salary was between €30 and €40. If you worked in a German [owned] bar working hours were shorter and payment was higher. But in Greek [owned] and Turkish [owned] bars the payment and the working conditions were bad to worse. (Polish female, now documented, interviewed in Austria)

For migrant women in the 'entertainment' industry, bad working conditions were related to a requirement by the employer for continuous alcohol consumption, table dancing, and prostitution. In all seven countries

Table 8.2 Distribution of Migrants by Sector of Employment and Ethnic Group of Current Employer

Current employer	Primary sector employment	Informal employment	Between primary and informal employment
Own community	13 (13.7%)	23 (26.8%)	3 (27.3%)
Other migrant community	3 (3.2%)	21 (24.4%)	2 (18.2%)
Local person	63 (66.3%)	39 (45.3%)	6 (54.5%)
Other	16 (16.8%)	3 (3.5%)	0 (0.0%)
Total	95 (100%)	86 (100%)	11 (100%)

Source: UWT, Field survey, 2007-2008.

in the study, construction and retail had more 'individual' forms of informal employment. Parts of the construction sector, in different proportions across Europe, traditionally operate in the informal economy. Workers and managers can be both migrants and locals. The most distinctive characteristic of the sector is its very high level of sub-contracting, which absorbs a considerable share of undocumented labour. Big companies recruit either through employment agencies or directly from the existing workforce. The use of forged documents to get a job on a site is a common practice.[8] The current economic climate appeared to have already altered recruitment into the sector. For example, in Spain, we found that undocumented workers had great difficulty in getting any work on construction sites. The dangerous nature of the work was felt to put Spanish employers at risk of imprisonment and high fines if detected employing undocumented migrants, and for this reason they were not willing to employ migrants who might be undocumented. Under these conditions access, to informal employment moved into the hotel and restaurant sectors.

Housekeeping, and especially elderly care, is another 'grey' area which is at present less evident in Northern Europe but of particular significance for Southern Europe, where it functions as a substitute to a weak welfare state. It is a relatively easy entry sector for migrant women without documents or knowledge of the host country language. We return to this issue in the next chapter.

Ways of Finding Work in the Informal Economy

Work in the informal economy is found mainly through networks of family and friends from the ethnic community, and we explore this issue of family in greater detail in Chapter 10. Our survey data showed that twice as many of those employed in the informal economy had found their last job through family contacts, as did those in the declared economy. It is inevitably the case that sectors of informal employment are particularly dependent on personal contacts as, given the nature of the employment situation, job vacancies are almost never advertised. This is even truer for the EU countries of Southern Europe, where the labour market is heavily networked and segmented and very few people find jobs through advertisements. It is also true to a degree for Northern Europe and although there is insufficient data, anecdotes suggest that work in the informal economy may also be accessed through family and co-ethnic networks.

Competition for Jobs Between Natives and Migrants in the Informal Sector

It is argued that the current crisis of capital has been accompanied by a trend toward the growth of inequality within the informal economy itself. This means that it reproduces external hierarchies, with local workers at the top, regularised migrants under them, and undocumented workers at the bottom. It is they who suffer from the worst working conditions and, above all, from the fewest opportunities of escaping from the informal sphere. Research on the informal economy in Denmark has shown a distinct internal hierarchy between migrants at the bottom and native Danes at the top of the irregular employment ladder. Undocumented migrants in Denmark are strictly confined to the informal economy. Lacking legal papers makes it impossible for them to have access to any public services without risking deportation (Rezai and Goli, 2007). Ethnic networks and 'migrant services' play a mediating role between the undocumented worker and regulated life in the country. Often there is a price to pay for their service:

> I am not stupid. I know that when you don't have permission to stay and work in a country then you don't pay tax but it costs you in another way—you pay other people who let you work without permission. You don't pay taxes to the government but you pay the same money to the one who secures your life. (Nigerian undocumented female interviewed in Denmark)

In Spain, direct competition between natives and immigrants was recorded in the informal niches of home care and in the restaurant sector. In the former, migrant women were usually paid less, but the remaining work conditions were identical. In the restaurant sector, the front-desk jobs were usually taken up by young Spaniards who were believed to be able to 'afford' being paid very little as they were still financially supported by their parents. In Austria, experts claimed that informal work was performed mainly by natives, even though the size of the sector was considerably smaller than in Southern Europe. In the construction and care sectors, undocumented migrants and Austrian citizens were found working side by side. A respondent we interviewed from the ICMPD spoke of the informal economy in Austria as socially accepted ('not even a minister has to resign if he hires an informal care worker'—a reference to the eventual resignation of a UK minister after she had been exposed as employing a worker without permission to work). He estimated that in Vienna alone, some 15,000 to 20,000 people were working in the informal cleaning industry. For him, another indicator of the importance of the informal employment in construction was the density of DIY ('do-it-yourself') stores in the country, pointing to a large-scale use of informal arrangements for small construction projects.[9]

Similarly, in agriculture, the available data suggests that the extreme flexibility of work organization that intensive agriculture demands has been satisfied through the informal employment of migrant workers without permits or, as with asylum seekers, with permits that do not allow them to work, in addition to the formal employment of migrant workers with seasonal permits. A Moroccan undocumented male worker in Italy commented as follows on the high demand for irregular migrants by employers in agriculture: 'From the experience I have in agriculture, they (undocumented migrants) work more; they really do a lot of work'.

Small manufacturing firms in Italy were a major employer of both undocumented migrants and local workers, and some undocumented migrants whom our Italian colleagues interviewed had even been introduced to them through their Italian colleagues. Indeed, the Italian union CGIL estimates that the shadow economy includes some two million Italian workers.[10]

Some workers expressed a preference for work in the informal employment. African legal migrants interviewed in the UK talked about their voluntary engagement in informal employment because of its freedom and untaxed income (enabling migrants to get higher 'cash' earnings). 'I want to be free. I don't want to be stuck in legal work', a young Moroccan man stated. Bauman (cited in Engbersen, 2001:223) calls it a development of 'life strategies' based on quality of life decisions as opposed to 'survival strategies'. However, such options do not apply to undocumented migrants. Similarly, local residents also engage in informal employment. Domestic work and hospitality (hotels and restaurants) are the sectors where locals, legal migrants, and undocumented migrants are found working side by side. As the informal market is not just a peripheral form of the formal labour market but rather a segmented market with its own hierarchies (Williams and Windebank, 1998), a discrepancy is registered between the wages paid to locals and those paid to migrants. Migrant women employed in domestic work in Barcelona were paid around €2 an hour less than what local women were being paid for the same work, with the latter earning around €8 to €10 an hour (Pajares and Leotti, 2008). It was also observed not only that more men than women participated in the informal sector but that they were likely to earn more than their female undocumented counterparts. Thus pay discrimination based on gender also seeped into the informal sector. Conversely, a recent study in London (Ahmad, 2008) found that smuggled migrants who entered the country illegally ended up working in butcher shops and cafes in fairly similar conditions to those of regular migrants from the same countries of origin.

MEASURES TO PREVENT INFORMAL EMPLOYMENT

Enforcement Mechanisms

Member States in Europe have looked across the Atlantic to the US experience, particularly in relation to enforcement. Since 27 March 2008, as a consequence of a new rule introduced by the Department of Homeland Security (DHS) and Department of Justice (DOJ), employers in the US with unauthorised immigrant workers have had to pay increased fines. This was the first increase in the level of the fines since 1999. The minimum penalty for knowingly hiring undocumented workers rose by 36 per cent, from

$275 to $375, and the maximum fine for a first-time offender rose by 45 per cent, from $2,200 to $3,200; a new maximum fine for repeat offenders, set at $16,000, was 45 per cent higher than the previous fine of $11,000. Immigration and Customs Enforcement (ICE) is the investigative branch of DHS (DHS was created in 2003) and is responsible for the enforcement of the US immigration law (Chishti and Bergeron, 2008; Terrazas, Batalova, and Fan, 2007).

In Austria, the Central Task Force for the Prevention of Illegal Employment (KIAB) is responsible for the identification of illegally employed workers, as well as for tax and social insurance fraud. Especially in the construction sector, the problem of fictitious companies avoiding taxes and social insurance contributions, as well as the problems of unpaid wages for undocumented foreign workers, is extensive. The Chamber of Labour, the body responsible for supporting workers in gaining their employment rights, has been supporting victims in making claims for the remuneration of unpaid wages. In 2004, it represented 2,300 employees (including undocumented migrants) who were victims of fictitious companies in the construction sector. Currently, combating social fraud is on top of the agenda of the social partners: in an amendment of the Austrian General Social Insurance Act (ASVG), the right of employers not to register an employee until the seventh day of her or his employment was removed. In future, the registration of employees for social insurance is obligatory from day one of employment. Until 2002, the Austrian labour inspectorate was responsible for checking worksites for the employment of undocumented migrants and documented their number by employment branch and nationality. Effective from July 2002, KIAB no longer retains data on the nationality of undocumented migrants. Catering (26 per cent), the building industry (21 per cent), and sub-contracting (17 per cent) are understood to be among the branches with the highest shares of undocumented labour. However, it must be borne in mind that the checks that are carried out apply only to enterprises and not to private households where many migrant workers, particularly women (see Chapter 9), work as live-in carers or domestic workers (Forschungs- und Beratungsstelle Arbeitswelt, 2007).

The latest amendment to the Foreigners Law in Spain introduced fines of up to €60,000 on employers of undocumented migrants and established that those working without current authorisation could be deported within 48 hours. Similarly, amendments to the UK immigration law of 29 February 2008 increased the financial and criminal sanctions on employers of undocumented workers (see also Chapter 5).

Government Initiatives

Here too it is useful to begin by looking at the US experience where the government has introduced an E-Verify Participation system, permitting employers to see whether newly hired workers are authorised to work by checking their names and social security numbers against a federal database. Although federal law does not mandate participation in the E-Verify, a new Arizona law requires all employers in the state to use it (Chishti and Bergeron, 2008). There have been some strong voices against the system, as the checks only determine who is not on the list and the records are often very incorrect (Bacon, 2008).

Belgium, the Netherlands, and Germany have implemented some of the most innovative initiatives in Europe in an attempt to facilitate the formalization of undeclared work. Rather than trying to eradicate it by tightened enforcement measures, these policy reforms seek to introduce new institutional arrangements, which can transfer undeclared work into the formal economy. For example, the Belgian government has introduced service vouchers as a means of paying for everyday personal services. This is essentially a wage cost subsidy for labour-intensive, low-skilled domestic work. A household can buy a voucher of €6.70 and uses it to pay for an hour's work, provided by a certified company (these can be commercial businesses; companies working in the social sector and public services). In addition to the €6.70, the registered company receives a government subsidy of €14.30. Workers paid with service vouchers have a 'service vouchers employment contract', which entitles them to social security rights and insurance against industrial accidents. At first, the contract between the agency and the unemployed person can be very short term and flexible. After six months, however, the company must offer a permanent contract for at least part-time employment, if the person has been previously registered as unemployed. The activities that an employee of these certified companies may do are restricted to domestic cleaning; washing and ironing; sewing; running errands; and preparing meals. The cost of the vouchers is partially tax-deductible.[11] The household can claim back 30 per cent of the price of the voucher on their tax return forms. Evaluation studies of the programme revealed that some 28,933 jobs had been created by the end of 2005, exceeding the government target of 25,000 jobs; some 25 per cent of the households using the service vouchers reported that the work most probably would have been done on an undeclared basis if there had not been vouchers (Renooy, 2007).

Belgium has experienced increased labour migration since the 2004 EU enlargement; much of this employment is outside the legal norms, especially in sectors such as construction and transport. In the summer of 2005 the social partners in the building sector, in co-operation with the federal government's Employment, Labour and Social Dialogue Service, set up an 'unfair competition' working party to address possible abuses related to labour migration from the new EU Member States. The labour inspection services are also increasing their efforts to combat fraud in the area (van Gyes, 2005). Another significant recent development concerns the institutionalisation of the fight against irregular work and social services fraud through several instruments. A law of 3 May 2003[12] provided a coordinated institutional framework for policies to combat irregular work and social services fraud through, for example, a focus on prevention measures, the presentation of propositions to ministers, and the establishment of recommendations for legal changes in relation to the fight against illegal work. Also, a law of 2006[13] introduced a new system of registration in order to better control the employment of migrants (self-employed; employees, students, or trainees) who come to Belgium for a short time for work. Declarations have to be made to the National Office of Social Security (ONSS) before the start of the work (Ouali, 2007).

In 2002, the German government adopted the Harz Committee's 'mini jobs' proposal, which was particularly geared at fighting undeclared work in the private household sector. The new regulations came into effect in April 2003, stipulating that employees with low-wage employment contracts earning up to €400 a month were exempt from paying contributions to the statutory employment, health, and pension insurance schemes out of their earnings. These are covered by the employers who pay a fixed percentage of 30 per cent of the wage for social security contributions. Since 2003, workers already in formal employment have been allowed to take up one parallel 'mini job' and receive the same preferential treatment. The social security contributions to be paid by employers of low-wage workers in private households were set at 12 per cent for mini job contracts; employers can offset some of the labour cost against their tax liability.[14] In order to facilitate the transfer from minor (mini jobs) to normal employment, the government introduced a transition income zone of €400 to €800, thus allowing gradual increase in employees' social security contributions (Ouali, 2007).

However, evaluating the outcomes of the aforementioned initiatives, Renooy (2007) argues that the schemes in Belgium and Germany, in which government subsidies lower formal wage costs for domestic work, are not a panacea for undeclared employment. As an alternative measure, in 2007, the Dutch government brought to an end its scheme that had previously helped households to use subsidized cleaners, replacing it with new tax rules on domestic services. These new rules allow households to employ domestic helpers for cleaning, cooking, washing, shopping, small repairs and maintenance jobs in and around the house, childcare, or gardening without the obligation to pay tax on wages, pay a social security premium, or register the worker at the tax and social security offices, as long as the employed person does not work more than three days a week. Not paying social security contributions means that the worker is not entitled to receive social benefits in case of unemployment, sick leave, or disability, and no retirement pension capital accrues. The theory behind this is that it removes any incentives on domestic workers to undertake undeclared work; it attracts more people with no educational qualifications to enter the labour market; and, by lowering the cost of domestic work, the labour market participation of the hiring person is enhanced.[15] These new rules were expected to make a significant contribution to the registered market for personal services in the Netherlands. In sum, these are interesting examples of government approaches that move away from tight enforcement in combating undeclared work, towards the elimination of those factors that are known to encourage it.

Unionising Undocumented Workers in the Informal Economy

Indisputably, organising migrant workers in unions is a major step forward in combating exploitation. Nevertheless, unions who choose to organise undocumented workers also face numerous challenges accessing undocumented workers. This is rooted in the very nature of undocumented migrant employment. For example, workers are often employed in sectors that have not been traditionally unionised, or they can be hard to reach because they are working in isolated places; unions can find that it is difficult to locate employers in order to intervene. The UWT study found that although both male and female undocumented migrants were often working in sectors where there were low levels of collective organisation, this was more likely to be the case for women. Male workers in the construction and manufacturing sectors could find themselves working alongside unionised workers and could sometimes benefit from the collective solidarities that such workplaces created. Women, on the other hand, working in the private care sector or in the sex industry were much less likely to find a collective way of improving their working conditions (McKay et al., 2009). Employers also use different strategies against workers to prevent them from joining a union. The US is a good example of such practices. The American Federation of Labor and Congress of Industrial Organizations (AFL/CIO) (cited in Bacon, 2008:96) claims that 'workers are routinely fired in 31 per cent of all US-union organising drives'. Bacon (2008:2) discusses the motivations behind the large-scale dismissals of migrant workers in the US in 2006. For the labour and immigrant-rights activists, the dismissals selectively targeted workplaces where people were organising unions, in an effort to enforce labour-protection laws, improve wages and benefits, or otherwise stand up for their rights. On the immigration raids at Smithfield Foods in the US in 2007, he states that 'according to many workers, those organising efforts, and not the twenty-one detained immigrants, were the raids' real target' (Bacon, 2008:14).

In some European countries, unions have shown strong commitment to organising undocumented workers. Chapter 6 offers examples of union initiatives in support of the regularisation of undocumented migrants in Europe. In Portugal, the Confederação Geral dos Trabalhadores Portugueses–Intersindical Nacional (CGTP–IN) has had a pro-immigrant worker policy since its inception in 1970. The union's database does not even distinguish between legal or undocumented workers so that members can have trust in a secure system. There are also some examples of unions that have undertaken concrete initiatives to protect undocumented workers. For instance, in Italy the Confederazione Generale Italiana del Lavoro (CGIL) has established a permanent relationship with the Associazione Studi Giuridici sull'Immigrazione (ASGI), an association of lawyers that works on immigrant issues; CGIL and ASGI organise seminars that provide union members with training on immigration issues. Similarly, the Athens Labour Centre (EKA) in Greece, through volunteer immigrant lawyers, provides undocumented workers with free consultancies on immigration and labour issues (Markova and McKay, 2008).

CONCLUSION

The existing different economic and welfare conditions in the seven partner countries appeared as an indicator both of the strength of the informal economy and of the presence of undocumented labour within it. Looking at the perspectives and developments in the underground economy in the EU, this chapter has identified several distinct features of the phenomenon of informal work. The underground economy is contextual. Its form, content, and dynamics are specific to the national and other contexts in which it is used and understood. The form, the content, and the dynamic of the phenomenon are situational. The underground economy refers to the experiences of those people who are subject to those definitional and operational categories, in this case specifically undocumented migrants themselves. The occurrence and development of the phenomenon is gradual, influenced by many factors such as migrants' length of residency, year of entry, gender, capitals, government policies, political and public discourse, among others. The phenomenon is conditional, referring to the character of the residency as being understood and dealt with by migrants themselves, and by the actual practice of formal intuitions as a formal and/or informal response to the structural need of the national economy in the era of globalisation.

There were some similarities observed in terms of sectors of operation, type of work undertaken, and the work experiences of those who are undocumented. Our research has shown that the seasonal nature of the work and its casual nature are important components of work in the informal sector. This is also work that is unwanted by local labour (at least under the conditions that are offered) and which is only accepted by undocumented workers because they have no alternatives. There is a suggested divergence in the trajectories of undocumented migrants, between the extremes at one end of the Italian model, wherein after a period of time, following a regularisation of their status, migrants may be able to move into the formal sector and particularly into trade union and collective organisation, and at the other end, the Danish model, where undocumented workers remain permanently excluded from the formal sector. The Belgian data indicates several governmental initiatives to combat underground economic activities. The Danish data shows that even a highly regulated and monitored and organised labour market cannot avoid the occurrence and development of underground economic activities. The consequence seems to be the growing importance of migrant networks as a form of reliance, which counteracts declared policies towards greater degrees of integration of migrants into mainstream society. The Italian data points to the development of a certain complementarity between the underground and regular economy and lower wages in both arenas. In Austria, semi-documented and undocumented labour is likely to fill the gaps that the welfare state does not cover. The UK data shows how mobility and the freedom of movement are identified as a positive feature of underground economic activities. Finally, the existence of an informal economy, in varying shares, in the studied countries, was more likely to provide employment opportunities for those without documents, although it was not the undocumented migrants who created or expanded this economy, once again validating Piore's (1979) argument that the informal economy is primarily demand-driven.

In the next chapter we turn to look specifically at the experiences of women migrant workers. Their stories are largely absent from the discourse on undocumented migration, yet, as we will show, they represent an ever-growing proportion of the undocumented migrant labour force.

9 The Feminisation of Undocumented Migration

> If I was a man I could easily work on a construction site and be earn-
> ing 'normally' like the other people too. But my documents and my
> Curriculum Vitae say: I am a women. Some people come and say: is
> this the wrong Curriculum or the wrong person? This is the problem
> with me. Now I am curious which jobs I can get here.
>
> (Ex-USSR, with residency but no right to work in Austria)

As it has been noted in the above extract from an interview, gender segregation in the labour market is prevalent in all European countries, impacting
on migrants and leading to different experiences and working conditions.
The gender approach to migration is a subject with a strong literature, not
only from an academic perspective but also from the perspective of NGOs
and advocacy organisations. However, the majority of this work is predominantly about legal migration; fewer studies have explored the dynamics of the feminisation of undocumented migration. Our work has located a
gender-based segregation in the labour market in all seven countries in the
UWT study. This had a specific effect on female undocumented migrants.
We found that women were much more likely to be in isolated employment
and that consequently this exposed them to specific disadvantages which
differed from those of men.

In this chapter we utilise the plethora of information that we have
aggregated from the findings of our research in the seven European countries with the intention of contributing further to an understanding of
migration processes from a gender perspective. The chapter concentrates
on the role of status and status change on influencing the outcomes of
female migration and also on their situation in the host country. Drawing data from the UWT qualitative interviews with international and
national experts, as well as interviews with migrant women, the chapter
argues that the current structure of the labour market is what primarily creates the conditions of particular disadvantage and exploitation of
female migrants, especially for female migrants with irregular status. The
chapter is divided into three sections.

The first section looks at the issue of 'illegality' from a gender point
of view. The main areas that have been identified in the literature include
'illegality' as linked to trafficking, 'illegality' in relation to employment in
the host country, and 'illegality' in terms of status transitions. The second
section gives an overview of the general characteristics of female migrants
through their testimonies and by using the data from the UWT database.
The final section concentrates on the domestic sector that predominately

recruits females and the attendant implications on women's choices, employment rights, and future prospects.

DECONSTRUCTING 'ILLEGALITY'——A GENDER PERSPECTIVE

In our view, 'illegality' and its exploitative consequences on individuals are equally experienced by male and female migrants, as well as by their families, when present. Such exploitation, however, follows gendered patterns. An international expert interviewee explained the gender differences:

> Male and female workers are exploited along the lines of their gender—there is not necessarily a double discrimination towards women, as men can be exploited in construction for physical labour and long hours, but women face different types of exploitation in hospitals, care, catering, tourism, domestic work, etc. (EU level trade union official)

Despite this gendered aspect of the labour market, which reflects general divisions in the domestic market in host countries, Piper (2006:139) has argued that the politics and policies that shape migration have ignored women's specific experiences,[1] in terms of migration flows and the gendered segregated labour market, the socioeconomic power structures, and sociocultural definitions of roles both in the home and host country. Similarly, 'illegality' has more specific (or different) consequences for female migrants, and three main areas can be identified in the literature. First, illegality as linked to trafficking, second in relation to employment in the host country, and third in terms of status transition.

'Illegality'—A Gendered Concept of Trafficking and Smuggling

The issue of women and trafficking is noted by Phizacklea (1998) and Agustin (2005) as being the main visible feature in the literature of gender and migration, especially in relation to trafficking for the purpose of prostitution (both cited by Schrover et al., 2008:11). The term 'trafficked' is used to describe 'illegality' for women who migrate against their will. 'Illegality' in the case of men is used with the assumption of them being smuggled by their own choice (ibid). Such a distinction separates women as victims and men as criminals, women as passive and men as active, in the decision to migrate with an undocumented status. But both descriptions use the term 'illegality' in connection with criminal behaviour, despite the fact that the majority of migrants are not criminals. Moreover this connection with criminal activity denotes a denial of migrants' humanity connected to fundamental rights apart from their status. Finally, such labelling may jeopardize the claims of asylum seekers who find themselves in an irregular situation (see Koser, 2005).

Although it is important to recognise that women and children can become the victims of trafficking or sex exploitation (PICUM, 2009:31), it is equally important to critically assess the focus of the trafficking debate itself. In the course of the interviews conducted with national experts, one commented that although the discourse on trafficking is highly politicised, the issue is more complex:

> States can keep the moral high ground and say they care about human rights (as they no longer can with refugees). There is an apparent common ground between the state, radical feminists and NGOs in trying to stop trafficking, with a chance to put labour exploitation on the agenda. But there is a problem of how to divide migrants into those who deserve help because they are exploited and those that are not and therefore don't deserve help. The whole point of labour immigration is that it can be exploited, so how do we draw the line between 'normal' exploitation and that which is unacceptable, and why are NGOs working with state to draw that line? The answer to labour exploitation is labour regulation not border controls. Trafficking is often used as shorthand for illegal migration ... also it separates out smuggled workers, who 'asked for it' so they don't get protection. The Trafficking Convention is not a human rights instrument, it isn't about protection, it is about law enforcement. (UK, academic expert)

The issue of trafficking can therefore be seen as contributing to particular state and political agendas, resulting in closer controls on women migrants (Andrijasevic, 2003; Erel, 2003).

Moreover, linking the issue of sex trafficking with the female 'victim' paradigm can restrict women who might want to migrate with the purpose of working in the sex industry. Such restrictions could have an effect not only on employment but also on the overall welfare of women, for example, access to specialist healthcare (Chauvin et al., 2009). Another national expert from a women's NGO made the point that not every woman who is smuggled across the border and is working in sex business is a victim of trafficking or forced to do this type of work: 'The public discourse on trafficking implies that this is a mass phenomenon; in fact I seldom come across victims of trafficking' (Austria, NGO national expert).

In the UWT research, undocumented women talked about trafficking or smuggling as a route of their migration, as one woman who had migrated from China recounted:

> I was smuggled into the UK in 2004. The journey from China lasted for almost a year. I have eight years of formal education in China; I was a factory worker. My husband was made redundant and the family decided for me to come and work in the UK; I paid 'an organiser' £20,000 to bring me to the UK; the family had to get a high interest

loan to finance my trip. When I arrived in the UK, I realised that £20,000 was a huge amount of money[2] that I may never be able to pay back, especially now that very few jobs are available to undocumented workers. The group that I was smuggled with into the UK had started from China on a train in 2003; then we had to walk for two months over the mountains in Siberia and then flew to Turkey; from there we continued on buses and trains to our destinations; not everybody was going to the UK; some went to Germany or Italy. The trip took a year as we had to wait in different countries for 'the organiser' to be informed that 'the road is clear for them to go'. Only three people came to the UK. Once in London, the organiser left us; we stayed homeless for two to three days sleeping in parks and helping each other. If we saw a Chinese face, we would approach them and ask for jobs. One person told us of a Chinese agency in London that could find us jobs and accommodation. We registered with the agency, paying a £200 fee and we all found jobs immediately; this was in 2004. (Chinese female undocumented, working in the UK)

This interviewee describes in detail her difficult journey as a smuggled person through two continents; she does not perceive herself as a victim of smugglers, but she recognises herself as a victim of poverty, as her purpose was to migrate to the destination country in order to improve her family's living conditions. The issue here is the financial exploitation of the interviewee by smugglers, the terms of which would apply equally to men in such circumstances, and indeed, as she makes clear in her account, both men and women made the journey with her.

'Illegality'—Gendered Segregation of the Labour Market

The gendered labour market and the challenges it poses for female migrants will be explored later in this chapter, but here we look at the specific link between 'illegality' and the gendered operations of labour markets. Social divisions in the labour market, occurring due to ethnicity, gender, and class, are areas that have been covered extensively in the literature on employment relations, related both to the formal and informal market environments. But in relation to the latter, particular aspects have been highlighted in the studies. So irregular work, which often provides a niche for migrant employment, is characterised by a standardised qualification profile (i.e., low-skilled jobs), seasonal employment or employment with a high labour turnover, labour-intensive jobs which are hard to mechanise, or generally a high fluctuation of workers and jobs with a relatively low risk of detection (Cyrus, 2004; Düvell, 2006; EMN, 2007:26).

Additional characteristics include employment in sectors with high labour costs exposed to intense competition (Schönwälder et al., 2004). In relation to these characteristics, certain differences between the structures of the labour market of each country should be taken into account. Despite the existence of these differences between countries, in the seven countries we surveyed we found areas of common ground, particularly in relation to the gender segregation of work (Krenn and Haidinger, 2009). Interviews with national experts showed that in all seven participating countries, undocumented migrant work was concentrated in the areas of construction, agriculture, hospitality, and the domestic and care sector.

This is not dissimilar to the work often available to all migrants, including those who are fully documented. Although agriculture, and to an extent hospitality, is a more gender-mixed area of work, the construction and domestic care sectors are highly gendered. This segregation creates specific circumstances for different work experiences with a particular gender focus. One national expert noted the following:

> Women's work problems are different from men's work problems because women work for a private person, they know their boss; can speak with her or him. For men working in the building industry, they are hired by subcontracting pseudo-firms they don't know even the name of these firms, or the name of their boss. (Belgium, legal officer working for an NGO)

Despite these differences, the interviewee suggests that an element of the exploitation of irregular work is present in both sectors, but the type of exploitation is gender specific and this creates a case for a gendered approach, in both understanding the issues and complexities and making policy-oriented suggestions and recommendations.

The concentration of women in the domestic sector creates more private and isolated work environments, usually accompanied by an unspecified job description, ill-defined working hours or rest time, but at the same time, as an interviewee pointed out, domestic care requires heavy general work which in other sectors would demand specific protections:

> Services are required that are not stipulated in the contract and are not financially recognized, such as giving medicines. Working hours are longer than they should be: often the right to one day off per week is not recognized and, in the case of live-in assistance, the working day is potentially around the clock, without this being recognized in financial terms. Furthermore, living with the family of the person cared for sharply limits the immigrant woman's social relations preventing—or at least hindering—her from getting out of work situations that are without protections and without recourse to trade unions. (Italy, lawyer working for an NGO)

Similarly, the issue of isolated working conditions that often prevent women from seeking external help was referred to by other experts, including one who worked for an organisation providing assistance to undocumented migrants:

Although women encounter specific problems, as an organisation we have more contact with men than women because women are very isolated and work usually in private houses. More men than women contact our organisation and ask for our services. (Belgium, legal official working for an NGO)

We would therefore argue that the sectoral and gendered segregation of the labour market not only creates the gendered conditions of exploitation but also affects access to legal advice on work-related issues to the disadvantage of women migrants.

'Illegality'—Gendered Approaches to Status Change

The processes that we identified in Chapter 3 as being involved in status transitions usually carry a gender bias together with a race and class bias. As has been noted by scholars like Kofman (2004), women's traditional routes to migration (to a greater extent than those of men) have been through family reunification schemes, joining members of their family or husbands in the host country.[3] This might have certain advantages, such as entering the host country with documents, but it also presents drawbacks. Additional to the fact that women under these circumstances are being 'tied in' to their families or husbands, their residence is dependent on the maintenance of family relationships, which may be particularly challenged as a consequence of migration. They may not always have permission to work and earn their living and may lose their status in the case of a separation or divorce. We have the case of a 24-year-old Turkish woman who, after finishing secondary school in Turkey, got married through an arranged marriage to a Turkish man with Austrian citizenship. She joined her husband in Vienna using the right to family reunification, meaning that her status was dependent on her marriage. She narrated her story as follows:

I came to Austria via an arranged marriage so my residence status was linked with that of my husband. I divorced him after three months and found myself working irregularly in the irregular market. But divorce was the only way to gain my own independent status. (Turkish female, now documented, working in Austria)

Although this case had a positive outcome,[4] such realities can be specifically harsh for women who experience domestic violence or abuse and do not speak the language of the host country or have knowledge of available help. Moreover, women who decide to remain in the host country after the breakup of a marriage are often faced with the dilemma of remaining within their ethnic and social networks or breaking free. Either decision can have its drawbacks, as cultural particularities may act as barriers. For example, when faced with the dilemma the above interviewee decided that it was easier to remain within the Turkish community in Austria but was obliged to re-marry as it was not considered 'proper' to be a divorcee. Such culturally specific constraints are usually linked to gender and reflect the overall position of women in the community. A woman's situation can also become precarious as a result of a change in her husband's or family status in the host country. For example, an interviewee from Armenia explained that she had gone to Bulgaria as a child with refugee status that she lost after secondary school. Although she had applied for legal status, her appeals were refused:

> I have married an Afghan refugee and we have two children. My husband has been arrested on suspicion of terrorism and he has been living in a detention centre for over a year. I had to go back to work in an Afghan restaurant in order to support my family. I found the job through my husband's connections. I work as an irregular as did my family before. (Armenian female, currently undocumented, working in Bulgaria)

This example also reveals that marriage can be a route to documented status in the host country but that the outcome is not always successful, even in the case of those women who have lived a large part of their lives in the host country. Although in this case it could relate to the political and economic transition period of Bulgaria or to the individual circumstances of her husband, it is nevertheless the case that the asylum laws have not treated women's experiences of persecution as seriously as men's (Crawley and Lester, 2004, cited in Askola, 2010).

A TYPOLOGY OF UNDOCUMENTED FEMALE MIGRANTS

General Characteristics

Current research has demonstrated the difficulty in obtaining accurate migrant data across Europe, a task complicated largely because there is no common strategy for the collection and interpretation of data (see Chapter 6). These factors reflect the difficulties of researching a phenomenon which is not clearly defined, as any of the findings can have a politically sensitive meaning. In terms of gender, the difficulty in determining the numbers remains the same; however, various studies have indicated that the number of women, including irregular women, has risen in recent years (Kofman, 2008; Triandafyllidou and Gropas, 2007; Zhelyazkova, 2008). As an EU-level trade union officer we interviewed noted, 'There are now almost as many female independent migrants [as opposed to dependants] as men'.

In our research we aimed to ensure that at least one in three of those migrants whom we interviewed, and who were or had been undocumented, were women. In fact we exceeded this target, with almost half (47 per cent) of our respondents being women, one third of which were undocumented at the time of the interview.[5] This allowed us to capture a wide range of specifically female experiences of undocumented migration. Countries of origin varied, but the majority were third-country nationals from Latin America, Africa, the former USSR countries, Turkey, China, and the Middle East. Indeed the country origins of the women whom we interviewed were as diverse as those of the men. In addition, their pathways to their destination country were equally as hazardous as those of the men. Some women who had come from Central and Eastern European countries had their residence status changed from undocumented to documented, as a result of their country of origin's accession to the European Union, either in 2004 or in 2007. In terms of age, the majority of our respondents were aged between 25 and 49, with few aged either over 50 or under 24. Again there were few differences between women and men, leading us to suggest that in terms of demography, there may not be great gender difference.

Most of the women interviewees had entered the seven countries in the study in the period between 2000 and 2007; however, 30 women in our seven-country sample—compared to 26 males—migrated between the years 1974 and 2000. The majority of the early women migrants had experienced status transitions. Below are two examples of early female migrants who had arrived during the 1970s. The first, a woman from Gambia at the age of 16, had arrived in Spain to join her husband who had migrated a year earlier:

> I remained under-documented for 18 years; that is I obtained a residence permit but not a work permit. During these years I gave birth to four children. I had to work and the only option was to become a cleaning lady but earn much less than the Spanish. (Gambian female, now documented, working in Spain)

A Chinese woman had arrived with her husband on a tourist visa in 1977 and decided to remain. She and her husband became documented after five years, and during this time they had to pay a 'diplomat' in order to obtain short stay permits. In the interview she gave an account of the first years of her migration:

> In the beginning it was terrible; we worked in our friend's restaurant. We had to eat leftovers from the customers. There was no hot water. We left and found a job in another restaurant with better conditions. We eventually opened our own restaurant. (Chinese female, now documented, working in Spain)

Female migrants who came later noted similar experiences of exploitation and status uncertainties although in some cases, as that of the Chinese woman above, they eventually had successful outcomes.

HUMAN AND SOCIAL CAPITAL

Although the concepts of human and social capital have been developed and critically assessed by economists and social scientists, this section will focus on the way the concepts were used in our project in relation to gender. In this sense, human and social capital was used to understand those personal qualities of respondents that would be potentially useful for them to enter the labour market in the host country. As the subject could be considered as personal and sensitive, involving cases of successes as well as failures, information on this area was established through the interpretation of a series of questions as well as through the narration of the migrant's life-story. The themes used to gain this information included educational background or other professional training, the command of the host country's language, and previous work experience. Related to the concept of social capital, the emphasis was on migrants' transitions through the use of networks and other support organisations, in relation to changes in their socioeconomic situations, their adaptation to new situations, and their ability to meet these changes. Moreover, the questions also focused on perceptions of how such experiences shaped the capacity of individuals to meet new challenges.

Human Capital

In terms of education, there were no great differences in the UWT sample between our male and female interviewees. Table 9.1 shows in more detail the education level of UWT participants. Whereas there was a higher percentage of men with a university degree, there was a higher percentage of women with a professional qualification.

The majority of all respondents had finished primary or secondary school. These results were not generally reflected in the types of jobs that the individuals ended up working in—as they were almost universally in low-paid and low-skilled employment. However, the issue of educational background and access to jobs is also linked to national policies on the

Table 9.1   Educational Level of Male and Female Migrants

	Educational level				
	Minimum	Secondary	University and above	Professional qualification	Total
Male	17(16%)	53(49%)	31(28%)	7(6%)	108(100%)
Female	22(23%)	42(43%)	16(16%)	16(17%)	96(100%)

Source: UWT Field survey, 2007–2008.

recognition of qualifications, an equally heated debate connected to migration (European Commission, 2008; Spencer, 2006:60). For example, in our sample, over two thirds of both men and women had acquired their qualifications in their home country. The refusal to recognise these diplomas and professional qualifications acted as a destabilising force not only for the migrants and their access to essential services but also for their access to jobs equivalent to their skills. Indeed in some cases the non-recognition of qualifications was a factor which limited their abilities to move out of poor work, to a greater extent than their status, as status was something that might be changed through government policy or a change in their personal situation (for example, through marriage), whereas there was less chance of qualifications being recognised, particularly the longer in the past that they had gained them.

We found that both male and female migrants experienced similar consequences of this discriminatory pressure to work in low-skilled jobs, independent of their background qualifications or work experience. However, what was even more discriminatory for women was the type of employment open to them: stereotyped as 'female' or suitable for women only, but providing in return low chances of social mobility in terms of gender equality, low payment, and harsh working conditions. These sectors, as already noted, are primarily in domestic and care jobs, hotels and restaurants, or the sex industry, as one migrant interviewed noted:

> Gender segregation in the shadow economy follows the same lines as in the regular labour market. I worked in various jobs in several sectors. But according to the allocation of female migrant workforce in the regular economy, I mainly worked in cleaning, private households, hotels and restaurants. (Slovakian female, undocumented, working in Austria)

Male interviewees also commented on their unequal access to jobs, but more in relation to their status than their gender:

> Work permits seem to have become more important in construction than some years ago. Holding documents makes it easier to find work—especially if you do not know the potential employer. In private households it is still not important if you have documents or not. (Ukrainian male, currently seeking asylum with no right to work, working in Austria)

Our research not only supports this statement but suggests that a differentiated treatment based on gender has meant that although the majority of men and women in our study were employed at the time of this research, women were only half as likely to be unemployed as men, suggesting that there may be a more ready availability of work in areas considered to be 'female jobs'.

This stereotyping of 'female' jobs goes one step further in relation to women, especially in the entertainment industry or indeed in any jobs that are directly related to serving a clientele, as the women we interviewed were clear that their bodies or looks were an asset for accessing jobs and in some circumstances provided them with a feeling of being in control and of independence, as one interviewee noted:

> I like it when customers are looking at me, just when I am entering the bar the customers pay me a compliment. I have this mentality. I like it when men look at me and I have the impression to be desired. And I underline my strengths. You can see my G-string when I bend down. I don't mind and the customers like it. I like to flirt. But I don't accept touches. (Polish female, now documented, working in Austria)

The same interviewee, who had worked many years as an undocumented migrant in this sector, noted how hard the conditions were for females in terms of the smoky atmosphere, drink, and the expectation for sexual services. For her the only solution was not for women to compete against one another to get work by accepting a lower wage but to 'stick together' and reject these conditions. Female interviewees were aware of such discrimination along gender lines, and they either had accepted it or had the resilience to continue until they found better employment (Morokvasic, 2007). But they also expressed their frustration with the situation. A domestic worker who is a qualified accountant noted:

> My employer is 'very correct'; she does not say that I am a 'cleaning lady/Putzfrau' . . . thanks. I don't care if she calls me 'putzfrau' or not. Household cleaning—no problem; I do not feel these words, this is not my language. But I thought about it hundreds of times. If I was a man I could easily work on a construction site and be earning 'normally' like the other people too. (Ex-USSR female, with residency but no right to work, working in Austria)

Another interviewee equally spoke of her discontent with her current job and her acceptance of a position that was much lower than her qualifications:

> I graduated from the French School of Hotel Management in Senegal and worked for seventeen years in the kitchens of the hotels of a major international chain; attaining the qualification of head chef . . . I decided to come to Venice because I like the city. At the beginning I sent my résumé to all the hotels in Venice and its hinterland. From only one I received a reply, which I still keep to this day and which said, 'We can't take you to work with us'. Currently I work as a cook for the cafeterias of public institutions . . . I [feel I have] failed because I have

a diploma and a degree in Hotel Management Structure, I worked my way up in Senegal to the rank of chef, and when I came here [to Italy] I turned all the way back down, because they didn't recognize anything I had done. In the future I would like to open a restaurant with ethnic cuisine, or work as a cook for a large family, or to go back to Senegal and open a restaurant there. (Senegalese female, currently with work permit, working in Italy)

Although the quote in this interview does not address gender directly, the interviewee referred to her disappointment at the downgrading of her career, as at home she had been able to reach a high position within her profession. Migration had a direct effect on her career chances, but at the same time she remained positive about her ability to create a new business for herself. This interviewee also discusses racism as a negative influence on her chances of job progress, both in society in general and among other workers, even if it appeared below the surface, noting, 'Relations with the other workers are good, even if you always see on their faces [that] they look at you in a different way. They see a person of colour as different.'

To conclude, the present structure of the labour market—even in countries that assume high levels of gender equality—leads to the assertion that there exist gendered recruitment and employment practices which fail to adequately utilise the qualifications and previous employment experiences of migrants in general, but of women in particular. As European economies emphasise the recruitment of skilled labour and the importance of the human capital that migrants bring with them, it appears that not only are the skills of migrants being wasted but, in terms of gender, the position of migrant women in society maintains the stereotyped roles of a paternalistic society that many women campaigned against throughout the 20th century. Migration thus does not challenge the gender divide but is forced to accommodate to it.

Social Capital

Although many of the migrants we interviewed, independent of gender, provided similar testimonies about their means of entry into the host country, if we look at the overall quantitative data on all 211 interviews, we observe certain differences between male and female migrants (as Table 9.2 shows) and some of these reflect their use of social capital.

The major area of difference highlighted in the table is in relation to marriage, where 11 women (11 per cent of all of our female interviewees) entered on that basis, compared to just less than one per cent of the male interviewees. Other studies have similarly linked marriage with female migration (Kofman, 2008). Examples of the marriages we found included

Table 9.2   Migrants' Modes of Entry into Host Countries

	Gender of respondents		
	Male	Female	Total
Smuggled/Clandestinely	39(72%)	15(28%)	54(100%)
Tourist visa/Visitor	39(45%)	47(55%)	86(100%)
Student visa	10(71%)	4(29%)	14(100%)
Work permit	6(33%)	12(67%)	18(100%)
Forged passport	5(100%)	0(0%)	5(100%)
Marriage/fiancé visa	1(8%)	11(92%)	12(100%)
Another way	12(55%)	10(45%)	22(100%)
Total	112(53%)	99(47%)	211(100%)

Source: UWT Field survey, 2007–2008.

family reunification, ethnic brides, and sham marriages. A second area of difference related to work permits, where women were twice as likely as men to have come through that route and this was mainly related to easier access to work permits for care jobs. Women however, were half as likely as men to have been smuggled into their destination country or to have come with false papers.

Female migrants had more frequently used contacts from family, ethnic associations, and local people for help to find employment or other forms of help such as housing, healthcare, or initial familiarization with the host country. What is particularly noticeable is that when looking for their first job, 23 per cent of the women in the sample mentioned help from relatives or families, 29 per cent help from friends from the same ethnic communities, four per cent help from friends from other ethnic groups, and 30 per cent help from local people. When asked about how they found their current job (which in the majority of cases was not their first job), there was a sharp decrease in their use of social capital with just seven per cent of women stating that they had been helped by family, 21 per cent by friends from the same ethnic community, six per cent by friends from other ethnic communities, and 41 per cent received help from local people. In addition, five per cent of women reported that they had found their current job through newspaper adverts:[6]

> When I moved to Spain at the beginning I received help only from relatives. I contacted the Romanian community but I did not receive any support. Any job offers come from my own social networks. I know now more local people than Romanians. (Romanian female currently documented, working in Spain)

Thus once women were more embedded in their destination country, their reliance on social networks declined significantly, from 56 per cent for their first job to 34 per cent in their most recent job. A developed work experience in the host country explains why women are more likely to form networks beyond, as well as within, their communities (Askola, 2010). This is also an indicator of the type of work that women do, as domestic workers in host country native homes, which allows them to network in a different, albeit more individual and isolated, way. It is also linked to the way job recruitment takes place in these sectors, being based mainly on word of mouth. Finally with regard to family connections, the sharp decrease in the number of women seeking family help to find a job once settled in the host country was due to their ability to form their own social networks, but it can also indicate a breakdown in family relations, especially in cases where entry to the country had been achieved through marriage.

EMPLOYMENT AND WORK CONDITIONS IN MIGRANT FEMALE EMPLOYMENT

The issue of employment and work conditions from a gendered perspective was raised earlier in this chapter. Here we concentrate on the domestic sector, which employs predominately women workers, and explain its impact on women's working conditions and employment prospects.

The Domestic Care Sector

Domestic work by migrants constitutes one of the key features in the feminisation of migration flows due to the large-scale demand for this work (Anderson, 2007; Phizacklea, 1998) particularly as a result of overall changes in the labour market, with more women working outside their homes and therefore needing support in the caring roles which traditionally were left to them to fulfil. Although this work is generally considered as low skilled and poorly paid, studies on remittances have found that women make significant contributions to the GDP of many developing countries (Ehrenreich and Hochschild, 2002).

The sector can also be considered as providing relatively constant employment, especially after the initial period of trust is established. This trust is very important, as an external employee commonly enters the private areas and aspects of private households in order to care for elderly relatives or children, as cleaners or in a combination of duties. From the point of view of the employer, it is beneficial to retain the same employee for as long as is needed.

> For undocumented people, especially women, domestic work offers advantages such as is to be protected against the police or any sort of control, being rent free, nothing to spend for eating, etc. This is helpful when you just arrive in a country and you need period for adaptation. (Ecuadorian female, undocumented, working in Belgium)

From the point of view of the employee, especially for migrants with undocumented status, this employment situation can appear also to be beneficial as it provides a 'protected' environment for work that is away from threats of deportation or prosecution, as the above interviewee emphasised.

Domestic work is most often reliant on social networks through organisations, churches, and private contacts used both by employers and employees. This type of employment nevertheless presents drawbacks for the same reasons as it appears to offer protection: it is a private workplace environment away from the protection of employment law, trade union organisations, and labour inspectors. For example, in the UWT interviews, when asked about trade union presence at work, only one third of female interviewees gave a positive response whereas two thirds of male respondents reported trade union contacts at work. This clearly relates to the fact that women's employment is more isolated, individual, and 'hidden' from the public sphere. Although demand for domestic work in itself might not be the problem, what is problematic for the women involved is the lack of legal protection, the low pay, and the poor conditions. This type of exploitation is also linked to wider societal issues; a lawyer whom our Italian colleagues interviewed pointed to the weak social position of elderly people who are in need of care. He stated:

> Improvements in the national contract of the domestic-work sector introduced since March 2007 have not affected the conditions of exploitation in force in this sector. These conditions are correlated with the crisis of welfare policies, which on the one hand make recourse to private forms of assistance necessary, and on the other adversely affect the elderly who receive assistance. Senior citizens more and more often live in conditions of marginality, with pensions that are too low and without the support of a family network: their poverty affects, in turn, the migrant woman workers, who are underpaid and are obliged to work in conditions of exploitation. (Italy, lawyer, male)

Some of these drawbacks, linked to working conditions, have been identified by earlier research (Anderson, 2007), and they have also been among findings of the UWT research.

Duties and Responsibilities

It is often unclear as to where the duties and responsibilities in relation to employment lie, particularly in the domestic sphere. At the same time, as the work usually involves multiple household tasks and responsibilities, it leaves very little free time for rest:

> If you are working there for 24 hours, when do you have time to attend a course? When do you have any time for yourself? You do not have any private sphere . . . we are not only the carers, we often have to be the hairdresser too—cutting the hair, hair drying; the cleaning lady—the

laundry, ironing, tidying up, shopping; the cook—you have to be very creative some times; the therapist: doing all the physical exercises with the patient; the gardener, if people have a garden; the waitress, if there are guests; the baby sitter, caring for the relatives' children. The overall task is working with the patients' bodies and souls. (Polish female, now documented, working in Austria)

Working in private homes, women interviewees often mentioned the lack of respect from their employers, at least the occasional accompaniment by verbal threats or abuse. The conditions under which such women must work has been catalogued in a number of high profile cases, but the account given to us of the experiences of a Ukrainian migrant sums it up:

It was very hot and I had the right to bathe once a week with cold water. It was terrible. I cried every day. Then when I began to understand the language [I realized that] she was continually telling me: 'You are the slave, I am the mistress.' I had to keep quiet. I couldn't talk back and I couldn't leave either, because I had debts . . . In the end I decided: 'Either I find another job or I go back to Ukraine, because no one can crush me this way like she does'. (Ukrainian female, currently with residence permit, working in Italy)

The Absence of Privacy

Many of the women who were interviewed in the course of the research referred to the absence of any privacy or private space in their work and the inability to separate work from private life. This was particularly linked to 24-hour care where the employee has to be available at any time to perform her duties on demand. Women spoke of a lack of privacy and the lack of a private space to rest. Some of the duties involved washing and dressing the patient, accompanying them to the toilet, and lifting them if they were not able to walk. One trade union officer from Italy summed up the conditions of workers in these circumstances:

The sector of domestic work and of family assistance presents multiple situations of irregularity: not only are the immigrant women often employed without contracts and without permits, but the working conditions themselves often fly in the face of all regulations. For example, in the employment relationships that involve living in the employer's home we find working days of 24 hours, without rest, without permits, without substitution, without vacations, without sick leave, etc. This situation also applies with regard to immigrant women with regular job contracts and with residence permits: they are regularized on the basis of contracts with minimum hours (25 hours a week) and with minimum wages (€500 a month), while the rest of their work is totally undocumented. (Italy, trade union official, female)

Women in this type of domestic care employment in their narratives to us have reported themselves as suffering from physical exhaustion or depression, even in cases that did not amount to mistreatment. Some had eventually required medical care, while others, after trying unsuccessfully to find another job, had developed strategies to enable them to cope with the overload of work, for example, by asking a colleague or friend to share the job and the responsibilities.

CONCLUSION

This chapter has looked at the feminisation of migration in relation to status. Although there is a large body of literature on gender migration, that on irregularity and gender is relatively limited. Utilising data from the UWT research the chapter has argued that exploitation, in terms of wages or working conditions, is present in most jobs employing migrants in general and undocumented migrants specifically. However, the existing segregation of the labour market, including the informal labour market along gender lines, is what creates work conditions that have particular relevance to women's employment. In this sense 'illegality' presents gender-specific features that are linked to the concepts of trafficking, employment, and the status transitions as examined in the first section.

Women's general migration experiences differ from those of men, as there is greater dependency on family or ethnic community networks as a way of entry into the country or as a way of finding the first job. However, as the data suggests, there are conditions which may permit women to create social networks with other ethnic communities or with indigenous communities that are independent of their own community networks and which enable them to use additional resources in job searches. But social networks, however constructed, remain especially important because the types of jobs available are based on networks, and recruitment is based on word of mouth and personal recommendations. As our interviews with migrant women have shown, for the domestic sector, employers use networks via organisations, church associations, or ethnic communities in order to recruit staff. However, even accounting for the existence of such networks, work experience in this sector is usually isolated and more individualised. The employment conditions encountered by female migrants are often harsh, with an absence of documents that set out their contractual terms and with the expectation of working long hours without rest breaks, while pay is at the minimum or below and union representation is rare.

The position of women cannot be discussed separately from their position within families. In Chapter 10 we turn specifically to the issue of undocumented family migration, looking at the additional difficulties encountered by migrants (and in particular by women) in relation to the care and support they provide to their families.

10 The Impact of Family on Undocumented Migration

> When I and my wife become legal in Belgium, I will ask my children to join me. I would like my daughter to study at the Brussels University, to study the Belgian culture.
>
> (Brazilian male, undocumented, working in Belgium)

As the interviewee quoted above demonstrates, migration status often defines the family situation of the migrant. The topic of family migration has become relatively neglected both in academic and policy-oriented research despite the fact that family migration constitutes one of the main entry routes into the host country. Two main reasons have been identified in migration literature for this under-representation of theoretical and empirical work on family migration and the consideration of family as less significant to the labour market.

The first relates to the predominance of economic theory in migration studies that focuses on human capital. This approach looks mainly at the economic outcomes of migration based on the individual and her or his participation in the labour market (Bailey and Boyle, 2004; Halfacree, 1995). Family is considered to represent a private sphere of activity, not measurable in economic terms (Zlotnik, 1995). As a result there has also been less concern with the non-economic aspects of family migration such as family formation, marriage, or quality of life. This concentration on the economic aspect of family migration has led observers to debate the rigour of the established theoretical understandings (Smith, 2004). Second, there has been an increasing interest in the gendered approach of migration and of migrant participation in the labour market, and consequently family has been considered as a secondary type of migration. Within this approach, emphasis has been placed on the issue of female dependants joining the male 'primary' migrant (Kofman, 2004) and the implication this might have on the migration status, labour market participation, and the overall integration of female migrants. But we have wanted to focus specifically on female migrants and their experiences of migration, family life, and work and life experiences.

It is beyond the purpose of the present chapter to fully explore what constitutes a family or to compare family patterns among the various countries, but it is accepted here that family structures are continuously evolving and changing the ways of living together. Definitions of family usually range from the narrow concept of 'immediate' family, which usually includes spouse and dependent children, to an extended one that may include any combination of the following: all unmarried children regardless of age; adopted children; fiancé/fiancée; parents; grandparents; grandchildren; aunts and uncles; nephews and nieces; cousins; siblings; and others. Both definitions, however, tend to conform to more traditional forms of marriage and only a few European states such as the Scandinavian countries, the Netherlands, and the UK allow entry to co-habiting or same-sex couples (Kofman, 2004). In relation to how we have used 'family', although it is accepted that a family can take many forms, the chapter discusses mainly family units as inclusive of children, as well as identifying other forms of family in the research. At the same time the notion of 'dependants' more often includes children, partners, older parents or grandparents, and in some cases other relatives. Kofman distinguishes four main categories of contemporary international family migration to Europe: family reunification, family formation, marriage migration, and family migration (Kofman, 2004, 2008). Although this typology refers to general family migration, it can also be used to explain the processes of family related migration in our own research. Research on family experiences has been limited especially at a country comparative level but also because findings suggest that irregular migrants, when accompanied by family members, are often faced with additional complexities in the host country and could be placed in more vulnerable situations. Our findings suggest that an increased number of female respondents have either initiated family migration or have played an equal role in the decision to migrate or have migrated alone in order to support a family which remained in the home country. As an additional factor, our research has found that for some female interviewees who have been divorced, marriage was essential in order to be accepted by their ethnic community in the host country.

Family migration is one of the main forms of migration to Europe, while two thirds of the total migration in the US involves families. Similarly, in Canada and Australia one third of migration is associated with families (Kofman, 2008). The OECD's International Migration Outlook 2008 showed that 44 per cent of migration to OECD counties in 2008 was family related, and this included family reunification and marriage migration such as entries of fiancés or recently married spouses (SOPEMI, 2008). The topic has recently attracted interest from sociologists, geographers, economists, and demographers and is increasingly becoming an interdisciplinary endeavour. This includes family movements at a sub-national level, between European states, or across wider international boundaries (Kofman, 2004; Smith and Bailey, 2006); a growing interest in transnational families (Bryceson and Vuorela, 2002); the dynamics of family networks as a linkage between home and host countries (Boyd, 1989); the impact of parent migration on family life; and the role of gender.

This chapter identifies types of family migration and the implications of migration policies and measures on family life or family formation. Although different states have imposed restrictions to control migration at various levels and to various degrees, existing statistics show that family related migration does occur in destinations considered to provide economic prosperity (or survival). Families migrate either through individual decisions or circumstances or with the help of social networks and often with the intention of settling permanently/semi-permanently in the host state. It is argued here that family related reasons often play a central role in the decision to migrate with or without documents and shape employment experiences, as individuals accept any kind of working conditions or pay in order to support their family. The chapter concludes that greater protection (in terms of status) and encouragement (in terms of involvement in the civic society) is needed for migrant families in order to enable integration and combat future disadvantage and discrimination that might be experienced from this group.

UWT FAMILY RELATED DATA

The chapter analyses primary data gathered in the seven UWT countries where, in relation to family situation, interviewees were asked to elaborate on their family status, existence of children, or if they travelled with other family members.

The majority of interviewees explained in great detail their family situation or spoke of incidents in their migration stories that were relevant to it as affected by their status or employment. Almost all interviewees talked about their existing families with reference to children who either migrated with them or were left back in the home country. In some cases a family would be separated, as one child might migrate with the parents in the host countries while the other(s) would remain in the care of relatives back home. As an additional factor, as noted in the previous chapter, is that for some female interviewees who have been divorced, marriage was essential in order to be accepted by their ethnic community in the host country. 'Because my divorced status contradicted with our traditions (defamation of my reputation) I was talked by my family into another marriage with a cousin of my father who lived in Turkey' (Austria, female interviewee, documented).

Families can play an important role in both ensuring that expected traditions are being followed and in providing contacts for the search of an 'appropriate' spouse. In some communities this is seen as an important part of living within a diasporic ethnic community on the host country.

FAMILY RELATED STATISTICS

The snapshot of data in Figure 10.1 shows that the average percentage of family migrants in some European countries is about 60 per cent, with France and Norway featuring the highest and the UK the lowest with 30 per cent. The

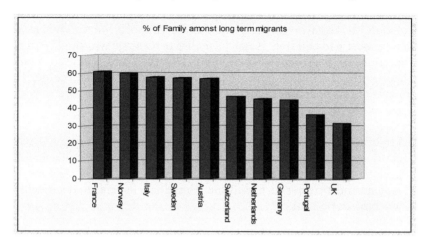

Figure 10.1 % of family among long-term migrants.
Source: Based on OECD, 2006.

figure includes only family members of economic and work permit migrants and not those entering on humanitarian grounds or through specific family related streams. It is worth noting that these proportions are affected by the scale of migration. In countries where migration numbers are low because migration entry is difficult, family reunion may show up as a higher proportion. Therefore the percentage may be a reflection of migration policies as well.

Findings from the UWT project are not very dissimilar. The following table shows the percentages of the family status of the 211 interviewees by gender.

Table 10.1 Family Status and Gender

	Gender of respondents	
	Male	Female
Single	(33%)	(25%)
Married with children	(46%)	(42%)
Married without children	(10%)	(6%)
Widowed with children	(1%)	(5%)
Co-habiting	(4%)	(3%)
Divorced/separated with children	(5%)	(12%)
Divorced/separated without children	(1%)	(5%)
Single parents	(1%)	(2%)

Source: UWT, Field survey, 2007–2008.

At the time of interviews, which took place throughout 2008, the majority of male and female migrants were in some form of a conventional family unit and most had children. A much smaller percentage was single parents, co-habiting, or widowed with children. Divorced and widowed women with or without children appeared more frequently to take the decision to migrate in comparison to males, and this may indicate a need to seek a change of life from a previous family situation:

> I migrated because I wanted to earn enough money and become financially independent. But also to be as far away from my ex-husband (a police officer) who was very possessive with me, he was jealous and violent and threatened to kill me. (Brazilian female, undocumented, working in Belgium)

Other findings from the UWT database suggest that female migrants are more likely to travel with another family member—57 per cent, compared to 42 per cent of males. However, a large proportion of women (44%) have travelled alone. In our sample the majority of the children reside with their parents in the host country: of female migrants, (64 per cent) had their children with them compared to 50 per cent of male migrants. The UWT research also illustrates the complexities of migration status for families.

Over 40 per cent of the migrants in the sample were undocumented at the time of the interviews; the remaining 60 per cent currently possessed a form of legal status, including indefinite leave to remain, work permit, acquisition of citizenship, student visa, dependent visa, or being a spouse of a host country national. However, it is important to note that

Table 10.2   Family and Legal Status

	Legal status of migrants		
	Undocumented	Semi-documented	Documented
Single	(11%)	(2%)	(16%)
Married with children	(12%)	(3%)	(28%)
Married without children	(2%)	(1%)	(6%)
Widowed with children	(1%)	(0%)	(2%)
Co-habiting	(1%)	(0%)	(2%)
Divorced/separated with children	(3%)	(2%)	(5%)
Divorced/separated without children	(1%)	(0%)	(2%)
Single parent	(1%)	(0%)	(1%)

Source: UWT, Field survey, 2007–2008.

all interviewees were undocumented at some point during their stay in the host country. The majority of respondents (over 70 per cent of the sample) reported that they had experienced a status change during their stay in the host country, either from being undocumented and then legalised or from losing their status and becoming undocumented. In terms of family situation, Table 10.2 shows that in both documented and undocumented categories, the majority of migrants were within some form of family, with or without children. Married migrants with children were much more likely to have travelled with family members (81 per cent in our sample) compared to married without children (57 per cent) or single (30 per cent). In the qualitative interviews, married respondents mentioned more frequently that they had travelled with their partner and at least some of their children. Single migrants reported that they had travelled with other members of their family such as parents, siblings, or uncles/aunts.

Finally, in relation to the destination country, family related migration among our sample had taken place mainly in Spain, Belgium, Bulgaria, and Italy. The least preferred countries were the UK and Denmark, and this decision could reflect the imposition of strict border controls and the trend to limit family reunification—although it could also reflect the wider migration access in these two countries.

TYPES OF FAMILY MIGRATION

Looking at the research interviews, what is noteworthy is first the centrality of family in the decision to migrate. This is not always based solely on the 'neat and rational actions' (Bailey and Boyle, 2004) of labour related reasons but also on personal circumstances: the desire to build a better future for family members and the motivation to secure adequate finances in order to form a family were considered as equally important for the interviewees. Second, some aspects of the family situation were attributed to the migration experience itself or to the uncertainties over changes in their status situation—for example, breaking a long-term engagement with a potential spouse at the country of origin.

Family Reunification

Broadly the term 'family reunification' refers to recognised state policies that enable family members such as spouses, children, parents, or others to join the primary migrant in the host country. Policies for family reunification are usually developed based on balancing the right for families to live together and the immigration controls that are in place in the destination country and often involve processes of a waiting period and certain conditions to be met before family reunification is granted—especially for migrants with subsidiary statuses (Kofman, 2008).

Internationally, although there is no accepted definition of 'family', the right to family reunification can be found in a number of treaties and conventions.[1] In the European Union the most recent EU Directive 2003/86/EC on the Right to Family Reunification has introduced, for the first time, a listing of family members that can be reunited with the sponsor and takes into consideration more contemporary forms of family structures. Consequently, EU countries have established their own procedures to accommodate family reunification related legislation.

Findings from our own research reflect this variation: all seven countries in the study had created their own frameworks for family reunification while also imposing their own restrictions. From the seven countries, the UK and Bulgaria had extended their policies to include asylum seekers and refugees. In the UK although the provisions have been expanded to cover a range of family forms, at the same time the measures are restrictive for other relatives such as grandparents. Some of these provisions are stricter than others and, for example, in Denmark certain mandatory conditions must be fulfilled before the issuing of time-limiting residence permits. Only after a number of years may applicants try for the conversion of a time-limited permit into a permanent one. In some countries this is a relatively new phenomenon, for example, in Spain where many wives and other members of family joined their husbands/fathers after 2000. In Austria there has been a decline in the numbers of first-time issued residence permits, to both sponsors and their dependants following the adoption of the Settlement and Residence Act (2005).

Family reunification as a process refers to migrants with a documented status who go through the legal channels in order to be joined by their family members. However, family reunion is also prominent among undocumented migrants. Our survey included interviews with 44 undocumented migrants, who were not single; 33 who had their families in the host countries and 19 who had travelled together with family members. The most regular family reunion pattern among undocumented migrants was for the family to migrate in stages; usually one member of the family migrated first, followed by a partner and other members, if present, at various stages. An undocumented migrant described the migration route:

> Initially my husband decided to join his mother who had lived in Belgium since 1999 because we had some marital problems. Then I followed and I live with him in Belgium. I am expecting a baby. Our other children are still in Brazil and will come later. I work as a domestic. I am illegal and try to find ways to regularise. My husband is also undocumented. (Brazilian female, undocumented, working in Belgium)

A documented status is still regarded by some as an important condition for them to reunite with their family. A male interviewee noted that a regularised status would help his family reunify but also provide better chances for his children both in terms of future prospects and in terms of integration: 'When I and my wife become legal in Belgium, I will ask my children to join me. I would like my daughter to study at the Brussels University, to study the Belgian culture' (Brazilian male, undocumented, working in Belgium).

Moreover, migration and a desired regularised status are viewed here by the interviewee as a means of upward social mobility for his children, and he talks about future prospects in terms of integration to the host society and education acquired in the host country.

Family Formation

This category refers to second or third generation children of migrant descent who bring spouses from the country of origin. This category can have a specific gender focus for females joining their husbands in the host country after an arranged marriage. And although such arrangements can provide a desirable solution for the individuals involved, they can also leave the individuals exposed and in a vulnerable position, especially in the absence of work permits. The following example of a female migrant living in her husband's house in Austria highlights this point:

> I was always at home. I felt in a crisis. In the household I was exploited like a servant. I became depressed. There was nobody. I didn't get on with my mother in law. . . . I was always at home for three months and became depressed. You know nobody and you don't go out. In the end I had to accept it. (Turkish female, documented, working in Austria)

This category can also be extended to include cases of family formation when two first generation migrants meet in the host country and form a family unit. Status irregularities and lack of protection could have adverse effects on individuals' lives. The following interview with a young undocumented couple in Belgium underlies the vulnerability of individuals in such situations but also shows the inflexibility of laws whose enforcement does not stop the individuals from re-entering the country without documents:

> I was arrested in a pub in Saint Gilles (Brussels) near my home by the local police force. Without any legal document, I was locked up in a centre while waiting for the next flight to Brazil. I should not have been expelled because my partner was at the end of her pregnancy and needed particular care as it was a pregnancy at risk. I arrived in Brazil and tried to find money to return to Belgium as soon as possible. In the end I had to run into debt to find money and pay for a plane ticket during the week of Christmas which was particularly expensive. As result, I lost the chance to earn money for a whole month. During this time, my partner remained alone and without money in Brussels. She was 'helped' by my boss who sent her the pay of a month (about €500)

and lent her approximately €150 for her daily expenses, while waiting for my return to Belgium. Since my return, I still try to make up for money I lost during this absence. My young woman survived thanks to the assistance of friends and migrant associations. (Brazilian male, undocumented, working in Belgium)

The preceding quote draws attention to the precarious situation that can develop when individuals with irregular status find themselves in need of help. Welfare protection appears to be minimal in this case when it is most needed. At the same time the interview indicates that border controls should become more flexible and considerate in these circumstances.

Marriage Migration

This category refers to the type of family migration where a permanent resident has been abroad for study, holidays, or work, and has met a partner and brought that partner to his or her (i.e., the permanent resident's) country of origin or country of permanent residence. The marriage could also be arranged. Similar to the other categories, restrictions have been imposed by countries in an effort to manage migration. For example, in Denmark, since 2005, foreign nationals with relatives in Denmark can be granted residence permits, but applicants must sign a 'declaration of integration' and spouses must be over the age of 24. In the UK, as noted by Gedalof (2007), marriages and family visits are presented as a serious problem or threat that needs to be managed (see, e.g., the title of the relevant chapter in the White Paper: 'Marriage/family visits and war criminals').

Our survey findings relate to this category in a broader way, where individuals migrate to other countries as a means of avoiding unwanted marriages. Findings also suggest that this affects mainly women[2] who experience prolonged gender discrimination in their home country and decide to leave with or without documents.

> The refusal of a forced marriage and massive physical violence by the males in my family made me leave my home country in order to save my life. I managed to escape the violent patriarchal structures, to cross Europe (without knowing the language), and to organise a regularised status despite the strong patriarchal structures within the ethnic minority community in Austria which I had either to circumvent or fight against. (Kurdish/Turkish female, documented, working in Austria)

Migration in such cases can be regarded as an emancipation experience for the individuals concerned. Women can gain 'freedom' to make their own decisions and choices. The above interviewee reported that once in Austria she got married, but because she had already gone through the whole process of gaining a residency, she felt more independent.

Family Migration

This category includes couples that are already married or co-habiting and take the decision to migrate together. However as the following interviewee noted, well-established social networks often play a pivotal role in assisting the newcomers in the host countries, especially when children are part of the initial migration and the parents are not regularised: 'For this job I was helped by people from my church. I don't want to insert an advert in the newspaper because it is dangerous; you never know who is calling' (Bosnian, female, undocumented, working in Italy).

Family migration can also bring unforeseen circumstances that can affect family life. In some cases migration is regretted and the need to go back to the home country increases, although this is not always possible because of financial or other constraints. There is a particular feeling of 'entrapment' in such situations, and when there are status irregularities, individuals do not seek help or help is limited or non-existent. The following interview illustrates this point:

> We came here to improve our lives and get out of poverty. I came with my wife first and then our children followed. One of our children had a car accident and was killed. My wife has not recovered from this loss and from the fact that we could not bury our daughter back home. She became depressed and I am unsupported in securing our financial survival and to become regularised. (Brazilian male, undocumented, working in Belgium)

These four types of migration do not represent neat categories that fully explain family related migration. Migration experiences can combine more than one type, revealing the complexities of migration processes in terms of status change, selection of destination (often determined by work availability and migration restriction policies), and family reunion processes. For example, a female interviewee described her journey this way:

> I first visited friends in Germany on a business visa. I decided to stay in Europe but Germany had very strict rules on undocumented migrants so I went to Italy where I acquired a permanent residence. Later I was joined by my partner and our child and together we have entered the UK. The permanent residence from Italy did not provide any protection in the UK and as a family we live with undocumented status and with constant anxiety that we will be discovered. (Filipino female, undocumented, working in the UK)

What we suggest, based on our research, is that independent of status requirements and state restrictions, people take their own risks to bring their family or form a family even under the most difficult circumstances.

THE IMPACT OF SHIFTING STATUS AND
WORK CONDITIONS ON FAMILY

One important consequence of frequent status transitions, and more specifically when status shifts towards irregularity, is linked to the vulnerability and disadvantage it creates for individuals. Most interviewees commenting on their residence and/or work status reported their constant stress in providing for their family, securing a future for their children but also worrying about the amount of time they could spend with their family. European societies are currently preoccupied with introducing work/life balance, family friendly hours and policies for the workforce, or in general reducing stress from everyday life. Such discussions can sound ironic, as little thought is given to the 'hidden' workforce and their families who are also part of European societies (despite their status) and have similar, if not worse, experiences as a result of their work conditions.

GENDERED EXPERIENCES OF FAMILY MIGRATION

UWT research found that there are not big differences between men and women and the ways that their status or status transition impacts on their family related experiences. In cases of family formation, again both male and female interviewees spoke of their need to secure their financial position and start a family. When a family was present, both men and women spoke of their need to secure their children's future and both felt responsible as main breadwinners for their family's welfare. If their children were back home, interviewees, independent of their gender spoke of their desire to secure their status and reunite the family. In many cases, when that was not possible they brought their children with them who, albeit undocumented, attended local schools, and efforts were made by the parent/parents to have them integrated in the society. But having the whole family present and with no ability to claim benefits, interviewees noted the need for one member to be in constant employment—often willing to take it at any cost.

> Belgium was our first choice because we have old friends here. We decided to leave Brazil, but because of growing violence in [the] São Paulo region and for a better future for our children. We bought airplane tickets by selling our car and borrowing some money. We work nonstop without holidays but we have problems with our lodgings as we had to move twice in three months. It is difficult to remain in the same place with undocumented status. We both work as cleaners. We find Belgium a good place for undocumented people because there are still provisions for health care and education. (Brazilian female and male undocumented, working in Belgium)

One difference, which has been identified in the research, between men and women's experiences of family migration relates to their employment security. As we have seen in Chapter 9, a large number of women find employment in private households as domestic workers, but there is high competition for these jobs and they often need to rely on private contacts. Having to care for their own family, women sometimes can experience additional pressure, as this interviewee described:

> After working for two years in Vienna, I decided to go back home to see my children. I wanted to bring them back with me but there were complications that delayed my journey back. During my absence my boss had to rely on another domestic worker. I was afraid that I would lose the job. The difference between my colleague (who I organised before leaving) and myself was that the woman was independent without children. (Ex-Soviet Union female, undocumented, working in Austria)

On the other hand, a male interviewee narrated his family migration experience and his position in the labour market differently:

> I am here with my wife but she cannot find work. We have to survive on €400 a month. I feel responsible for my family and I have to send money to my children when possible. My family and the dependants I have to care for are a burden at the moment for my possibilities to legalise . . . I could have applied as a key worker somewhere else but I have to care for my family and this is the highest priority. (Ex-Soviet Union male, undocumented, working in Austria)

Balancing the need for legalisation with the responsibility of supporting a family has been described in this interview as an additional pressure for people with undocumented status.

The research also revealed the harsh realities for some individuals who decide to make the journey to Europe under whatever migration status they can get and the effects this can have an impact on their family life. An interviewee from China explained her feeling of entrapment as her separation from family members had become semi-permanent:

> As an undocumented migrant in the UK, I had to move from job to job in order to avoid deportation. Most of these positions have been badly paid and involved long working hours. I took the journey alone and was smuggled in the UK. My husband followed a year later. I have not seen my children for eight years and only speak to them on the phone as me and my husband have a debt of £34,000 to pay back to the people that helped us migrate. (Chinese female, undocumented, working in the UK)

Such separation may come with lasting consequences for the family especially when it takes place in the early years of children's lives, as Erel found in her work with Turkish women immigrants in Germany whose children were left in the care of grandparents back in Turkey (Erel, 2002).

In general, the majority of migrants from our sample were in employment during the research period. The greatest number of these was among divorced people with children. There was an almost equal distribution between those working in declared and undeclared work, but undeclared work was again much higher for divorced people with children. In both cases the majority of interviewees were females working in the unregulated domestic care sector. Many migrants in the UWT sample (around 35 per cent) work in casual employment, but the proportion is again higher for migrants with children (38 per cent for married with children and 47 per cent for divorced with children). The majority of interviewees were either receiving a monthly salary or cash-in-hand pay. Again there was a higher proportion of migrants with children (either married or divorced) who received cash-in-hand, were self-employed on their own account, or were self-employed working through an agency. Finally, people with families in our data were more aware of trade union activities, and more were in contact with trade unions than single people, both male and female. The majority of interviewees, however, indicated that they did not know about the existence or function of trade unions.

It can be argued that working conditions for both single people and those with families tend to be similar, according to the UWT data, although some differences have been highlighted in this chapter. Our findings suggest that people with families and children could be working under more precarious conditions, but overall it is their legal status that plays a more determined role in the levels of exploitation experienced by migrants in terms of pay rate, working hours, and harsh working environment.

CONCLUSION

The chapter has looked at family related migration and, as there is a relative lack of research on undocumented migrants, the UWT project has contributed some important findings. The chapter reviewed the reasons for the also relatively under-theorised subject of family migration. A gender focus was adopted, as findings suggest a strong link between gendered processes of migration and the presence of family.

Using Kofman's basic typology, we also examined the complexities of defining contemporary forms of family and family. All four categories—family reunification, family formation, marriage migration, and family migration—are part of the undocumented migrant experiences and were present in our research, but we have expanded the definition to encompass additional outcomes of family related migration.

Considering the growth in family related international migration and the fact that many of those interviewed in our research did have children or expected to have them, live with partners, or had been at some stage married, points to the centrality of family decisions in defying legal restrictions and seeking improved living conditions. It is therefore necessary to further encourage both academic and policy related research on the issue and for states to adopt measures in support of migrant family life and integration as part of eliminating future disadvantage.

11 Europe's Undocumented Migrants
Here to Stay

> Anyway, you see, we very often have the experience of much more
> freedom in foreign countries than in our own. As foreigners we can
> ignore all those implicit obligations, which are not in law but in the
> general way of behaving. Secondly, merely changing your obligations
> is felt or experienced as a kind of freedom.
>
> (Michel Foucault, cited in Rabinow, 2000: 123)

Michel Foucault, in an interview with Stephen Riggins (cited in Rabinow,
2000), focuses on one of the elements that continue to drive migration
(including that which is undocumented) but one that sometimes is under-
played by migration researchers. He highlights that migration is also about
the expression of the hopes and aspirations of individuals who desire to
experience life beyond the narrow confines of their own environments.
Foucault is not normally regarded as a migrant. He was a French citizen, a
leading academic and theorist, and certainly not someone who experienced
the deprivations of many of the migrants we have discussed in this book.
However, he spent several years working outside France, and his experience of the freedoms he encountered, through the very act of moving to a
different country, is something that many migrants, including those who
are undocumented, share. This view is supported by much of the theory
and practice in relation to migration, which demonstrates that migration
has the capacity to serve both economic needs and life experience needs.
And we would add to this by emphasising that these benefits do not go only
to those who migrate; in our view, migration provides wider benefits to
citizens, in countries of destination as well as in countries of origin. As we
set out at the beginning of this book, migration has taken place throughout
human history and without it many of the innovations and advances that
humanity has benefited from would not have occurred.

However, our conclusions in relation to migration and to state controls
on those who enter suggest that the construction of a precarious and vulnerable workforce is the intended consequence of migration laws, and the
extent to which there can be an effective challenge to this, by workers across
status, is a question to be addressed. This is of course exactly what immigration controls are aimed at preventing. Anderson (2010:301) has recently
made the point that such controls 'combine with less formalised migratory processes to help produce precarious workers that cluster in particular
jobs and segments of the labour market'. We have recorded some examples of trade unions taking up the demands of undocumented migrants

for employment rights or for regularisation, and although the number of initiatives is not very large, the links that are made between undocumented migrants and a wider labour movement are, we think, a fundamental requirement for breaking the barriers that immigration controls encourage.

Our conceptualisation of migration as bringing rewards that are beyond monetary ones makes it even clearer why state policies that aim to keep undocumented people out, or to expel them once they become undocumented, are unlikely to be successful. This is why we have continually stressed that states need to develop policies that are based on the realities of migration today. Merely stating that migration must be limited and that borders will somehow be effectively policed is unworkable and has been shown to be so.

We wanted also to use this concluding chapter to emphasise how a convergence of policies in relation to undocumented labour within Member States, represents a movement towards a Europeanisation of migration, favouring intra–Member State migration, at the expense of third-country migration. What we mean by this is that as Member States bring their laws closer into conformity with one another and with EU-level directives, the pathways for migration, open to third-country nationals, are closing fast. This has encouraged a fundamental break with previous political positions, particularly in countries like the UK and Belgium, which have had a long history of migration to them from countries that previously were linked by colonial ventures. As Europe tightens its borders, in a belief that it can satisfy most of its labour market needs through the accession of key states into the European Union, it is closing routes of entry to those who have well-acknowledged existing ties. The UK has already tightened rules on entry through marriage, targeting third-country nationals. In doing this it denies to its own black and minority ethnic citizens the right to select partners from where they want, or the right to bring elderly relatives or young family members to live with them. We believe that this policy agenda will foster increasing resentments and hostilities and that they risk promoting tensions within Member States, particularly between established and new migrant groups, as well as between migrants and indigenous populations, feeding into nationalist and xenophobic discourses, with the potential, ironically, of destabilising the European Union project, rather than strengthening it. We would submit instead that it needs to be acknowledged that common histories are more relevant that common skin colours. We also assert that undocumented migrants should be recognised as representing an important component of Europe's labour force and that this requires of states, as a minimum, that they give equal employment rights to such migrants and that they recognise them as having access to the same fundamental rights that Europe promotes.

This in turn leads us to address employment and the workplace, the main focus of this book and of our work on the UWT project. We believe that the workplace represents a key area of integration and we draw on the work of Estlund (2003), who argues that of all the places where adults interact, the workplace is likely to be the most demographically diverse. She further states that it is the one space in the US unaffected by white flight, making it the best location in which to challenge racial and ethnic divisions. However, our study shows that because undocumented migrants hold a marginal position in the labour market, this narrows their range of choices of workplace and thus makes it less likely that they will find themselves in the type of racially diverse workplaces that Estlund draws hope from. The fact that undocumented migrants are increasingly forced into the shadows of the labour market, as the stories we have highlighted demonstrate, reduces their opportunities to integrate within wider society and to construct bridges between themselves and documented workers, whether migrant or local. This opens them up to discrimination and creates a gulf between the interests of the majority of workers and those of the undocumented. It makes developing solidarity, including ethnic solidarity, more challenging, particularly where there is over-reliance on co-ethnic employers, and can give voice to racist and xenophobic sentiments. For although all migration is a focus of these sentiments, those who are hostile to migration find it easier to voice their hostility by focusing on the undocumented.

However, there are some developments at odds with this scenario and which present a more positive picture. For example, the current economic climate in Europe and in North America pushes both migrants and locals into work on the peripheries of the labour market whilst paradoxically assisting in the creating of more diverse workplaces. In addition changes in the labour market which we have highlighted in this book mean that there are increasingly blurred boundaries between informal and formal sectors/jobs. At the same time we can also draw inspiration from the undocumented themselves, in their actions throughout Europe and North America, who work on building solidarity within their own sections of the workforce while also reaching out to any movements which they identify as supportive. The actions of the *sans-papiers* in France and in Belgium; of undocumented migrants in Naples who organised against particularly exploitative employment; and the organisation by undocumented migrants in the UK of the 1 May demonstrations of 2006 and 2007 are but a few examples. Looking beyond Europe, the actions of undocumented migrants in the US demonstrate how dependent the economy is on undocumented labour. Bacon (2008:121) reminds us of the potential of even those who seem to be without power to organise themselves, citing one undocumented migrant:

> What do we do while we're waiting for work on the corner every morning? We're learning to live with each other, telling jokes and stories, playing games, arguing about football, a hundred interactions. We're learning to organize ourselves to the rhythm of our happiness and sadness. We're creating a culture of liberation.

One of the major difficulties, in making these links, is the differential position that undocumented migrants have in many European countries, in relation to employment rights, as immigration status also determines access to employment rights. This means that those who are undocumented have no rights at work that they can effectively pursue. Generally their employers are not bound to pay them the national minimum wage, to provide holidays and holiday pay, to pay sick pay, or indeed to provide adequate protection to women who are pregnant or on maternity leave. An essential step, we would suggest, is the separation of immigration and employment rights, where currently entitlement to the latter is removed when immigration rules are breached. This would represent a major step forward for many undocumented migrants, while at the same time it would take away the economic advantage that employers gain from hiring those without employment rights. Indeed it could be argued that without this advantage, employers would be less likely to turn to undocumented migrants for labour if such workers could nevertheless enforce the same rights at work as documented workers.

A second issue is in relation to sanctions on employers. Although it may seem an obvious response that those who employ individuals illegally should be prosecuted for their actions, in truth sanctions do not work in this way. As we have emphasised, employers actually use the existence of sanctions to reduce the wages and conditions of undocumented migrants and indeed can benefit from the presence of a sanctions-focused policy to rid themselves of workers who are seen as troublesome or as potential worker organisers. Iskander (2007) in her work on the *sans-papiers* movement in France describes mainly the garment industry in Paris and shows that those without documents worked in a sector which required flexibility and where learning was developed on the job and where time and skills could overcome disadvantage, regardless of status. These were jobs in the informal labour market but nevertheless seen as 'good' jobs. But the legal changes imposing sanctions on employers forced people out into the suburbs where opportunities to improve their skills were limited and where the work was more precarious. This created an 'all-or-nothing situation': migrants either had work permits and access to jobs or they had neither. She notes:

> The 'sans papiers' were not calling for the state to improve the informal labour markets and undeclared employment practices that the Pasqua laws and the crackdown on undeclared work transformed so profoundly, if indirectly. They were petitioning the state for access to employment relationships that would remain beyond the purview of state control and to the social networks that would ensure their quality. (2007:318)

The experience in the US is similar and indeed as long ago as 1979, Michael Piore made the point that sanctions did no more than encourage employers to exploit more in order to protect their profits (1979:184).

Regularisation and the granting of legal status is the primary way for undocumented migrants to achieve equal employment rights, and we also want to take the opportunity to reflect briefly again on the experiences of regularisation. We have demonstrated that regularisation has been used in some countries systematically to address concerns over the growth of undocumented migrants, but we have also noted that policies promoting regularisation are under attack from the European Commission, supported by many EU Member States and that therefore there is less likelihood of further large-scale regularisations, like those we have witnessed in Spain and Italy. Although these had not necessarily permanently removed the predicament of undocumented migration, as regularised migrants often fell back into irregularity, they showed that it was possible to integrate large numbers of previously undocumented migrants with no noticeable negative impact on the economy or on society more generally. But the problem is that if regularisation is no longer to be available to Member States and if closed borders are the preferred model, we need to reflect on what the alternatives might be. Is Europe really committed to the deportation of somewhere between one and eight million undocumented migrants (depending on what figures are referred to)? Alternatively, is it time to consider a range of options from earned amnesties to the complete abandonment of migration controls?

Notes

NOTES TO CHAPTER 1

1. In March 2011, as this publication went to press, the European Parliament adopted a Resolution on 'Reducing health inequalities in the EU' in which it calls on Member States to tackle health inequalities in access to health care for undocumented migrants.
2. Just over $5 USD an hour.

NOTES TO CHAPTER 2

1. The countries that made up the EU15 were Austria, Belgium, Denmark, Finland, France, Germany, Greece, Ireland, Italy, Luxembourg, Spain, Portugal, Sweden, the Netherlands, and the UK.
2. During the wars, foreign nationals (internees) were deported or isolated in camps in order to eliminate the threat of espionage. There were significant casualties among internees when ships carrying them were hit by enemy fire, most notably the sinking of the Arandora Star by the German navy, as it was carrying more than 1,200 Italian and German internees from the UK to Canada.
3. For a more extensive discussion on civic and ethnic national identity and the formation of new states, see Smith (1995).
4. For example, see the 2005 riots in France: http://news.bbc.co.uk/1/hi/world/europe/4413964.stm
5. For more information on the data, see http://www.oecd.org/document/57/0,3 343,en_2649_39023663_45634233_1_1_1_1,00.html. (Accessed: 14 December 2010).

NOTES TO CHAPTER 3

1. In the remaining eight cases, they were always undocumented and had not experienced any status change.
2. At the end of 2007 the UK government announced that work permits for senior care workers would be removed where their rate of pay fell below a fixed level, regardless of whether that rate was available to UK workers. As a result many workers were dismissed by employers who were not in a position to pay the declared rate and despite the fact that they could continue lawfully paying UK workers at less than that rate.

NOTES TO CHAPTER 4

1. The WLRI team consisted of the three authors together with Tessa Wright, Janet Emefo, Steve Jefferys, and Leena Kumarappan.

4. In the interviews that we conducted, undocumented migrants frequently referred to themselves as 'illegal'. We believe that their use of the term was as much an attempt to explain to themselves, as much as to anyone else, why they were trapped in situations of such hardship. It was a way of detaching themselves from their situation. This is not to imply that they believed that they had alternatives that they could have exercised to escape their situation, but it demonstrates how status was for some a more acceptable explanation of their predicament than for example, that it was as a result of racism, sexism, or xenophobia.
5. We used a system provided by London Metropolitan University called Livelink.

NOTES TO CHAPTER 5

1. Principally the UN Convention Relating to the Status of Refugees and the 1967 Protocol together with the International Convention on the Protection of the Rights of All Migrant Workers and Members of Their Families, 1990.
2. For example, SEC(2008)2026/27 'managing immigration effectively means addressing also different issues linked to the security of our societies and of immigrants' themselves. This requires fighting illegal migration and criminal activities related to it, striking the right balance between individual integrity and collective security concerns'.
3. The principle of non-refoulement, which is recognised in international law, requires of a state that it protects the fundamental rights of all persons and in particular that it does not return persons to persecution or danger. See *UNHCR Note on the principle of non-refoulement*: http://www.unhcr.org/cgi-bin/texis/vtx/refworld/rwmain?docid=438c6d972 (Accessed: 2 December 2010).
4. Cases C-261/08 and C-348/08 Zurita García and Choque Cabrera.
5. On 30 August 2009 the Italian government 'returned' 75 migrants to Libya, even though it included 15 women and three children who were most likely from Eritrea or Somalia (*PICUM newsletter*, August/September 2009). This is understood to have been the first forced repatriation coordinated by FRONTEX (*PICUM newsletter*, July 2009).

NOTES TO CHAPTER 6

1. See Chapter 5 for an analysis of EU regulation.
2. It was first proposed by the Parliamentary Assembly (2007).
3. This term was used during the 2005 regularisation programme in Spain.
4. See the definition by the Parliamentary Assembly (2007), p.6 and the one in the REGINE study by Baldwin-Edwards, M. and Kraler, A. (2009), p.7.

NOTES TO CHAPTER 7

1. Legalisation programmes are defined as state measures applied for a specific period of time aimed at granting legal status to undocumented migrants, usually in employment, who satisfy certain conditions.
2. Regularisation mechanisms form part of the regular migratory framework of a state and as such they are permanent measures.
3. Migration flows are defined as the patterns of movement of people from country to country or region to region at any given time. Migration stock, on the other hand, is the number of people born in a country other than that in which they live.

4. The figure derives from an estimate based on the 2001 Census by subtracting an estimate of foreign-born population residing legally.
5. The Partido Popular party is a centre-right party and the largest opposition party in Spain.

NOTES TO CHAPTER 8

1. The term 'urban traditional sector' was used instead of the underground economy because the theory was developed at a time when the underground economy was still thought of as not significant enough for a separate study.
2. Interview with migration expert, 12 September 2007.
3. Interview with Jeff-Dayton Johnson, OECD economist, 28 February 2008.
4. Interview with Martin Baldwin-Edwards, 29 February 2008.
5. Interview with migration expert, 12 September 2007.
6. Interview with migration expert, 29 November 2007.
7. Interview with Martin-Baldwin Edwards, 29 February 2008.
8. Interview with a manager from the construction sector in the UK, 23 February 2008.
9. Interview with Austrian migration expert, 12 September 2007.
10. Interview with CGIL migration expert, 20 June 2007.
11. http://www.eurofound.europa.eu/areas/labourmarket/tackling/cases/be004.htm (Accessed: 3 December 2010).
12. MB 10 June 2003.
13. Loi-programme (I) du 27 décembre 2006, Moniteur belge du 28 décembre 2006, 3ème édition.
14. http://www.eurofound.europa.eu/areas/labourmarket/tackling/cases/de003.htm (Accessed: 3 December 2010). http://www.eurofound.europa.eu/areas/labourmarket/tackling/cases/nl001.htm (Accessed: 3 December 2010).

NOTES TO CHAPTER 9

1. Although Piper also notes that there is a growing recognition in policy debates of results produced through gender research (Piper, 2006:139).
2. At the time of this individual's migration, the exchange rate was approximately £1 to €1.50.
3. The right to family reunion is recognised by the Treaty of the European Communities (Art. 36, para. 3a).
4. The positive outcome in this case was that the interviewee managed to gain her own residency, not linked to a marriage. The interviewee also commented that being part of an ethnic community gave her access to jobs and, albeit exploited in terms of working conditions, she was not unemployed.
5. Almost an equal proportion of male respondents were also undocumented during the time of the research.
6. Similar trends can also be observed in the UWT database for men but at much less noticeable rates.

NOTES TO CHAPTER 10

1. Examples of legal provisions for family reunification and the protection of family life as a fundamental right are included in the 1948 Universal Declaration of Human Rights (UDHR), the 1966 International Covenant on Civil and Political Rights (ICCPR), the 1989 UN Convention on the Rights of the Child (CRC), and the 1990 International Convention on the Protection of

the Rights of All Migrant Workers and Members of Their Families. More information on legal provisions for family migrants can be found on the International Organization for Migration website: www.iom.int.

2. However, two interviews in Bulgaria revealed that an Albanian and a Syrian man had migrated in order to escape arranged/forced marriages. In the case of the Syrian, a forced marriage had already taken place with a close relative. The interviewee noted that as a result the couple had given birth to two severely handicapped children. He explained that he could no longer live in that situation and decided to leave his country (but he supported the children financially).

Bibliography

Abella, M. (2000) 'Migration and employment of undocumented workers: do sanctions and amnesties work?' in Cinar, D., Gacher, A., and Waldrauch, H. (eds.), *Irregular dynamics, impact, policy options,* Vienna: European Centre for Social Welfare Policy and Research, pp. 205–215.

Adepoju, A. Van Noorloos, F. Zoomers, A. (2011) 'Europe's migration agreements with migrant-sending countries in the global south: a critical review' *International Migration* 48(3):42-75.

Ahmad, A. N. (2008a) 'The labour market consequences of human smuggling: "illegal" employment in London's migrant economy', *Journal of Ethnic and Migration Studies,* 34(6):853–874.

Ahmad, A. N. (2008b) 'The romantic appeal of illegal migration: gender, masculinity and human smuggling from Pakistan', in Schrover, M., Van der Leun, J., Lucassen, L., and Quispel, C. (eds.), *Illegal migration and gender in a global and historical perspective,* Amsterdam: Amsterdam University Press, pp. 127–150.

Alcoff, L. (1991) 'The problem of speaking for others', *Cultural Critique,* 20:5–32.

Anderson, B. (2007) 'A very private business—exploring the demand for migrant domestic workers', *European Journal of Women's Studies,* 14(3):247–264.

Anderson, B. (2008) *'Illegal immigrant', victim or villain,* COMPAS Working Paper No. 64, University of Oxford.

Anderson, B. (2010) 'Migration, immigration controls and the fashioning of precarious workers', *Work, Employment and Society,* 24(2):300–317.

Andrijasevic, R. (2003) 'The difference borders make: (il)legality, migration and trafficking in Italy among Eastern European women in prostitution', in Ahmed, S., Castaneda, C., Fortier, A., and Sheller, M. (eds.), *Uprootings/regroundings: questions of home and migration,* Oxford: Berg, pp. 251–272.

Apap, J., de Bruycker, P., and Schmitter, C. (2000) 'Regularisation of illegal aliens in the European Union—summary report of a comparative study', *European Journal of Migration and Law,* 2:263–308.

Arango, J. and Finotelli, C. (2009) 'Country study: Spain' in Baldwin-Edwards, M. and Kraler, A. (eds.), *REGINE: Regularisations in Europe. Study on practices in the area of regularisation of illegally staying third-country nationals in the Member States of the EU, Appendix A: Country studies,* Vienna: ICMPD, pp. 83–93.

Askola, H. (2010) '"Illegal migrants", gender and vulnerability: the case of the EU's Returns Directive', *Feminist Legal Studies,* 18(2):159–178.

Augustin, L. (2005) 'Migrants in the mistress's house: other voices in the "trafficking" debate', *Social Politics: International Studies in Gender, State and Society,* 12(1):96–117.

Bacon, D. (2008) *Illegal people: how globalization creates migration and criminalizes immigrants,* Boston: Beacon Press.

Bade, K. (2003) *Migration in European history* (A. Brown, Trans.), Malden, MA: Blackwell.

Bailey, A. J. and Boyle, P. (2004) 'Untying and retying family migration in the New Europe', *Journal of Ethnic and Migration Studies*, 30(2):229–242.

Baldaccini, A. (2009) 'The return and removal of irregular migrants under EU law: an analysis of the Returns Directive', *European Journal of Migration and Law*, 11:1–17.

Baldwin-Edwards, M. (2008) 'Illegal migration: a theoretical and historical approach', *Third World Quarterly*, 29(7):1449–1459.

Baldwin-Edwards, M. and Kraler, A. (eds.) (2009, January) *REGINE: Regularisations in Europe. Study on practices in the area of regularisation of illegally staying third-country nationals in the Member States of the EU*, Vienna: ICMPD, http://ec.europa.eu/home-affairs/doc_centre/immigration/docs/studies/regine_appendix_a_january_2009_en.pdf (Accessed: 30 November 2010).

Beyer, G. (1981) 'The political refugee, 35 years later', *International Migration Review*, 15(1/2):26–34.

Biffl, G. (2002) 'Estimation on the extent of the informal economy in Austria' (Schätzung des Ausmaßes der Schwarzarbeit in Österreich), in Biffl, G. (ed.), *Integration of foreigners and their effects on the labour market in Austria* (Arbeitsmarktrelevante Effekte der Ausländerintegration in Österreich), Vienna: WIFO/Austrian Institute for Economic Research, pp. 362–364.

Black, R. (2003) 'Breaking the convention: researching the "illegal" migration of refugees to Europe', *Antipode*, 35(1):34–54.

Bloch, A. (2004) 'Labour market participation and conditions of employment: a comparison of minority ethnic groups and refugees in Britain' *Sociological Research Online* 9(2).

Bloch, A. (2007) 'Methodological challenges for national and multi-sited comparative survey research', *Journal of Refugee Studies*, 20(2):230–247.

Boeri, T. and Garibaldi, T. (2002) *Shadow activity and unemployment in a depressed labour market*, CEPR Discussion Paper No. 3433.

Bohning, W. R. (1996) *Employing foreign workers: a manual on policies and procedures of special interest to middle and low income countries*, Geneva: International Labour Organisation.

Bonney, N. and Love, J. (1991) 'Gender and migration: geographical mobility and the wife's sacrifice', *Sociological Review* 39:335–348.

Bourdieu, P. (1991) *Language and symbolic power*, Cambridge, MA: Harvard University Press.

Bourdieu, P. (1998) *Acts of resistance: against the new myths of our time*, Cambridge: Polity Press.

Bourne, R. (1916) 'Trans-national America', *Atlantic Monthly*, 118:86–97.

Bouteillet-Paquet, D. (2003) 'Passing the buck: a critical analysis of the readmission policy implemented by the European Union and its Member States', *European Journal of Migration and Law*, 5:359–377.

Bowcott, O. (2010) 'EU border agency says fewer illegal migrants spotted in last year' *The Guardian*, 25 May 2010.

Boyd, M. (1989), "Family and personal networks in international migration", *International Migration Review*, Vol. 23 No. 3, pp. 638-70.

Boyle, P. J., Feng, Z., and Gayle, V. (2009) 'A new look at family migration and women's employment status', *Journal of Marriage and the Family*, 71:417–431.

Bramwell, A. and Marrus, M. (1988) *Refugees in the age of total war*, London: Routledge.

Brubaker, R. (1998) 'Migrations of ethnic unmixing in the "New Europe"', *International Migration Review*, 32(4):1047–1065.

Bryceson, D. F. and Vuorela, U. (2002) *The transnational family: new European frontiers and global networks*, Oxford: Berg.

Butcher, M. (2009) 'Ties that bind: the strategic use of transnational relationships in demarcating identity and managing difference', *Journal of Ethnic and Migration Studies,* 35(8):1353–1371.

Cangiano, A. (2010, November) *UK data sources on international migration and the migrant population: a review and appraisal,* COMPAS, University of Oxford.

Castles, S. (2007) 'Twenty-first century migration as a challenge to sociology', *Journal of Ethnic and Migration Studies,* 33(3):351–371.

Castles, S. and Miller, M. (2009) *The age of migration: international population movement in the modern world* (4th ed.), New York: Guilford Press.

Cavalcanti, T. V. (2002) 'Labour market policies and informal markets', *mimeo, Universidade Nova de Lisboa,* Faculdade de Economia.

Chamberlain, M. (1997) 'Gender and the narratives of migration', *History Workshop Journal,* (43):87–108.

Chaudhuri, T. D. (1989) 'A theoretical analysis of the informal sector', *World Development,* 17(3):351–355.

Chauvin P., Parizot, I., and Simonnot, N. (2009) *Access to healthcare for undocumented migrants in 11 European countries,* 2008 Survey report, Médecins du Monde European Observatory on Access to Healthcare.

Chishti, M. and Bergeron, C. (2008, March 17) *Virtual border fence given mixed assessment in the first test,* Washington, DC: Migration Policy Institute, http://www.migrationinformation.org/USfocus/display.cfm?id=675 (Accessed: 3 December 2010).

Chiswick, B. (1988) 'Illegal immigration and immigration control', *Journal of Economic Perspectives,* 2(3):101–115.

Chiswick, B. and Miller, P. (1999) 'Language skills and earnings among legalized aliens', *Journal of Population Economics,* 12(1):63–89.

Cholewinski, R. (2006) *Irregular migrants: access to minimum social rights,* Council of Europe.

Cholewinski, R., Perruchoud, R., and MacDonald, E. (eds.) (2007) *International migration law: developing paradigms and key challenges,* Cambridge: Cambridge University Press.

Chou, M. (2006) *EU and the migration development nexis: what prospects for EU-wide policies,* Working Paper No. 37, Compas, Oxford.

Cillo, R. and Perocco, F. (2007) *Italy country report,* http://www.undocumented-migrants.eu/londonmet/library/t78243_3.pdf (Accessed: 3 December 2010).

Cobb-Clark, Deborah A, and Sherrie A. Kossoudji. (1999). 'Did Legalization Matter for Women? Amnesty and the Wage Determinants of Formerly Unauthorized Latina Workers.' *Gender Issues*: 3-14.

Collins, F. L. (2009) 'Connecting "home" with "here": personal homepages in everyday transnational lives', *Journal of Ethnic and Migration Studies,* 35(6):839–859.

Council of Europe Assembly (2007) *Regularisation Programmes for irregular migrants.* Report Committee on Migration, Refugees and Population. Rapporteur: Mr John Greenway, United Kingdom, European Democrat Group, Doc 11350, http://assembly.coe.int/Mainf.asp?link=/Documents/WorkingDocs/Doc07/EDOC11350.htm (Accessed: 27 November 2007).

Cyrus, N. (2004) *Aufenthaltsrechtliche Illegalität in Deutschland. Sozialstrukturbildung—Wechselwirkungen—Politische Optionen* (Illegal residency in Germany. Social structure formation—Interaction—Policy options). Bericht für den Sachverständigenrat für Zuwanderung und Integration, Berlin, http://www.forum-illegalitaet.de/Materialien/04_Expertise_Sachverst_ndigenrat_Cyrus.pdf (Accessed: 21 November 2010).

Dahinden, J. and Efionayi-Mäder, D. (2009) 'Challenges and strategies in empirical fieldwork with asylum seekers and migrant sex workers' in Van Liempt, I. and Bilger, V. (eds.), *The ethics of migration research methodology: dealing with vulnerable immigrants,* Brighton: Sussex Academic Press, pp. 98–117.

De Bruycker, P. (ed.) (2000) Les regularisations des étrangers illégaux dans l'union européenne. (Regularisations of illegal immigrants in the European Union), Brussels: Bruylant.

De Wenden, C. (2007) 'The frontiers of mobility' in Pécoud, A. and de Guchteneire, P. (eds.), *Migration without borders: essays on the free movements of people,* UNESCO, pp. 51–64.

Dench, S., Hursfield, J., Hill, D., and Akroyd, K. (2006) *Employers' use of migrant labour,* London: Home Office.

Dentler, A. (2008) *Why do some states draw upon amnesties for irregular migrants while other do not? A comparison between Spain and the United Kingdom,* Migration Studies Unit Working Paper No. 2008/04, London: London School of Economics and Political Science.

Diner, H. R. (2001) *Hungering for America, Italian, Irish and Jewish foodways in the age of migration,* Cambridge, MA: Harvard University Press.

Doeringer, P. and Piore, M. (1971) *Internal Labor Markets and Manpower Analysis.* New York: Sharpe.

Dorigo, G. and Tobler, W. (2005) 'Push pull migration laws', *Annals of the Association of American Geographers,* 73(1):1–17.

Düvell, F. (ed.) (2006) *Illegal immigration in Europe,* Houndmills: Palgrave/Macmillan.

Dzengozova, M. (2009) 'Belgium' in Baldwin-Edwards, M. and Kraler, A. (eds.), *REGINE: Regularisations in Europe. Study on practices in the area of regularisation of illegally staying third-country nationals in the Member States of the EU, Appendix A: Country studies,* Vienna: ICMPD, pp. 14–24.

Ehrenreich, B. and Hochschild, A. R. (eds.) (2002) *Global woman: Nannies, maids and sex workers in the new economy,* London: Granta Books.

Engbersen, G. (2001) 'The unanticipated consequences of panopticon Europe: residence strategies of illegal immigrants', in Guiraudon V. and Joppke C. (eds.), *Controlling a new migration world,* London: Routledge, pp. 222–246.

Ennaji, M. (2003) 'Illegal Migration from Morocco to Europe', Paper presented at the MeroMed Seminar, International Metropolis Project, 10-12 December 2003, Milan."

Enste, D. H. and Schneider, F. (2006) 'Schattenwirtschaft und irreguläre Beschäftigung: Irrtümer, Zusammenhänge und Lösungen', in Jörg, A. and Bommes, M. (eds.), *Illegalität: Grenzen und Möglichkeiten der Migrationspolitik* (Illegality: limits and possibilities of immigration policy), Wiesbaden, Germany: VS Verlag für Sozialwissenschaften, pp. 35–59.

Entorf, H. and Moebert, J. (2004, January/February) 'The demand for illegal migration and market outcomes', *Intereconomics,* 39:7–10.

Erdemir, A. and Vasta, E. (2007) *Differentiating irregularity and solidarity: Turkish immigrants at work in London,* COMPAS Working Paper No. 42, University of Oxford, http://www.compas.ox.ac.uk/fileadmin/files/pdfs/WP0742-Vasta.pdf (Accessed: 3 December 2010).

Erel, U. (2002) 'Reconceptualizing motherhood: experiences of migrant women from Turkey living in Germany' in Bryceson, D. and Vuorela, U. (eds.), *The transnational family: new European frontiers and global networks,* Oxford: Berg pp. 127–1462.

Estlund, C. (2003) *Working together: how workplace bonds strengthen a diverse democracy,* New York: Oxford University Press.

"Euro-African Partnership for Migration and Development (2006) *The Rabat Action Plan,* http://www.realinstitutoelcano.org/materiales/docs/RabatDeclaration_ActionPlan.pdf. (Accessed: 2 December 2010).

European Commission (1997) *Treaty of Amsterdam,* http://www.eurotreaties.com/amsterdamtreaty.pdf. (Accessed: 2 December 2010).

European Commission (1998) *Vienna Action Plan,* http://eur-lex.europa.eu/smart-api/cgi/sga_doc?smartapi!celexapi!prod!CELEXnumdoc&lg=EN&numdoc=31999Y0123(01)&model=guichett. (Accessed: 2 December 2010).

European Commission (2002) *Action plan on illegal migration to combat illegal migration and trafficking of human beings in the European Union,* http://europa. eu/rapid/pressReleasesAction.do?reference=MEMO/05/153&format=HTML&a ged=0&language=EN&guiLanguage=en. (Accessed: 2 December 2010).

European Commission (2005) *The Hague Programme,* http://europa.eu/rapid/ pressReleasesAction.do?reference=MEMO/05/153&format=HTML&aged=0 &language=EN&guiLanguage=en. (Accessed: 2 December 2010).

European Commission (2006) *Policy priorities in the fight against illegal immigration of third-country nationals,* COM(2006)402 FINAL.

European Commission (2009) *The Stockholm Programme,* http://www.se2009.eu/ polopoly_fs/1.26419!menu/standard/file/Klar_Stockholmsprogram.pdf.

European Union (2006) *Consolidated Version of the Treaty on European Union,* http://eur-lex.europa.eu/LexUriServ/LexUriServ.do?uri=OJ:C:2006:321E:0001 :0331:EN:PDF (Accessed: 2 December 2010).

European Commission. (2008) *A common immigration policy for Europe: principles, actions and tools* (COM(2008) 386 final), http://eur-lex.europa.eu/ LexUriServ/LexUriServ.do?uri=SEC:2008:2026:FIN:EN:PDF (Accessed: 28 November 2010).

European Commission. (2009, November 23) *CLANDESTINO project: final report,* http://www.epim.info/docs/documents/clandestino-final-report_-november-2009.pdf (Accessed: 13 December 2010).

European Commission. (2010) *First annual report on immigration and asylum* (COM(2010) 214) http://www.emn.fi/files/238/CSWP_-_SEC(2010)_535.pdf (Accessed: 2 December 2010)

European Council on Refugees and Exiles. (2007) 'Weekly update of 15 September 2007', http://www.ecre.org (Accessed: 13 December 2010).

European Migration Network (EMN). (2007) *Illegally resident third country nationals in EU Member States: state approaches towards them, their profile and social situation,* EMN synthesis report, http://ec.europa.eu/home-affairs/ doc_centre/immigration/docs/studies/emn_synthesis_report_illegal_immigration_final_january_2007.pdf (Accessed: 20 November 2010).

Evans, Y. (2008) *Papers please: the impact of the civil penalty regime on the employment rights of migrants in the UK,* London: Migrant Rights' Network.

Fields, G. S. (2004) 'Dualism in the labour market; a perspective on the Lewis model after half a century', *The Manchester School,* 72(6):724–735.

Fondazione ISMU. (2007) *Dodicesimo rapporto sulle migrazioni, 2006,* Milan, Italy: FrancoAngeli.

Forschungs- und Beratungsstelle Arbeitswelt (FORBA). (2007) *Austria country report,* Vienna: FORBA, http://www.undocumentedmigrants.eu/londonmet/ library/x81059_3.pdf (Accessed: 3 December 2010).

Freedman, J. (2008) 'Women, migration and activism in Europe', *Amnis,* 8.

Gann, L. and Duignan, P. (1975) *Colonialism in Africa, 1870–1960,* Cambridge University Press.

Gans, H. (1962) *The urban villagers,* New York: Free Press.

Garson, J. P. (2000) 'Amnesty programmes: recent lessons', in Cinar, D., Gächter, A., and Waldrauch, H. (eds.), *Irregular migration: dynamics, impact, policy options,* Vienna: European Centre for Social Welfare Policy and Research, pp. 217–224.

Gayle, V., Boyle, P., Flowerdew, R., and Cullis, A. (2008) 'Family migration and social stratification', *International Journal of Sociology and Social Policy,* 28:293–303.

Gedalof, I. (2007) 'Unhomely homes: women, family and belonging in UK discourses of migration and asylum', *Journal of Ethnic and Migration Studies,* 33(1):77–94.

Gentleman, A. (2010) 'The asylum seekers who survive on £10 a week', *The Guardian,* 16 June 2010, http://www.guardian.co.uk/uk/2010/jun/16/asylum-seekers-survive-on-streets (Accessed: 10 November 2010).

Ghosh, B. (1998) *Huddled masses and uncertain shores*, International Organisation for Migration, Geneva.

Global Commission. (2005) *Migration in an interconnected world: new directions for action*, http://www.gcim.org/attachements/gcim-complete-report-2005.pdf (Accessed: 2 December 2010).

Gordon, I., Scanlon, K., Travers, T., and Whitehead, C. M. E. (2009) *Economic impact on the London and UK economy of an earned regularisation of irregular migrants to the UK,* London: Greater London Authority.

Gordon, J. (2007) 'Transnational labor citizenship', *Southern California Law Review,* 80:503.

Guiraudon, V. (2006) 'Enlisting third parties in border control: A comparative study of its causes and consequences', in Marina Caparini, M. and Marenin, O. (eds.), *Borders and security governance,* Vienna and Geneva: LIT Verlag/DCAF, pp. 79–97.

Haidinger, B. (2006) 'Transnational contingency: the domestic work of migrant women in Austria' in Walsum, S. and Spijkerboer, Th. (eds.), *Women and immigration law in Europe: new variations on feminist themes*, London: Routledge.

Halfacree, K. (1995) 'Household migration and the structuration of patriarchy: evidence from the USA,' *Progress in Human Geography,* 19(1):159–182.

Honohan, I. (2008) 'Reconsidering the claim to family reunification in migration', *Political Studies,* 57:768–787.

Horst, H. A. (2006) 'The blessings and burdens of communication: cell phones in Jamaican transnational social fields', *Global Networks,* 6(2):143–159.

Humphries, J. (2010) *Childhood and child labour in the British industrial revolution*, Cambridge: Cambridge University Press.

International Labour Office (ILO). (2001) *Stopping forced labour,* Geneva: International Labour Office.

Institute of Public Policy Research (ippr). (2006) *Irregular immigration in the UK: an ippr fact file,* London: ippr.

International Organization for Migration (IOM). (2000) *World migration report,* Geneva: IOM.

International Organization for Migration (IOM). (2005) 'Feminization of migration', World Migration Report Series, No. 3. Geneva: IOM.

Iskander, N. (2007) 'Informal work and protest: undocumented immigrant activism in France, 1996–2000', *British Journal of Industrial Relations,* 45(2):309–334.

Kay, D. and Miles, R. (1992) *Refugees or migrant workers: European volunteer workers in Britain, 1946–1951,* London: Routledge.

Kennan, G. (1957) *American diplomacy, 1900–1950,* New York: Mentor Books.

King, R. (ed.) (1995) *Mass migration in Europe: the legacy and the future,* Chichester, UK: Wiley.

King, R. (1996) 'Migration in a world historical perspective', in van den Broek, J. (ed.), *The economics of labour migration,* Cheltenham: Elgar, pp. 7–77.

King, R. (2002) 'Towards a new map of European integration', *International Journal of Population Geography,* 8:89–106.

Kofman, E. (2004) 'Family-related migration: a critical review of European studies', *Journal of Ethnic and Migration Studies,* 30(2):243–262.

Kofman, E. (2008) 'Gendered migrations, livelihoods and entitlements in European welfare regimes', in Piper, N. (ed.), *New perspectives on gender and migration,* New York: Routledge, pp. 59–100.

Kofman, E. and Meetoo, V. (2008) 'Family migration' in International Organization for Migration (ed.), *World migration 2008: managing labour mobility in the evolving global economy,* Geneva: IOM, pp. 151–172.

Kofman, E., Phizacklea, A., Raghuram, P., and Sales, S. (eds.) (2000) *Gender and international migration in Europe,* London: Routledge.

Koser, K. (2005, September) *Irregular migration, state security and human security,* Paper prepared for the Policy Analysis and Research Programme of the Global Commission on International Migration, Global Commission on International Migration.

Kossoudji, S. A. and Cobb-Clark, D. A. (2004) 'IRCA's impact on the occupational concentration and mobility of newly-legalised Mexican men' in Zimmermann, K. and Constant, A. (eds.), *How labour migrants fare,* Berlin: Springer-Verlag, pp. 333–350.

Kovacheva, V. and Vogel, D. (2009) *The size of the irregular foreign resident population in the European Union in 2002, 2005 and 2008: aggregated estimates,* Hamburg Institute of International Economics (HWWI), Database on Irregular Migration, Working Paper No. 4, http://www.irregular-migration.hwwi.net/Working_papers.6113.0.html (Accessed: 2 December 2010).

Kraler, A. (2009, January) 'Austria' in Baldwin-Edwards, M. and Kraler, A. (eds.), *REGINE: Regularisations in Europe. Study on practices in the area of regularisation of illegally staying third-country nationals in the Member States of the EU, Appendix A: Country studies,* Vienna: ICMPD, pp. 4–13.

Krenn, M. and Haidinger, B. (2008, November) *Un(der)documented migrant labour—characteristics, conditions and labour market impacts,* http://www.undocumentedmigrants.eu/londonmet/library/y23633_3.pdf (Accessed: 30 November 2010).

Labour Research Department (LRD). (2010, August) 'Using immigration law to break our unions?' *Labour Research,* pp. 9–11.

Ladas, S. (1932) *The exchange of minorities: Bulgaria, Greece and Turkey,* New York: Macmillan.

Lammers, E. (2005) 'Refugees, asylum seekers and anthropologists: the taboo on giving' *Global Migration Perspectives, Paper No. 29,* Global Commission on International Migration.

Lee, E. (1966) 'A theory of migration', *Demography,* 3(1):47–57.

Lenoel, A. (2009, January) 'United Kingdom' in Baldwin-Edwards, M. and Kraler, A. (eds.), *REGINE: Regularisations in Europe. Study on practices in the area of regularisation of illegally staying third-country nationals in the Member States of the EU, Appendix A: Country studies,* Vienna: ICMPD, pp. 102–123.

Levinson, A. (2005) *The regularisation of unauthorised migrants: literature survey and country case studies,* Oxford: Centre on Migration, Policy and Society, University of Oxford.

Lewis, W. A. (1954) 'Economic development with unlimited supplies of labour', *The Manchester School,* 22:139–191.

Loyaza, N. V. (1994) *Labor regulations and the informal economy,* Policy Research Working Paper No. 1335, World Bank Working Policy Research Department, Macroeconomic and Growth Division.

MacDonald, J. S. and MacDonald, L. D. (1964) 'Chain migration, ethnic neighbourhood formation and social networks', *Millbank Memorial Fund Quarterly,* 41(1):82–97.

Mandaville, P. (2009) 'Muslim transnational identity and state responses in Europe and the UK after 9/11: political community, ideology and authority', *Journal of Ethnic and Migration Studies,* 35(3):491–506.

Markova, E. (2001) *The economic performance of Bulgarian illegal and legalised immigrants in the Greek labour market,* PhD thesis, Athens: Department of Economics, University of Athens.

Markova, E. (2009) 'The role of the researcher' in Van Liempt, I. and Bilger, V. (eds.), *The ethics of migration research methodology: dealing with vulnerable immigrants,* Brighton: Sussex Academic Press, pp. 141–154.

Markova, E. and McKay, S. (2008) *Agency and migrant workers; literature review,* Report for the Commission on Vulnerable Employment, http://www.

vulnerableworkers.org.uk/wp-content/uploads/2008/08/literature-review-final. pdf (Accessed: 3 December 2010).

Marrus, M. R. (1985) *The unwanted: European refugees in the twentieth century,* New York: Oxford University Press.

Massey, D. S. (1990) 'The social and economic origins of immigration', *Annals of the American Academy of Political and Social Science,* 510:60–72.

Massey, D. S., Alarcón, R., Durand, J., and González, H. (1987) *Return to Aztlan: the social process of international migration from Western Mexico,* Berkeley: University of California Press.

Massey, D. S., Goldring, L., and Durand, J. (1994) 'Continuities in transnational migration: an analysis of nineteen Mexican communities', *American Journal of Sociology,* 99(6):1492–1533.

Mazower, M. (1995) *After the war was over,* London: Longman.

McDowell, L. (2003) 'Workers, migrants, aliens or citizens? State constructions and discourses of identity among post-war European labour migrants in Britain', *Political Geography,* 22:863–886.

McKay, S. (ed.) (2008) *Refugees, recent migrants and employment: challenging barriers and exploring path ways,* New York: Routledge.

McKay, S. (2009) 'Existing in a twilight world', *Labour Research.*

McKay, S., Markova, E., Paraskevopoulou, A., and Wright, T. (2009) *The relationship between migration status and employment outcomes,* UWT final project report, www.undocumentedmigrants.eu, (Accessed 14 December 2010).

McKay, S. and Snyder, P. (2009) 'Methodological challenges in researching the working experiences of refugees and recent migrants', in McKay, S. (ed.), *Refugees, recent migrants and employment,* New York: Routledge, pp. 35–49.

Meng-Hsuan, C. (2006) *EU and the migration-development nexus: what prospects for EU-wide policies,* COMPAS Working Paper No. 37, University of Oxford.

Mestheneos, E. (2006) 'Refugees as researchers: experiences from the project "Bridges and fences: paths to refugee integration in the EU"' in Temple, B. and Moran, R. (eds.), *Doing research with refugees: issues and guidelines,* Bristol: Policy Press, pp. 21–36.

Migration Watch (2005) 'The Illegal Migrant Population in the UK', Briefing Paper 9.15 *Migration Trends,* 28 July 2005.

Monastiriotis, V. and Markova, E. (2009) *Maximising the benefits of migration in a small island economy: the case of the island of Rhodes in Greece,* Report prepared for the John Latsis Foundation, London: London School of Economics and Political Science.

Morokvasic, M. (2004) '"Settled in mobility": engendering post-wall migration in Europe', *Feminist Review,* 77:7–25.

Morokvasic, M. (2007) 'Migration, gender, empowerment' in Lenz, I., Ullrich, C., and Fersch, B. (eds.), *Gender orders unbound: globalisation, restructuring and reciprocity,* Opladen, Germany: Verlag Barbara Budrich, pp. 69–98.

Moses, J. W. (2006) *International migration,* London: Zed Books.

Mottura, G. and Rinaldini, M. (2009) 'Migrants' paths in the Italian labour market and in the migrant regulatory frameworks: precariousness as a constant factor', in McKay, S. (ed.), *Refugees, recent migrants and employment,* London: Routledge, pp. 84–101.

National Archives. (2008) *Convincing the colonies: how did Britain try to keep the support of the people of West Africa?* http://www.nationalarchives.gov.uk/ documents/education/ww2-propaganda.pdf (Accessed: 4 November 2010).

OECD. (1994) *Trends in international migration,* Paris: OECD.

OECD. (2006) *Women and men in OECD countries,* Paris: OECD.

OECD Secretariat. (2000) 'Some lessons from recent regularisation programmes', in OECD (ed.), *Combating the illegal employment of foreign workers,* Paris: OECD, pp. 53–69.

Orrenius, P. and Zavodny, M. (2004) *What are the consequences of an amnesty for undocumented immigrants,* Working Paper No. 2004–10, Federal Reserve Bank of Atlanta.

Ouali, N. (2007) *UWT country report: Belgium,* http://www.undocumentedmigrants.eu/londonmet/library/q65044_3.pdf (Accessed: 3 December 2010).

Pajares, M. and Leotti, P. (2008) *UWT Thematic report: the relationship between status and migration transitions,* http://www.undocumentedmigrants.eu/londonmet/library/j12442_3.pdf (Accessed: 4 December 2010).

Papademetriou, D. (2005, September) *The regularization option in managing illegal migration more effectively: a comparative perspective,* Policy Brief No. 4, September 2005, Washington, DC: Migration Policy Institute.

Papademetriou, D. and Martin, P. L. (1991) *The unsettled relationship: labour migration and economic development,* Westport, CT: Greenwood Press.

Papademetriou, D., O'Neil, K., and Jackimowicz, M. (2004) *Observations and regularization and the labour market performance of unauthorized and regularized immigrants,* Hamburg: HWWA.

Papademetriou, D. and Somerville, W. (2008) *Earned amnesty: bringing illegal workers out of the shadows,* Policy paper, London: CentreForum, http://www.centreforum.org/assets/pubs/regularisation-web.pdf (Accessed: 13 December 2010).

Passel, J. (2007) *Unauthorised migrants in the United States; estimates, methods and characteristics,* OECD Social, Employment and Migration Working Paper No. 57.

Peixoto, J., Sabino, C., and Abreu, A. (2009) 'Immigration policies in Portugal: limits and compromise in the quest for regularisation', *European Journal of Migration and Law,* 11:179–197.

Perocco, F. (2010, July) 'Immigrant women workers in the underground economy between old and new inequities', *International Review of Sociology,* 20(2):385–390.

Petrakou, H. and Tatlidil, E. (2003) 'Dimensions of female immigration in the European Union and Greece' in Tatlidil, E. and Fokiali, P. (eds.), *Greek–Turkish approaches: revealing women's socio-economic role,* Athens: Atrapos pp. 125–14.

Phizacklea, A. (ed.) (1983) *One way ticket: migrant and female labour,* London: Routledge.

Phizacklea, A. (1998) 'Migration and globalization: a feminist perspective', in Koser, K. & Lutz, H. (eds.), *The new migration in Europe: social constructions and social realities,* London: Macmillan, pp. 21–39.

PICUM (2009) Newsletter, July 2009.

PICUM (2010) Newsletter, July 2010.

PICUM. (2009) *The exploitation of undocumented migrant women in the workplace,* Report on a global workshop organised by PICUM and the United Methodist Women Immigrant/Civil Rights Initiative, Athens: PICUM.

Piore, M. J. (1979) *Birds of passage: migrant labour and industrial societies,* New York: Cambridge University Press.

Piore, M. J. (1980) 'Dualism as a response to flux and uncertainty', in Berger, S. and M. Piore (eds.), *Dualism and discontinuity in industrial society,* Cambridge: Cambridge University Press, 23–54.

Piper, N. (2006) 'Gendering the politics of migration', *International Migration Review,* 40(1):133–164.

Portes, A. (1997, September) *Globalisation from below: the rise of transnational communities,* Working Paper No. WPTC-98–01, Princeton, NJ: Princeton University.

Portes, A. and Borocz, J. (1989) 'Contemporary immigration: theoretical perspectives on its determinants and modes of incorporation', *International Migration Review,* 23(3):606–630.

Rabinow, P. (ed.) (2000) *Essential works of Foucault 1954–1984, Ethics* (Vol. 1), London: Penguin.

Ravenstein, E. G. (1889, June) 'The laws of migration', *Journal of the Royal Statistical Society*, pp. 241–301.

Renooy, P. (2007) 'Undeclared work: a new source of employment?' *International Journal of Sociology and Social Policy*, 27(5/6):250–256.

Reyneri, E. (2001) *Migrants' involvement in irregular employment in the Mediterranean countries of the European Union*, ILO International Migration Papers No. 41.

Reyneri, E. (2003) *Illegal immigration and the underground economy*, National Europe Centre Paper No. 68, University of Sydney.

Rezai, S. and Goli, M. (2007) *UWT Country report: Denmark*, http://www.undocumentedmigrants.eu/londonmet/library/s15990_3.pdf (Accessed: 3 December 2010).

Rivera-Batiz, F. L. (2004) 'Undocumented workers in the labour market: an analysis of the earnings of legal and illegal Mexican immigrants in the United States', in Zimmermann, K. and Constant, A. (eds.), *How labour migrants fare*, Berlin: Springer-Verlag, pp. 307–332.

Rogers, S. (2002) 'There were no parades for us', *The Guardian*, 6 November 2002, http://www.guardian.co.uk/uk/2002/nov/06/britishidentity.military (Accessed: 30 November 2010)

Ruhs, M. and Anderson, B. (2006) *Semi-compliance in the migrant labour market*, COMPAS Working Paper No. 30, University of Oxford.

Ruhs, M. and Anderson, B. (2008) *The origins and functions of illegality in migrant labour markets: an analysis of migrants, employers and the state in the UK*, COMPAS Working Paper No. 30a, University of Oxford.

Ruspini, P. (2009, January) 'Italy' in Baldwin-Edwards, M. and Kraler, A. (eds.), *REGINE: Regularisations in Europe. Study on practices in the area of regularisation of illegally staying third-country nationals in the Member States of the EU, Appendix A: Country studies*, Vienna: ICMPD, pp. 70–82.

Russel, S. S. (1997) *International migrations: implications for the World Bank*, HRO Working Paper No. 54, Washington, DC: World Bank.

Ryan, L., Sales, R., Tilki, M., and Siara, B. (2009) 'Family strategies and transnational migration: recent Polish migrants in London', *Journal of Ethnic and Migration Studies*, 35(1):61–77.

Saint-Paul, G. (1996) *Dual labour markets: a macroeconomic perspective*, Cambridge, MA: MIT Press.

Sandell, S. H. (1977) 'Women and the economics of family migration', *Review of Economics and Statistics*, 59(4):406–414.

Sassen, S. (2001) *The global city: New York, London, Tokyo*, Princeton, NJ: Princeton University Press.

Sassen, S. (2002) 'Women's burden: counter-geographies of globalization and the feminization of survival', *Nordic Journal of International Law*, 71(2):255–274.

Schönwälder, K., Vogel, D., and Sciortino, G. (2004) *Migration and illegality in Germany: the AKI research review in brief*, Berlin: Wissenschaftszentrum.

Schrover, M., Van der Leun, J., Lucassen, L., and Quispel, C. (2008) *Illegal migration and gender in a global and historical perspective*, Amsterdam: Amsterdam University Press.

Silverman, N. A. (2005) *Deserving of decent work: the complications of organising irregular workers without legal rights*, COMPAS Working Paper No. 21, University of Oxford.

Sinke, S. (2006) 'Gender and migration: historical perspectives', *International Migration Review*, 40(1):82–103.

Sjaastad, L. (1962) "The costs and returns of human migration", *Journal of Political Economy*, 70S:80–93.

Smith, A. (1995) *Nations and nationalism in a global era,* Cambridge: Polity Press.

Smith, D. (2004) 'An "untied" research agenda for family migration: loosening the "shackles" of the past' *Journal of Ethnic and Migration Studies,* 30(2):263–282.

Smith, D. and Bailey, A. (2006) 'International family migration and differential labour-market participation in Great Britain: is there a "gender gap"?' *Environment and Planning* 38:1327–1343.

Smith, S. J., Kramer, R. G., and Singer, A. (1996) *Characteristics and labor market behavior of the legalized population five years following legalization,* Washington, DC: Department of Labor.

Sohler, K. (2009, January) 'France' in Baldwin-Edwards, M. and Kraler, A. (eds.), *REGINE: Regularisations in Europe. Study on practices in the area of regularisation of illegally staying third-country nationals in the Member States of the EU, Appendix A: Country studies,* Vienna: ICMPD, pp. 1–40.

SOPEMI. (2007) *International migration outlook,* Paris: OECD.

Spencer, S. (ed.) (2006) *Refugees and other new migrants: a review of the evidence on successful approaches to integration,* Report commissioned by the Home Office, COMPAS, University of Oxford.

Stalker, P. (2002) 'Migration trends and migration policies in Europe', *International Migration Quarterly Review,* 40(5):151–178.

Stark, O. (1991) *The migration of labor,* Boston: Blackwell.

Stola, R. (1992) 'Forced migrations in Central European history', *International Migration Review,* 26(2):324–341.

Straubhaar, T. (1988) 'International labour migration within a common market: some aspects of EC experience', *Journal of Common Market Studies,* 27(1):45-62.

Swedish Presidency. (2009) *The Stockholm Programme: An open and secure Europe serving and protecting the citizen,* Council of the European Union, http://www.se2009.eu/polopoly_fs/1.26419!menu/standard/file/Klar_Stockholmsprogram.pdf (Accessed: 2 December 2010).

Temple, B. (2001) 'Crossed wires: interpreters, translators and bilingual workers in cross-language research', *Qualitative Health Research,* 12(6):844–854.

Temple, B. and Edwards, R. (2006) 'Limited exchanges: approaches to involving people who do not speak English in research and service development', in Temple, B. and Moran, R. (eds.), *Doing research with refugees: issues and guidelines,* Bristol: Polity Press, pp. 37–54.

Temple, B. and Moran, R. (eds.) (2006) *Doing research with refugees: issues and guidelines,* Bristol: Polity Press.

Terrazas, A., Batalova, J., and Fan, V. (2007, October) *Frequently requested statistics in the United States,* Migration Information Source, http://www.migrationinformation.org/USfocus/display.cfm?id=649 (Accessed: 3 December 2010).

Todaro, M. P. (1969) 'A model of labor migration and urban unemployment in less developed countries', *American Economic Review,* 59(1):138–148.

Todaro, M. P. and Maruszko, L. (1987) 'Illegal migration and US immigration reform: a conceptual framework', *Population and Development Review,* 13(1):101–114.

Triandafyllidou, A. (2010) 'Irregular migration in Europe in the early 21st century' in Triandafyllidou, A. and Gropas, R. (2007) *European immigration. A sourcebook,* Aldershot: Ashgate.

Triandafyllidou, A. and Ilies, M. (2010) 'EU irregular migration policies' in Triandafyllidou, A. (ed.), *Irregular migration in Europe—myths and realities,* Aldershot: Ashgate, pp. 1–41.

Tsoukalas, K. (1977), *Dependence and reproduction: the social role of educational mechanisms in Greece (1830–1922),* (Exartisi kai Anaparagogi. O koinonikos rolos ton ekpaideutikon michanismon stin Ellada (1830–1922), Athens: Themelio.

Turner, S. (2008) 'Studying the tensions of transnational engagement: from the nuclear family to the World-Wide Web', *Journal of Ethnic and Migration Studies*, 34(7):1049–1056.

UWT. (2008) *Undocumented migration glossary*, http://www.undocumentedmigrants.eu/londonmet/library/h11625_3.pdf (Accessed: 3 December 2010).

UWT. (2009) *Final report: the relationship between migration status and employment outcomes*, http://www.undocumentedmigrants.eu/londonmet/fms/MRSite/Research/UWT/UWT%20FINAL%20REPORT%20Revised%2021%20November%202009mw.pdf (Accessed: 30 November 2010).

Van Eijl, C. (2007) 'Tracing back "illegal aliens" in the Netherlands, 1850–1940', in Shrover, M., Van der Leun, J., Lucassen, L., and Quispel, C. (eds.), *Illegal migration and gender in a global and historical perspective*, Amsterdam: Amsterdam University Press, pp. 39–56.

Van Gyes, G. (2005) 'Social partners concerned by labour migration from central and eastern Europe', EUROnline, 22 September 2005, http://www.eurofound.europa.eu/eiro/2005/09/feature/BE0509303F.htm (Accessed: 13 February 2008)

Van Noorloos, A. F. and Zoomers, A. (2010, June) 'Europe's migration agreements with migrant-sending countries in the Global South: a critical review', *International Migration*, 48(3):42–75.

Vasta, E. (2004) *Informal employment and immigrant networks: a review paper*, Working Paper No. 2, University of Oxford.

Vecchio, D. C. (2006) *Merchants, midwives, and laboring women: Italian migrants in urban America*, Urbana: University of Illinois Press.

Warhurt, C., Lloyd, C., and Dutton, E. (2008) 'National minimum wage, low pay and the UK hotel industry: the case of room attendants', *Sociology*, 6:1228–1236.

Widgren, J. (1994) *Multinational co-operation to combat trafficking in migrants and the safeguarding of migrant rights*, Discussion paper presented at the 11th IOM seminar on Migration, 26–28 October 1994, Geneva.

Wihtol de Wenden, A. (2007) *The frontiers of mobility*, Paris UNESCO: New York, Berghahn Books.

Williams, C. C. and Windebank, J. (1998) *Informal employment in the advanced economies—implications for work and welfare*, London: Routledge.

Wills, J., Datta, K., Evans, Y., Herbert, J., May, J., and McIlwaine, C. (2010) *Global cities at work—new migrant divisions of labour*, London: Pluto.

Woodbridge, J. (2005) *Sizing the unauthorised (illegal) migrant population in the United Kingdom in 2001*, Home Office Online Report 29/05.

Zanfrini, L. (2006) *Italian policy on irregular migrants in the labour market and the shadow economy*, Report for the ad-hoc meeting of CDMG experts on policies on irregular migrants, CDMG 66, Strasbourg: Council of Europe.

Zhelyazkova, A. (2008, December) *Female migrants—the new nomads in old Europe: the gender specific dimensions of migration*, UWT Thematic report, WLRI, http://www.undocumentedmigrants.eu/londonmet/library/q68458_3.pdf (Accessed: 13 December 2010).

Zlotnik, H. (1995) 'Migration and the family: the female perspective', *Asia and Pacific Migration Journal*, 4(2/3):253–271.

Zlotnik, H. (2003) 'The global dimensions of female migration', *Migration Information Source*, Washington, DC: Migration Policy Institute.

Index

For Product Safety Concerns and Information please contact our EU
representative GPSR@taylorandfrancis.com
Taylor & Francis Verlag GmbH, Kaufingerstraße 24, 80331 München, Germany

www.ingramcontent.com/pod-product-compliance
Ingram Content Group UK Ltd.
Pitfield, Milton Keynes, MK11 3LW, UK
UKHW021432080625
459435UK00011B/240

* 9 7 8 0 4 1 5 8 5 1 8 0 0 *